Resurrection and Responsibility

"*The resurrection concerns the very nature of our faith in Christ, the meaning of our life, and our responsibility in the world.*"

—Thorwald Lorenzen

Resurrection and Responsibility

*Essays on Theology, Scripture, and Ethics
in Honor of Thorwald Lorenzen*

Edited by
KEITH D. DYER *and* DAVID J. NEVILLE

☙PICKWICK *Publications* • Eugene, Oregon

RESURRECTION AND RESPONSIBILITY
Essays on Theology, Scripture, and Ethics in Honor of Thorwald Lorenzen

Copyright © 2009 Wipf and Stock Publishers. All rights reserved. Except for brief quotations in critical publications or reviews, no part of this book may be reproduced in any manner without prior written permission from the publisher. Write: Permissions, Wipf and Stock Publishers, 199 W. 8th Ave., Suite 3, Eugene, OR 97401.

Pickwick Publications
A Division of Wipf and Stock Publishers
199 W. 8th Ave., Suite 3
Eugene, OR 97401

www.wipfandstock.com

ISBN 13: 978-1-60608-461-8

Cataloging-in-Publication data:

    Resurrection and responsibility : essays on theology, scripture, and ethics in honor of Thorwald Lorenzen / Edited by Keith D. Dyer and David J. Neville.

    xiv + 276 p. ; 23 cm. Includes bibliography of Thorwald Lorenzen.

    1. Lorenzen, Thorwald, 1936-. 2. Jesus Christ—Resurrection. 3. Christian Ethics. I. Title.

BT 481 R472 2009

Manufactured in the U.S.A.

Contents

Foreword / vii

Abbreviations / xi

Introduction: The Christian Spirituality of a Baptist Theologian—*Frank Rees* / 1

Part One: Theological Explorations

1. Friendship, Faith, and Theology—*Graeme Garrett* / 17
2. Out of Bounds: Christian Spirituality in a World of Differences—*Elizabeth Green* / 35
3. The Resurrection of Christ and the New Earth —*Jürgen Moltmann* / 51
4. *Totus homo*: Augustine on Resurrection—*Tarmo Toom* / 59

Part Two: Scriptural Expositions

5. Mission in Matthew: Relating to the Resurrected Christ —*Isam E. Ballenger* / 79
6. Creation Reclaimed: Resurrection and Responsibility in Mark 15:40–16:8—*David J. Neville* / 95
7. The Raising of Lazarus in John 11: Sign-Reading via Paul Ricoeur's Narrative Hermeneutics—*David M. Hunter* / 116
8. Paul and Embodied Resurrection: Rethinking 1 Corinthians 15—*Keith D. Dyer* / 136

Part Three: Ethical Engagements

9. Human Rights in Early Christian Perspective: The Distribution of Wealth—*E. Glenn Hinson* / 165

Contents

10	The Challenge of the State-Church System to Religious Liberty and Human Rights—*Per Midteide* / 185	
11	*Ethos*, Compassion, and Human Rights: A Foundation for Homiletical Ethics—*David Albert Farmer* / 206	
12	From Terri Schiavo toward a Theology of Dying—*D. Dixon Sutherland* / 225	

Bibliography of Works by Thorwald Lorenzen / 247
Contributors / 253
Scripture Index / 259
Author Index / 268
Subject Index / 273

Foreword

WHO IS THORWALD LORENZEN? This question is capable of being answered in any meaningful sense only within the context of friendship, and the editors of this collection of studies are grateful to be able to call—and to call upon—Thorwald their friend. Graeme Garrett's essay on "Friendship, Faith, and Theology" explores more fully the dynamic of genuine friendship, but here we acknowledge and give thanks for the enrichment of life that has resulted from residing within the ambit of Thorwald Lorenzen's circle of friends.

Although details of a person's life do not necessarily convey a great deal about his or her passions and proclivities, they nevertheless provide a sense of a person's commitments, interests, and orientation in life. To that end, then, we provide the following brief overview of Thorwald Lorenzen's life-experience thus far.

Thorwald Lorenzen was born in Hamburg, Germany, on August 20, 1936. As a young boy, he experienced some of the horror of World War II. His primary and secondary education occurred in Hamburg and Güstrow, after which he completed an apprenticeship in industrial commerce. After working for almost two years as a commercial clerk, in 1958 he made the decision to travel to Australia, where he found work in the industrial sector of New South Wales. During the early 1960s, he completed a Bachelor of Arts at the University of Sydney and ordination studies at Morling College, before being ordained to Christian ministry by the Baptist Union of New South Wales on July 8, 1966. He continued his theological studies at the International Baptist Theological Seminary in Rüschlikon, Switzerland, earning the Bachelor of Divinity degree in 1968 and the Master of Theology degree in 1969, before pursuing doctoral study at the University of Zurich, where he completed a dissertation on John 21 under the supervision of Eduard Schweizer.

Since his ordination as a Baptist pastor, Thorwald Lorenzen has been committed to the teaching, preaching, pastoral, and prophetic dimensions of Christian ministry. During the early 1970s, he taught New Testament at Southeastern Baptist Theological Seminary in Wake Forest, North Carolina, after which he took up the position of Associate Professor (1974–1982) and then Professor (1982–1995) of Systematic Theology and Ethics at the International Baptist Theological Seminary in Rüschlikon. There he passed on to students from all over the world his passion for theology integrated into the whole of life. During the winter semester of 1994–1995, he was also Visiting Professor for Ecumenical Theology at the Roman Catholic Faculty of Theology in Lucerne, Switzerland. Frank Rees's introductory essay on "The Christian Spirituality of a Baptist Theologian" explores the various facets of Thorwald's particular embodiment of a "sacramental," "evangelical," and ecumenical Baptist theologian.

As Rees notes, Thorwald Lorenzen has left his mark as both preacher and pastor in addition to his considerable legacy as a scholar and human-rights advocate. During 1965–1966, he served as Pastor of Avalon Baptist Church in Sydney, and he returned to full-time pastoral work in 1995, when he was called to serve as Senior Minister of Canberra Baptist Church, from which he retired in 2005. But in between these two periods of pastoral ministry in Australia, he served as interim pastor for significant periods of time in both Switzerland and the United States. For Thorwald Lorenzen, theology must always be lived out in both the church and the wider world.

As a conference speaker, Thorwald Lorenzen has been invited to speak in many countries, both those in which he has lived and worked and in others, including Poland, Denmark, Romania, the former Yugoslavia, Portugal, Spain, Puerto Rico, and the United Kingdom.

Among Thorwald Lorenzen's central theological concerns and commitments, one would have to name the centrality of the resurrection of the crucified Christ, the church and ecumenical relations, the nature of faith and discipleship, and Christian social responsibility, especially with respect to justice matters, human rights, and ecology. His publication list reveals how dominant such themes have been across his academic career. Numerous essays and two books explore the reality and significance of the resurrection, the beating heart of his life-affirming theology: hence the theme of this collection of studies.

His theological commitments are also reflected in other roles and responsibilities. From 1975 to 1990 and again from 1995 to 2000, he was a member of the Human Rights Commission of the Baptist World Alliance, and he chaired this same body during 1985–1990 and 1995–2000. During the late 1980s (1986–1989), he cochaired the Joint Commission of the Baptist World Alliance and the Lutheran World Federation. Between 1985 and 1990 and again in 1994–1995, he was the official representative of the Baptist World Alliance at the United Nations in Geneva. From 1992 to 1995, he was Secretary of the European Baptist Theological Teachers' Conference, and during 1994–1995 he also chaired the European Baptist Federation's Task Force for Religious Liberty and Human Rights. He has served on the Ethics Committee of the John James Hospital in Canberra, chaired the Reconciliation network ("Journey of Healing") in the Australian Capital Territory (2000), and during the period from 2000 to 2002 he was chair of the Australian Capital Territory Churches Council and its Executive. From 1997 to 2006 he was on the Board of Directors for the Australian Centre for Christianity and Culture, and since 2006 has served on the Centre's Council. Until recently, he was general editor of *International Theological Studies: Contributions of Baptist Scholars*, published by Peter Lang, and from 1995 to 2001 he was an advisory editor for *Pulpit Digest*.

We have both had the privilege of preparing some of Thorwald Lorenzen's lectures and papers for publication. What stands out in his writings is a profound commitment to faithful discipleship to Jesus Christ, holistic mission, and personal integrity. Also noteworthy is his creative and flexible facility with the English language—the result, at least in part, of the fact that he learned English in adulthood. His commitment to discerning the Word of God in Scripture and to conveying it into ever-new situations is reflected in his capacity to speak and write in ways that convey faithfully and meaningfully both the irresistibility and implications of God's gracious communication to humanity.

Alongside this impressive list of accomplishments and at the heart of his life and ministry, Thorwald Lorenzen has also been a family man. In Sydney on January 8, 1966, he married Jill Thyrd, with whom he has had two children, Christina and Stephan, who in turn have brought seven grandchildren into their lives. The Lorenzen home has always been a vibrant center for hospitality. No matter where they might happen to be residing, Jill and Thorwald are exemplary hosts and practitioners of open-table fellowship. The food, the wine, the stories, and the encouragement flow abundantly, and the guest list will often consist of a delightful mix of ethnic, social, and religious backgrounds, including the eminent visitor,

Foreword

the liveliest teenager, and the loneliest student on campus. This should come as no surprise concerning our theologian of the resurrection, whose commitment has been to follow the one made known in the breaking of bread (Luke 24:35).

It remains to express our acknowledgments to those who have contributed to the publication of this volume. Our thanks go first to our fellow contributors for sharing with us the vision of producing these studies as an expression of gratitude for what each of us has learned from Thorwald Lorenzen. In particular, we thank Graeme Garrett for his editorial assistance. Together we represent the many mentors, colleagues, students, and friends who could have made worthy contributions to this volume. Sincere thanks too to Pickwick Publications for publishing these studies, and especially to our editor, K. C. Hanson, for his editorial oversight and guidance. Finally, and most importantly, we express heartfelt thanks to Lynne and to Sonia, who have supported the project from the outset and provided advice and encouragement along the way. They too delight in knowing Thorwald and Jill, and they echo our thanks and appreciation.

Keith Dyer and David Neville
December 2008

Abbreviations

OLD TESTAMENT

Gen	Genesis
Exod	Exodus
Lev	Leviticus
Num	Numbers
Deut	Deuteronomy
Josh	Joshua
Judg	Judges
1–2 Sam	1–2 Samuel
1–2 Kgs	1–2 Kings
1–2 Chr	1–2 Chronicles
Neh	Nehemiah
Esth	Esther
Ps/Pss	Psalms
Prov	Proverbs
Eccl	Ecclesiastes
Song	Song of Songs
Isa	Isaiah
Jer	Jeremiah
Lam	Lamentations
Ezek	Ezekiel
Dan	Daniel
Hos	Hosea
Obad	Obadiah

Abbreviations

Mic	Micah
Nah	Nahum
Hab	Habakkuk
Zeph	Zephaniah
Hag	Haggai
Zech	Zechariah
Mal	Malachi

NEW TESTAMENT

Matt	Matthew
Rom	Romans
1–2 Cor	1–2 Corinthians
Gal	Galatians
Eph	Ephesians
Phil	Philippians
Col	Colossians
1–2 Thess	1–2 Thessalonians
1–2 Tim	1–2 Timothy
Phlm	Philemon
Heb	Hebrews
Jas	James
1–2 Pet	1–2 Peter
Rev	Revelation

APOCRYPHA AND SEPTUAGINT

Bar	Baruch
1–2 Esd	1–2 Esdras
1–2 Macc	1–2 Maccabees
Sir	Sirach
Tob	Tobit
Wis	Wisdom of Solomon

Abbreviations

APOSTOLIC FATHERS

Barn.	*Barnabas*
1–2 Clem.	*1–2 Clement*
Did.	*Didache*
Herm. *Mand.*	Shepherd of Hermas, *Mandate*
Herm. *Sim.*	Shepherd of Hermas, *Similitude*
Herm. *Vis.*	Shepherd of Hermas, *Vision*
Ign. *Smyrn.*	Ignatius, *To the Smyrnaeans*
Pol. *Phil*	Polycarp, *To the Philippians*

JOURNALS, PERIODICALS, AND SERIES

AB	Anchor Bible
ABQ	*American Baptist Quarterly*
ABRL	Anchor Bible Reference Library
BETL	Bibliotheca Ephemeridum theologicarum Lovaniensium
BZNW	Beihefte zur Zeitschrift für die neutestamentliche Wissenschaft und die Kunde der älteren Kirche
CBQ	*Catholic Biblical Quarterly*
CTM	Calwer theologische Monographien
ER	*Ecumenical Review*
ERT	*Evangelical Review of Theology*
ExpTim	*Expository Times*
ITQ	*Irish Theological Quarterly*
JAAR	*Journal of the American Academy of Religion*
JBL	*Journal of Biblical Literature*
JES	*Journal of Ecumenical Studies*
JSNT	*Journal for the Study of the New Testament*
JSNTSup	Journal for the Study of the New Testament: Supplement Series

JSOTSup	Journal for the Study of the Old Testament: Supplement Series
JTS	*Journal of Theological Studies*
KKTS	Konfessionskundliche und kontroverstheologische Studien
MF	*Ministerial Formation*
NIGTC	New International Greek Testament Commentary
PTMS	Princeton Theological Monograph Series
RevExp	*Review and Expositor*
SBS	Stuttgarter Bibelstudien
SBT	Studies in Biblical Theology
SemeiaSt	Semeia Studies
SJT	*Scottish Journal of Theology*
SNTSMS	Society for New Testament Studies Monograph Series
SP	Sacra pagina
STR	*Seinan Theological Review*
TG	*Theologisches Gespräch*
TS	*Theological Studies*
TZ	*Theologische Zeitschrift*
WBC	Word Biblical Commentary
ZNW	*Zeitschrift für die neutestamentliche Wissenschaft und die Kunde der älteren Kirche*
ZTG	*Zeitschrift für Theologie und Gemeinde*

OTHER ABBREVIATIONS

BWA	Baptist World Alliance
EBF	European Baptist Federation
NRSV	New Revised Standard Version (Bible)
WCC	World Council of Churches
WEB	World English Bible

Introduction

The Christian Spirituality of a Baptist Theologian

Frank Rees

Thorwald Lorenzen is a Baptist theologian. Some might consider that description almost an oxymoron. Baptists are not known throughout the contemporary church for their contributions to theology, especially to the discipline of Systematic Theology. However much that may be so, Lorenzen truly is a Baptist theologian. His work as a theologian is a rich gift to us all, not least the various Baptist communities around the world.

At the heart of his work as a theologian is a distinctive perspective that pervades his life as a pastor, a theologian and as a participant in church life around the world. This perspective I want to name a "Christological spirituality." To begin to explain what this means in Lorenzen's thought and in his contribution as a Baptist theologian, we begin with the baptismal character of the life of faith.

A BAPTIST THEOLOGY FOR A BAPTIZED COMMUNITY

The first time I heard Thorwald Lorenzen preach was at a baptismal service, during a series he undertook as the visiting speaker for a large Baptist church in the eastern suburbs of Melbourne. This church saw itself as the flagship of conservative evangelical witness in the Baptist Union of Victoria, and the fact that Lorenzen was invited to preach there was itself remarkable. That he did so with such a warm reception bears witness to his extraordinary ability to relate right across the spectrum of Christian experience. On this occasion, his sermon was on the theme, "Baptism, an evangelical sacrament." In a conversation later that same week, he reflected with me on the unusual conjunction of those words, "evangelical" and "sacrament." These are words that do not usually go together for Baptists, but he was keen to invite his audience to see what they might have to offer us. That he continued to wonder about these ideas out loud with me, a theological student, is another measure of the person. His approach to ministry is to invite others into his explorations and reflections and to encourage us to find our own voices, in conversation with him and with the theological and biblical traditions.

At that time, Lorenzen was participating in a number of ecumenical conversations and was writing about the distinctive contribution Baptists might have to make to the common life of the whole church. In a number of articles, he wrote of the distinctive Baptist understanding of baptism and its relation to ecumenicity.[1] Similarly, he wrote on the theme of baptism and church membership, reminding Baptists of the theological and spiritual depth of their baptismal experience and the identity of the church arising from our baptism.[2] Here again, we see his willingness to engage where others fear to tread. Ecumenicity is not, for Lorenzen, something that negates the specific character and contribution of each branch of the Christian family. Rather, it is precisely as each tradition offers its gifts to the common table that the unity of the whole is discovered and celebrated. Hence, Lorenzen worked on the theme of baptism, and his preaching on baptism as "an evangelical sacrament" reflected this commitment.

The term "sacrament" may be broadly defined as an element, process, ritual, or event within our historical life through which God acts towards human beings. Sacraments are the means by which God's saving, healing, and liberating purpose becomes effective for us. Baptists have traditionally not used this term, sometimes because of a desire to move away from what they have seen as "magical" overtones in other churches' understandings of sacraments or sometimes because they have wished

---

1. Thorwald Lorenzen, "Anabaptists and Discipleship," *European Baptist Press Service* (Sept 12, 1978): 2–4; also in *The Australian Baptist* (Nov 1978): 4–5; *Slowo Prawdy* 12 (1978): 26–27; *Nigerian Baptist* (Jan 1979): 29–30; *DC*, de christen Weekblad van de Baptistengemeeten, No. 46 (1978): 1–2. See also his "Baptists and Ecumenicity with Special Reference to Baptism," *RevExp* 77 (1980) 21–45, and a different paper with the same title, "Baptists and Ecumenicity with Special Reference to Baptism," *ER* 32 (1980) 257–73.

2. Thorwald Lorenzen, "Baptism and Church Membership: Some Baptist Positions and their Ecumenical Implications," *JES* 18 (1981) 561–74; "A Baptist Response," in *Unity in Each Place — In All Places — : United Churches and the Christian World Communions* (ed. Michael Kinnamon; Faith and Order Paper 118; Geneva: WCC, 1983), 25–34.

to emphasize more everyday aspects of our lives as disciples and thus have downplayed the special nature of these events or rituals. All meals and all gatherings and all relationships are to be occasions for knowing God's presence, so the events of baptism and communion are, from this perspective, less special. Rather, they serve as symbols of the wider presence of Christ in all our lives. In addition, Baptists have mostly chosen to call these two special rituals of the church "ordinances" rather than sacraments, to emphasize that in these events we are following the explicit example and instruction of Jesus. Thus, for Baptists and for many like-minded groups, baptism and the Lord's Supper are ordinances in which disciples follow the example of Jesus and commit themselves to continuing obedience to him.[3]

When we turn to the conjunction of "sacrament" with "evangelical," we see the distinctive strength of Lorenzen's contribution, both to theology and to Baptist churches' understanding of their own heritage and ecclesiality. There continues to be a lively discussion about the meaning of the term "evangelical," especially when it is made into a proper noun. A number of contributors claim to identify essential ingredients for a theology or spirituality worthy of that term, while others have sought to "revision" evangelical theology.[4] I would suggest that Lorenzen's use of the term seeks specifically to focus upon the New Testament idea of *gospel*, the good news of Jesus Christ. Rightly, he follows the insight of Rom 1:18, where the content of the gospel is not words or propositions but a living presence. The gospel is not simply *about* Jesus Christ but is rather the creative and redemptive power of his living presence. So for Lorenzen the word "evangelical" alludes to the good news of the living presence of the risen Jesus. But this emphasis can only be sustained through a close link with the historical

3. For a detailed historical treatment of Baptists' understanding of sacraments, with particular reference to baptism, see Stanley J. Fowler, *More Than a Symbol: The British Baptist Recovery of Baptismal Sacramentalism* (Studies in Baptist History and Thought 2; Carlisle: Paternoster, 2002).

4. In particular, Stanley Grenz described his work as a systematic theologian in terms of "revisioning" evangelical theology. See Stanley J. Grenz, *Revisioning Evangelical Theology: A Fresh Agenda for the 21st Century* (Downers Grove, IL: InterVarsity, 1993), and *Renewing the Center: Evangelical Theology in a Post-Theological Era* (Grand Rapids: Baker Academic, 2000). Other expressions of the contemporary quest to characterize evangelical theology include Gary Dorrien, *The Remaking of Evangelical Theology* (Louisville: Westminster John Knox, 1998); and Alister McGrath, *A Passion for Truth: The Intellectual Coherence of Evangelicalism* (Leicester: Apollos, 1996).

life and death of Jesus of Nazareth. The story of the historical Jesus must be told if the gospel is to retain its power to save. Still, that story alone is not sufficient for the evangelical mission. More than that story is the reality of the living Christ, the crucified *and* resurrected one. In this gospel, this evangelical witness, Jesus is not only an exemplary person, whose moral life and teachings provide a pattern for Christian life today. Faith as obedience is not enough. Indeed, it is most likely to lead to forms of self-deception, moral superiority, or burn-out, since in the end it is fuelled by the moral commitment of believers but not sufficiently grounded in a continuing spiritual relationship with Christ.

Central to the possibility of effective and genuine evangelical witness are the sacraments, perhaps especially the Lord's Supper. Here, believers are gathered into the living body of the risen Christ, "participating" in that life, the body and blood of Christ, his continuing presence and self-giving. Here, Christ is not only remembered but known. Here is communion, fellowship, participation.

To declare that baptism is an evangelical sacrament is to recognize that believers, both as individuals and in community, are gathered into the living body of Christ and thus become part of the good news. We participate in the life of Christ. We do not merely re-enact Jesus' baptism. Rather, we are immersed into his continuing life. His Spirit gathers us from death to life, raising us into the new creation that has come into the world through Jesus' life, death, and resurrection. This is "evangelical," good news, as it declares an end to the dominion of sin and death, washes away the old order, and opens before us the reality of God's reign, the fulfilment of Jesus' own promise and commitment. Baptism as an evangelical sacrament is, then, a perpetual act of God, which takes place within history and yet reaches out beyond this life and death into the new creation. It is, too, an act of the believing, responsive community as it places its trust in the reality of God's saving presence in the here and now and commits itself to live into the promised new creation.

Finally, Lorenzen's understanding of baptism as an evangelical sacrament clearly addresses the tendency of many evangelical groups to turn baptism into an event focused on the subjective experience of the individual. Lorenzen's theology squarely sets baptism in its appropriate historical context—the life of the church. Indeed, understood in this way, baptism defines the life of the church. This is what the church is— the community of this evangelical life, this participation in the presence of the crucified and risen Christ, reaching out in hope and joy for the coming of his promised salvation.

Before leaving this theme, it is crucial to identify one further aspect of Lorenzen's theology. The idea of baptism as an evangelical sacrament was set forward in a sermon. Lorenzen's sermons are always based upon clear and careful biblical exegesis. In the first part of his career, he was both a New Testament professor and a professor in Systematic Theology. The crucial connection here is between the life of the sacraments and the enlivening reality of the Word of God. In the theology of the Reformers, it is the Word of God that enables the elements of the created order to be sacraments, the mediums of God's saving presence. While this is true of bread and wine, and the water of baptism, it is also comprehensively so for the church itself. Without the enlivening Word, the church cannot be the church. Hence Lorenzen's commitment to biblical studies and to preaching as the outworking of a genuinely evangelical theology. His life as theologian and pastor has been one of enabling communities to be centered around the living Christ, who is known in word and sacrament, so that the community itself may participate in that living word of good news.

BIBLICAL FAITH AS CHRISTIAN ETHICS

In his early years of teaching at the International Baptist Theological Seminary in Rüschlikon, Lorenzen's title included three disciplines. He was a Professor in Systematic Theology, New Testament, and Theological Ethics. This was not so much a sign of omniscience as a clear indication of the integration of disciplines in his theological work. Christian faith must express itself not only as ideas to be believed but as values to be lived. Along with his close friend and colleague Athol Gill, Lorenzen placed a strong emphasis on Christian life as discipleship. The New Testament does not call people to be "Christians" so much as disciples of Jesus. Lorenzen's work as a Christian ethicist derives from his exploration of a radical life-style of discipleship.

To illustrate the integration of theology, biblical studies, and ethical implications in Lorenzen's thought, I would like to draw upon one of Lorenzen's recent publications, a series of studies in the first volume of *The Pastor's Bible Study*.[5] In one section of this work, Lorenzen offers five

---

5. David Albert Farmer, gen. ed., *The Pastor's Bible Study*, vol. 1 (Nashville: Abingdon, 2004).

studies on "Christian Faith and Power." Beginning with a recognition that power is a reality in all of life, he argues that it is both a promise and a problem. Power may be creative or destructive. More than that, there may be power in weakness, as well as weakness in power.

The studies explore five biblical themes through related passages:

1. "The Transfiguration of Power (Rev 5:1–14)." Here we find the contrasting images of power, the lion and the lamb. Christians are called to a new song, the vision of all creation made new in Christ, and to live within this song.

2. "Money Is Power (Mark 10:17–31, Luke 19:1–10)." Here, a new paradigm of power is offered. Money is power in the worldly paradigm, but when set within the transfiguring presence of God's reign, as in the example of Zacchaeus, money is turned towards the love of God and love of one's neighbor.

3. "Christians, Governing Authorities, and Context (Rom 13:1–10)." This study explores the questions of loyalty and obedience to the temporal powers of the state. While Paul calls Christians to observe the law and pay their taxes, "the content and context of the text make it clear that obedience to the state must be seen in the context of one's relationship to Christ. Any obedience to the law and to the government is not blind and is not absolute."[6]

4. "Christians, Governing Authorities, and Obedience (Rev 13:1–18)" continues this theme, drawing upon the image of "the beast," suggesting that "even an evil and powerful state . . . is not outside the realm of the providence by which God sustains, guides, and accompanies human history."[7] So Christians need to know where their fundamental allegiance lies and where their security rests. Here Lorenzen identifies a fundamental basis for engagement in Christian witness in the face of "the powers of this world," calling for and defending the rights of all God's children.

5. "Christians, Governing Authorities, and Conflict (1 Pet 2:13–17, Mark 12:13–17, Acts 5:17–42)." These passages together remind us that governing authorities can become evil, but Christians

---

6. Thorwald Lorenzen, "Christian Faith and Power," in *The Pastor's Bible Study* 1:202.

7. Lorenzen, "Christian Faith and Power," 204.

are called to pray for them and to live in the world obeying God rather than human authorities. In contrast to the common understanding, which sees Jesus as saying that people should always obey "Caesar," careful exegesis shows that through examining the blasphemous inscription on the denarius coin, Jesus calls his followers to recognize the limitations of Caesar's claim and to render to God the things that are God's.

In these studies we see one crucial dimension of Lorenzen's understanding of Christian life as discipleship. Just as a proper understanding of Jesus cannot divorce him from his place in history, neither can Christian spirituality be separated from responsible participation in the life of the world, including the world of political power. Even more so, this calls for an engagement of protest, in the light of God's promise to and for the world. Jesus does not call his disciples out of the world but to serve God's reign within the world, including caring for those dispossessed and disempowered by the machinations of human systems. It is typical of Lorenzen's approach to Christian lifestyle that he does not begin with individualist questions of private morality. Rather, he goes directly to the difficult structural issues within which those other questions must be set, issues of political power and the wider question of God's purposes in and for the world. But here his purpose is not ideological. Rather, by identifying the theological foundations of ethics in the reign of God, he is able to direct our attention to God's concern for those who are disempowered, whose rights and hopes are denied.

What we see here is also evident in other publications at a more scholarly level. Through his academic work, in his leadership of the Baptist World Alliance Commission on Ethics and Human Rights, and in his pastoral role, there has been continuity in Lorenzen's contribution. This is not merely a continuity of subject matter and themes, for these in turn arise from a continuity I have called his "Christological spirituality." His conviction is that the continuing mission and ministry of the crucified and risen One deeply intersect with the life of the world. Faith does not take us out of the world but rather enables us to live into the life of the world as God's creation, with the promise and hope of new creation through Christ. This life and hope is the gospel. It is a vision of salvation that calls forth discipleship in lives of worship and service.

THE CHRISTOLOGICAL CENTER: WHO IS THIS JESUS WE FOLLOW?

Several years ago, when delivering the commencement address at Whitley College, Lorenzen said: "Theology is the servant of the church. Its function and dignity is to help the church to be the church: salt and light for the world. Its function is to try to help keep Christian faith Christian."[8]

One of the most significant dimensions of Lorenzen's career as a theologian is his commitment to theology and to the church, both as an academic teacher and as a pastor. As a pastor he sought always to be a theologian, and as a theologian he sought always to be a pastor. His theological corpus expresses his commitment to the church, calling the church to be the church, to remain "Christian." This objective is only possible, however, when we maintain a radical and clear focus on the Christological center of our faith. Here, I believe, we see the heart of Thorwald Lorenzen, Baptist theologian and pastor, in his Christological spirituality. In an article on "Jesus Christ and Spirituality," Lorenzen identifies the basic themes of his entire theological and pastoral contribution. One paragraph shows the tenor of the whole:

> Since Jesus Christ came into the world to bring life, Christians are therefore agents of change, and Christian spirituality must empower Christians to change things in the direction of truth, freedom and justice. Christian spirituality derives from the awareness that Jesus Christ in the power of the Spirit is impinging upon us, drawing us into the truth, freedom and justice that God has established by raising Jesus from the dead.[9]

Here we see the immediate linkage Lorenzen makes between the resurrection of Jesus and the enabling of the Spirit, not only to know the presence of Jesus but to empower Christians to live into God's reign of truth, freedom, and justice. These are central characteristics of Lorenzen's Christological spirituality.

In reflecting theologically upon these dimensions of Christian discipleship, I find it helpful to identify several crucial elements that were clearly enunciated by the German New Testament theologian,

---

8. This commencement address was later published under the title "Discerning the Spirits," *St Mark's Review* 195 (2004) 8–14.

9. Thorwald Lorenzen, "Jesus Christ and Spirituality," 86, in *Faith and Freedom: Christian Ethics in a Pluralist Culture* (ed. David Neville and Philip Matthews; Adelaide: ATF Press, 2003), 81–94.

Ernst Käsemann. In identifying these elements from Käsemann, I mean to suggest that Lorenzen's theology superbly fulfills the requirements Käsemann enunciated. Käsemann was concerned to identify a viable Christology for people facing the many challenges of the later twentieth century.[10] The challenge was to find a pattern of discipleship that mediated between an escapist piety and an impious liberalism. In his essay, "Was Jesus a liberal?" Käsemann poses the matter directly: "May a church or a denomination continue to call itself Christian if its devout members have ceased to be liberal, and its liberal members can no longer be regarded as devout?"[11] He goes on to argue that Jesus was a "liberal" in relation to much of his own cultural and religious heritage. But this liberalism is not what defined him: "He was unique in that he remained, lived and died, acted and spoke, in the freedom of being a child of God."[12]

In an incisive later chapter, Käsemann addresses the need for a theology of resurrection truly grounded in Christology. His specific concern here is the popular "existentialist" interpretation of resurrection faith, which all too easily reduces faith to an enthusiasm in the present experience of Christian persons. This will not do because it misplaces Jesus Christ himself. Käsemann asserts that a theology of resurrection must begin with Christology and remain with it. In doing so, it "must become a theology of the cross," or else, like the Corinthian difficulty, it becomes "a wrong-headed enthusiasm."[13] On the other hand, a theology of the cross must not itself collapse into an ethical or ideological program, without the inner dynamic of the risen Christ. For Käsemann, the continuous dangers are that Christian faith will collapse into a mystical, "other-worldly" enthusiasm or an ethical, ideological focus without a spiritual foundation.

Käsemann's New Testament theology was shaped by the desire to steer between these dangers. He insisted on holding together a definite, historical link with the person of Jesus of Nazareth, the crucified One.

---

10. See particularly Ernst Käsemann, *New Testament Questions of Today* (trans. W. J. Montague; London: SCM, 1969), especially "New Testament Questions of Today" and "The 'Jesus of History' Controversy," and also Ernst Käsemann, *Jesus Means Freedom* (trans. Frank Clarke; London: SCM, 1969).

11. Käsemann, *Jesus Means Freedom*, 20.

12. Ibid., 41.

13. Ibid., particularly 72–75.

Without this historical anchor, Christian faith collapses into existential piety. But the heart of Christian faith cannot be linked only to the historical Jesus. The "liberal" acknowledgement of the "mythical" elements in the gospel witness is essential, to take us beyond the literal and historical, to the presence of the living Christ, without which faith has no present and no future. The Lord must be known as an historical figure *and* as the eschatological one, whose presence ever and anew calls women and men to faith and discipleship.

My contention is that these same theological dynamics characterize Lorenzen's theology, though in his own distinctively Baptist way and against a broader framework of scholarship and theological debate. I am not meaning to suggest that Lorenzen has derived his focus from Käsemann's work, though no doubt the latter was one of the influential sources in the context where Lorenzen studied and taught. Rather, I am suggesting a commonality of focus upon the necessity of a Christian spirituality, enabling an appropriate and empowering discipleship today. As with Käsemann, so for Lorenzen, the presence of the historical Jesus, once crucified and now risen and calling us to faith, is central to theology and to the life of the church. Furthermore, with his friend, Athol Gill, Lorenzen sees the importance not only of the death and resurrection of Jesus, but of the life he lived, which led to that death, a life of mission to the outcast and proclamation of good news to the poor. This spirituality guides theology and the church, and is essential if we are to remain "Christian."

Fundamental to all this, then, is the reality of Jesus Christ's resurrection, a theme central to Lorenzen's theological work.

RESURRECTION FAITH

It is no accident that Thorwald Lorenzen has published two books on the theme of resurrection.[14] This has been the work of his life. From this theological foundation, all else proceeds. At the beginning of *Resurrection and Discipleship*, we read:

> When we speak about the resurrection of Jesus Christ we are dealing not with *a* question of faith, but with *the* question of the

14. Thorwald Lorenzen, *Resurrection and Discipleship: Interpretive Models, Biblical Reflections, Theological Consequences* (Maryknoll, NY: Orbis, 1995; Eugene, OR: Wipf & Stock Publishers, 2004), and *Resurrection, Discipleship, Justice: Affirming the Resurrection of Jesus Christ Today* (Macon, GA: Smyth & Helwys, 2003).

Christian faith. The resurrection is not merely an object of faith, and it is not merely a credal statement to accept; it is the *origin* and *ground* of faith. Here the *nature* and *content* of faith, what Christian faith actually *is*, is decided.[15]

The argument for the centrality of resurrection faith for all Christian theology is carefully developed in a broad and well researched work, which demonstrates the systematic connections between the rising of Jesus and the character and possibility of Christian life today. But the same argument can also be presented in a shorter form, with a closer linkage to the mission for justice which characterizes the life of discipleship.

In Lorenzen's resurrection theology we see the same dynamics we have already noted in the work of Käsemann and in the life of the baptized community. First, there is an essential emphasis on the historical foundations of resurrection faith. Jesus' rising from death is an historical event, but exactly what this means and how it is to be known requires careful consideration. This consideration makes up the first part of the earlier book, where four approaches to the character of the resurrection are examined. "Traditional" approaches to the resurrection, exemplified in the work of Carl Henry and Wolfhart Pannenberg, offer what appears to be a straightforward historical account of events. But in the end, these approaches find it difficult to explain exactly what they mean by "history" and are found to be so much concerned with facts or "proof" that the dimension of faith is effectively excluded. Other models, such as the "liberal" approach of Rudolf Bultmann, the "evangelical" thought of Karl Barth and Edward Schillebeeckx, and the "liberationist" approach represented by Jürgen Moltmann and Jon Sobrino are examined in turn. In each of these chapters, the arguments, strengths, and weaknesses of the writers and their respective "models" are clearly outlined. Through it all, Lorenzen seeks to explore the nature of the *event* of the resurrection. In the end, his conviction is that these questions cannot be answered without engaging with the New Testament witness itself.

Here we see the very best of Lorenzen's work, as he brings together his immense abilities as exegete *and* theologian. The resurrection can only be understood in the way the New Testament speaks of it, as an "act of God." The accounts of the appearances of the risen Christ are considered, carefully distinguishing different possible meanings of the

15. Lorenzen, *Resurrection and Discipleship*, 1.

term "appearing." Then, after examining Paul's testimony, he returns to the foundational witness of Mary, noting the "great and tragic" irony that whereas Jesus first appeared to a woman, for most of its history the church has denied the equality of women and men and refused proper recognition to the ministry of women.

Next Lorenzen asks how Christian experience of the Spirit is related to the resurrection of Christ. Here we see the immediate practical relevance of what he terms the priority of Christology over soteriology and ecclesiology. The Spirit is not to be identified with our experience of salvation, nor is it the Spirit of the Church (alone). Essentially it is the Spirit of the crucified Christ and bears witness to Christ, and thus is the means of our salvation and our life in the community of faith.

Interestingly, it is only after all these considerations that Lorenzen examines the significance of the empty tomb narratives. Here he explores a range of ideas of "resurrection" and "body," offering a rigorous assessment of the historical basis of the empty tomb traditions and what significance they may have for us today. Whereas some recent scholarship has tended to downplay the significance of the empty tomb traditions, Lorenzen argues for their importance. There may have been an original apologetic purpose, but the theological meaning Lorenzen finds here emphasizes that faith in the risen Christ is a flesh-and-blood reality, in the here and now. The empty tomb stands against every docetic temptation to shift Christ and our faith into some ephemeral, other-worldly mystique, an escape from the demands of discipleship today.

The third section of the book, called "Response: The Nature of Faith in the Risen Christ," is pivotal to the book's purpose. Here Lorenzen outlines what he calls the dialectic of Christian knowing, which, to my mind, is crucial to his entire purpose. On the one hand, he insists that the resurrection is an historical reality, but on the other he maintains that it cannot be known except through the life of faith. It is therefore crucial to explain the nature of this faith. Drawing upon the elements of word, promise, remembering, and witness, Lorenzen seeks to explain the character of Christian faith in general and resurrection belief in particular. But none of these elements is an inward or merely intellectual phenomenon. The response of resurrection faith is worked out in discipleship, through worship, praxis, and knowledge.

Thus, this book and its later development, *Resurrection, Discipleship, Justice*, work out the implications or consequences of this theology of resurrection. Yet the term "consequences" is a little misleading, in that for Lorenzen these are not separate from a theology of resurrection. They are part of its meaning. Without this worship, praxis, and knowledge, without justice and discipleship, a theology of resurrection is an empty claim. It collapses, in the ways Käsemann also suggested, into an inward piety, without outward significance, or into an ideological framework without the vitality to sustain its commitments. Only if resurrection faith is indeed knowledge of and participation in the life of the risen Christ, through "discipleship and justice," is it truly resurrection faith.

There is, then, finally, interdependence between the resurrection of Jesus and our own faith in the risen One. In Lorenzen's words, "The resurrection of Jesus Christ and our faith in him must be distinguished from each other, but they cannot be separated."[16] A few pages later, he explains that the resurrection calls for discipleship "so that the identity of Christian faith is preserved," while discipleship needs the resurrection "so that its liberating manifestation of the gospel is not reduced to the moralism of a merely human activity."[17] It is crucial, then, to emphasize that we do not by our discipleship or any other human efforts "create" the reality of Christ's resurrection, nor can we prove it or establish it as such. Yet we are called to enter into its verification, and in this sense we are part of its truth. Here we see the immense significance of what I have called Lorenzen's Christological spirituality. This is no mere theory, nor is it about a privatized inwardness. Rather, this spirituality and this Christology together press towards life in the world, a life characterized by the Spirit of the risen Christ. This life is described by Lorenzen in terms of an "all-encompassing salvation." The resurrection of Jesus brings not only forgiveness of sins but also liberation for the downtrodden and God's promised justice for the oppressed. These indications of resurrection praxis give rise to the wider dimensions of Lorenzen's theological work, his commitment to the social, ethical, and political implications of Christian discipleship.

Thorwald Lorenzen's work as a theologian is always grounded in a biblically informed, practical, and faithful engagement with the issues and challenges of his situation, both local and international. Just as for Lorenzen theology serves the church, so too his theology calls the church to the praxis of a Christological spirituality. For this, we owe him

---

16. Lorenzen, *Resurrection and Discipleship*, 232.
17. Ibid., 235.

a deep and abiding debt of gratitude, best expressed in our own attempts to follow that pathway.

Part One

Theological Explorations

1

Friendship, Faith, and Theology

Graeme Garrett

"I believe that within the sphere of ... freedom friendship is by far the rarest and most priceless treasure."

—Dietrich Bonhoeffer[1]

ON THE FACING PAGE of Karl Barth's *Die Kirchliche Dogmatik I/1* are the words "meinem Freund Rudolf Pestalozzi" ("to my friend Rudolf Pestalozzi"). The attribution is not incidental for the theology that follows, as the story of this friendship shows.[2] Theology takes place through engagement with a long-standing tradition reaching back to the words of scripture. The defining figures in this tradition loom large in every generation's development of its theological ideas. But the appropriation and re-interpretation of the tradition rarely takes place apart from a living conversation with particular friends. This is true in my own experience. God, it seems, is best found in life shared with others similarly devoted to listening for God, and speaking to God and about God. Thorwald Lorenzen has been such a friend on my journey. I am not alone in that. In tribute to his capacity for friendship and what it has contributed to the lives of many, I want to reflect on friendship as a theme in theology and on the place friends hold in our human dealings with God.

The remarkable friendship between Dietrich Bonhoeffer and Eberhard Bethge is an illuminating narrative through which to conduct

---

1. Dietrich Bonhoeffer, *Letters and Papers from Prison* (trans. Reginald Fuller et al.; London: SCM, 1971), 193.

2. Eberhard Busch, *Karl Barth: His Life from Letters and Autobiographical Texts* (trans. John Bowden; London: SCM, 1976), 75, 105–6, 145, 212.

the investigation. This friendship changed the landscape of world theology. Here is compelling evidence of how friendship contributes directly to theological thought and faithful discipleship.

A RARE AND PRICELESS TREASURE

Bonhoeffer was twenty-nine and Bethge twenty-six years old when they met on the shores of the Baltic Sea near Zingst at the end of April 1935. Bethge was with a group of twenty-three candidates in training for ministry at one of the illegal seminaries established by the Old Prussian Union Church to replace those closed down by the Reich Church government. On the face of it, they appeared an unlikely pair. Bonhoeffer was Director of the seminary. He hailed from the intellectual aristocracy of Berlin and was confident, erudite, authoritative, and well connected. Bethge was of country origin, son of a Lutheran pastor, born in the little village of Warchau in the district of Magdeburg near Brandenburg, without, as he says, any preparation or ambition "beyond that of an honest community country pastor."[3] Ten years later, at the time of Bonhoeffer's execution on April 9, 1945, the two were firm friends whose intimate thoughts, expressed in the now famous *Letters and Papers from Prison*, were set to become the most transformative theological texts of the post-war period.

The full story of this friendship is yet to be told.[4] But one thing is clear. More than sixty years after his death, Bonhoeffer's thought remains a seemingly inexhaustible source of renewal for Christian life and thought across the world. A major reason for this is Eberhard Bethge. Without Bethge's devotion to the preservation, editing, publication, and continuous re-interpretation of his friend's writings, without his superb biography,[5] "we would not know or understand Bonhoeffer in the way

---

3. Christian Gremmels and Wolfgang Huber, eds., *Theologie und Freundschaft. Wechselwirkungen. Eberhard Bethge und Dietrich Bonhoeffer* (Gütersloh: Kaiser/ Gütersloher, 1994), 17.

4. Gremmels and Huber, eds., *Theologie und Freundschaft*, especially the chapters by Bethge, "Mein Freund Dietrich Bonhoeffer" and "Der Freund Dietrich Bonhoeffer und seine theologische Konzeption von Freundschaft," 11–50. See also Eberhard Bethge, *Friendship and Resistance: Essays on Dietrich Bonhoeffer* (Geneva: WCC; Grand Rapids: Eerdmans, 1995), and John W. de Gruchy, *Daring, Trusting Spirit: Bonhoeffer's Friend Eberhard Bethge* (Minneapolis: Fortress, 2005).

5. Eberhard Bethge, *Dietrich Bonhoeffer: Theologian, Christian, Contemporary* (trans. Eric Mosbacher et al.; London: Collins, 1970).

we do today."⁶ Friendship is the medium through which the voice of Bonhoeffer continues to speak.

Bethge can mediate Bonhoeffer's theology in death because he was an integral part of the conversation that formed the theology in life. The nature of the conversation between the friends is plain for all to see in the letters they exchanged during the time of Bonhoeffer's imprisonment. Nothing is off limits—nothing too trivial to be of interest, nothing too weighty to be a burden. Family, love, gifts, books, ideas, emotions, weather, war, daily life, fear, hope, death, friendship itself—nothing is left unexplored, *un-talked-about*. The correspondence reveals the unique character of this friendship and the harrowing circumstances in which it was played out. But part of its enduring fascination is that all of us can recognize here the twists, stops, starts, and repetitions of our own talk with close friends. If we wish to see how friendship shapes life and thought, there is no substitute for studying the concrete details of the correspondence itself. But Bonhoeffer sums up its general import in a striking passage from a letter to Bethge dated Christmas Day 1943.

> The mind's hunger for discussion is much more tormenting than the body's hunger for food, and there is no one but you with whom I can talk about some things and in one way. A few pregnant remarks are enough to touch on a wide range of questions and clear them up. This ability to keep on the same wavelength, to play to each other, took years to cultivate, not always without friction, and we must never lose it.⁷

For Bonhoeffer, constructive theological thought and enduring Christian discipleship arise from, or at least are enhanced by, talk with a specific person. Of course Bonhoeffer had many friends. But *this* friendship had particular characteristics won through a long period, not without struggle. Central to it was the capacity to facilitate imaginative thinking through a mutual, almost playful, exchange of ideas. All the classic Bonhoeffer themes—discipleship, community, religionless Christianity, world come of age, God at the center, not the margins, of life—are sifted through the give and take of talk. Bonhoeffer is clearly

---

6. De Gruchy, *Daring, Trusting Spirit*, xv. See also Werner Simpfendörfer, "'Er freut sich hoch über des Freundes Stimme'. Eberhard Bethge als Hermeneut," in Gremmels and Huber, eds., *Theologie und Freundschaft*, 51–88: "We owe the rich legacy of Dietrich Bonhoeffer exclusively to this friendship" (55).

7. Bonhoeffer, *Letters and Papers from Prison*, 177–78.

the primary force of articulation. But Bethge is not just an ear. He is an independent voice ("on the same wavelength"). As such, he is a catalyst that stimulates theological creativity.

Not only did Bethge's friendship contribute essentially to the formulation of Bonhoeffer's theological ideas and then to their dissemination to a wider world. The relationship also gave rise to Bonhoeffer's late and remarkable reflections on the nature of friendship—this "rarest and most priceless treasure"—and its theological significance.

A NECESSARY FREEDOM

Friendship is at best a minor theme in Bonhoeffer's early writings. Of course, he deals with personal relationships in *Sanctorum Communio*, *Life Together*, and *Ethics*,[8] but the focus at that time was mainly on the "brotherhood" [sic] of fellow believers in the church or on marriage and family ties. Where they rate a mention at all, friends tend to be discussed along with issues connected with family relations and obligations. Only in the late writings, especially the letters from prison after 1943, does friendship become a clear theme in its own right. This is no accident. At a time of threat, separated from family and loved ones, Bonhoeffer's relationship with friends, and particularly with Eberhard Bethge, became crucial for his sense of identity and well being. Bonhoeffer never had the opportunity to write an extended treatise on friendship in the classic style of an Aristotle, Cicero or Montaigne, although the influence of that tradition echoes in his thinking. His reflections tumble out in fragments, with tantalizing brevity and often in the midst of other matters of pressing concern. Yet, like so much of Bonhoeffer's later thought, taken together these unfinished jottings are deeply moving and ring true to that human togetherness that goes by the name of friendship.[9]

---

8. Dietrich Bonhoeffer, *Sanctorum Communio: A Dogmatic Inquiry into the Sociology of the Church* (trans. William Collins; London: Collins, 1967); *Life Together* (trans. John W. Doberstein; London: SCM, 1970); *Ethics* (trans. Neville Horton Smith; London: Collins/Fontana, 1963).

9. For the main sources of Bonhoeffer's concept of friendship, see Gremmels and Huber, eds., *Theologie und Freundschaft*, 30–32. I will be concerned mainly with the material in the letters.

What Friendship Is Not (Quite)

"It is by no means easy to classify friendship sociologically," Bonhoeffer remarks.[10] There are close relationships between human beings in various spheres of life that have friend-like characteristics but which, in his judgment, do not finally merit the name, for example, *kinship* (marriage and the family), *brother-/sisterhood* (shared faith in the life of the *sanctorum communio*), and *comradeship* (collegial connections in work or politics). These three kinds of relationship may well display elements that overlap with friendship proper—affection, loyalty, support and so on. However, "Marriage, work, state, and church all have their definite, divine mandate," he argues, which friendship does not.[11] They exist as discrete but connected spheres of sociality, based ultimately in the creative and redemptive action of God, through which society is propagated, sustained, ordered and addressed by the truth. As such, these relationships have sociologically supported forms, institutionally codified functions, and are largely determined by interests, aims and goals that have a public and even legal standing that pure friendship lacks—or rather transcends. Put in poetic terms:

> Not from the heavy soil,
> where blood and sex and oath
> rule in their hallowed might,
> where earth itself,
> guarding the primal consecrated order,
> avenges wantonness and madness—
> not from the heavy soil of earth,
> but from the spirit's choice and free desire,
> needing no oath or legal bond,
> is friend bestowed on friend.[12]

The "not" here is important. Approaching a description of friendship via comparison with friend-like relationships which are in the end *not* exactly friendships stands in a long tradition. Aristotle famously classified friends into three types, differentiated by what attracts the people concerned and binds them into the relationship.[13] He called

10. Bonhoeffer, *Letters and Papers from Prison*, 192.
11. Ibid.
12. Ibid., 388.
13. See Aristotle, *Nicomachean Ethics*, 1156a10–24; also Paul J. Wadell, *Friendship and the Moral Life* (Notre Dame: University of Notre Dame Press, 1989), 46–69.

these friendships of pleasure, friendships of usefulness or advantage, and friendships of character or goodness. The first two he regarded as friendship in a *secondary* sense; indeed, one gets the sense that Aristotle finally held such relationships to be friendships only in a diminished or analogous form. These relationships are determined by what can be derived from them by way of interest or advantage for the participants. They have an instrumental value. Only the third form is pure friendship—an end in itself. Friends rejoice in each other. The relationship of affection, trust and communication they depend upon brings their lives to greater fulfillment in shared goodness and deepening virtue. Life itself, not some activity or interest within it, is the point. We become who we are (or can be) in relation to the other who is friend.[14]

Bonhoeffer is more restrictive in his use of the term "friend" than Aristotle. Kinship, comradeship, brother-/sisterhood, in his conception, fit somewhere within Aristotle's categories of friendships of pleasure or advantage. Though he nowhere uses the term, something like Aristotle's "character friendship" is friendship proper for Bonhoeffer. And that has to do *not* with soil, blood, sex and oath, but with "the spirit's choice and free desire."

What Friendship Is

Bonhoeffer nowhere offers a definition of friendship after the well-known Ciceronian model.[15] This is partly because of the fragmentary nature of his reflections on the theme. But it also has to do with his increasing sense of the elusiveness of friendship in the field of human social connections. As we have seen, for Bonhoeffer friendship "cannot be compared with the treasures of the mandates [work, state, marriage, church], for in relation to them it is *sui generis*; it belongs to them as the cornflower belongs to the cornfield."[16] The cornflower is self-sown, not

---

14. For a wonderful contemporary discussion of friendship in these terms, see Graham Little, *Friendship: Being Ourselves with Others* (Melbourne: Scribe, 2000).

15. "For friendship is nothing else than an accord in all things, human and divine, conjoined with mutual goodwill and affection, and I am inclined to think that, with the exception of wisdom, no better thing has been given to man by the immortal gods" (Cicero, *Laelius on Friendship*, vi.20). I owe this reference to Janet Martin Soskice, "Friendship," in *Fields of Faith: Theology and Religious Studies for the Twenty-first Century* (ed. David F. Ford et al.; Cambridge: Cambridge University Press, 2005), 167, n.2.

16. Bonhoeffer, *Letters and Papers from Prison*, 193. Bonhoeffer develops the image of the cornflower in the poem, "The Friend," in ibid., 388–89.

deliberately planted; fragile, not supported by the main crop; unique, not belonging to the dominant group.

From a reading of the prison letters, one can easily list the qualities a friend must have. These include (in no special order) trust, understanding, commitment, love, honesty, self-sacrifice, courage, loyalty, forgiveness, support, counsel, common purposes, and open conversation. We probably all agree that without qualities like these, friendship either would not exist or could not survive. But many, if not all, of them can be found in the social context of the mandates, and so, according to Bonhoeffer, do not isolate the *sui generis* nature of the friend. I want therefore to look briefly at three other characteristics that Bonhoeffer stresses in his discussion: singularity, reciprocity, and freedom.

Singularity

Bonhoeffer never speaks, like Aristotle, of friendships of pleasure or advantage, still less of work friends, social friends, or family friends. There is a level of intimacy, personal trust and commitment in friendship as he conceives it that involves selection and particularity. Friendship is a bond that shies away from the plural toward the singular. In response to a letter of Bethge's, in which he wished his friend the blessing of "good, stimulating friends," Bonhoeffer replied:

> You wished me, among other things, good, stimulating friends. That is a good thing to wish, and today it is a great gift. But the human heart is created in such a way that it seeks and finds refuge in the singular rather than the plural. That is the claim, the limit and the richness of genuine human relationship, to the extent that it touches on the area of individuality and to the extent that it rests essentially on loyalty. There are individual relationships without loyalty and loyalty without individual relationships. Both are to be found in the plural. But together (which is seldom enough!) they seek the singular, and happy is he who "succeeds in this great luck."[17]

Repeatedly in the letters, Bonhoeffer makes reference to the fact that "there is no one but you" with whom he can speak candidly and with

---

17. The letter was written on Bonhoeffer's birthday in 1941. See Bethge, *Friendship and Resistance*, 87–88. The quotation at the end comes from Schiller's "Ode to Joy" used by Beethoven in the finale of the Ninth Symphony.

absolute trust.[18] No doubt this has much to do with the circumstances of the times. Resistance to Hitler was a dangerous and, for Bonhoeffer, lethal course of action in the end. Complete trustworthiness in the sharing of sensitive information was a requirement of survival. Understandably, friendships were restricted and entered into with some caution. But beyond the contingency of the times, deep friendship always retains the character of a singular relationship ("the human heart is created in such a way..."). The singularity arises from history. Friendship is a bond forged across time. The quality of the relationship is built up through a thousand meetings, wide-ranging talk, adventures shared, journeys made, burdens carried, joys celebrated, letters exchanged. The prison correspondence documents it all. Bonhoeffer recognizes this as both the "limit" and the "richness" of friendship. It is *limit* because only a select few can enter the inner circle in any one life. This implies exclusion of others. But it is *richness* also. In true friendship, one human soul is opened to another in a way that enables both to discover truth, to transform meaning, and to find the courage to live.

Reciprocity

Friendship is a two-way street. To be a friend is to have a friend and vice versa. It makes no sense to say, "I am *his* friend but he is not mine."[19] Mutuality between equals is strongly prized in all classical discussions of friends. Cicero speaks of "accord in all things ... conjoined with *mutual* goodwill and affection."[20] Goodwill and affection, along with most of the characteristics of friendship Bonhoeffer mentions such as loyalty, understanding, honesty, courage, etc., can conceivably be expressed by one person in relation to another without them necessarily being returned in kind. But where that is the case, whatever the relationship may be, it is not friendship.

Central to the mutuality of the Bonhoeffer/Bethge friendship is conversation, shared *talk*. The existence of the letters themselves is the greatest witness to this. But there is specific acknowledgement as well.

> [T]he work is giving me great pleasure. Only I wish I could talk it over with you every day; indeed, I miss that more than you

---

18. Bonhoeffer, *Letters and Papers from Prison*, 129, 130, 173, 177.
19. Soskice, "Friendship," 169.
20. Cicero, *Laelius on Friendship*, vi.20 (my emphasis). Cf. note 15 above.

think. I may often have originated our ideas, but the clarification of them was completely on your side. I only learnt in conversation with you whether an idea was any good or not. I long to read to you some of what I've written. Your comments on details are so much better than mine.[21]

Not only are the springs of intellectual life primed and purified in the mutuality of talk, but all of life is opened for deeper appreciation and reinterpretation. In weakness: "you are the only person who knows how often *accidie, tristitia*, with all its menacing consequences, has lain in wait for me." In renewal: "I know that we have shared spiritually, although not physically, in the gift of confession, absolution, and communion . . ." In joy: "a happy moment springing from the freedom of a lightsome, daring, trusting spirit, is a friend to a friend."[22]

But friendship is not all affirmation and accord. A friend is someone we don't always agree with or approve of. Bonhoeffer speaks of "the endurance tests of such a friendship"[23] and of the fact that "I have sometimes made life hard for you."[24] Honest mutuality cannot be otherwise. Friends fight hard at times to find a deeper accord.

Freedom

As Bonhoeffer and Bethge circled the idea of friendship, they gradually came to see freedom as the heart. On January 2, 1944, Bethge wrote to Bonhoeffer, again contrasting marriage and friendship. Marriage is "recognized outwardly," he argued, and even if it becomes unstable, the wider community "finds it the right thing that much should and must be undertaken for it." But "friendship—no matter how exclusive and how all-embracing it may be—has no *necessitas* . . ."[25] This sentence prompted Bonhoeffer's single most significant meditation on the subject of friendship, in his letter of January 23, 1944: "I very much agree with what you say in this connection about friendship which, in contrast to marriage and kinship, has no generally recognized rights, and therefore depends entirely on its own inherent quality."

21. Bonhoeffer, *Letters and Papers from Prison*, 130; also 160.
22. Ibid., 129, 388.
23. Quoted by de Gruchy, *Daring, Trusting Spirit*, 62, from a letter to Bethge, February 1, 1941, in Bonhoeffer, *Werke*, Vol. 16 (Gütersloh: Kaiser/Gütersloher, 1996), 125.
24. Bonhoeffer, *Letters and Papers from Prison*, 129.
25. Ibid., 181.

Then, musing whether friendship might be placed as a sub-category of culture and education, he goes on:

> They belong, not to the sphere of obedience, but to the broad area of freedom, which surrounds all three spheres of the divine mandates. The man who is ignorant of this area of freedom may be a good father, citizen, and worker, indeed even a Christian; but I doubt whether he is a complete man and therefore a Christian in the widest sense of the term ... Who is there, for instance, in our times, who can devote himself with an easy mind to music, friendship, games, or happiness? Surely not the "ethical" man, but only the Christian. Just because friendship belongs to this sphere of freedom ("of the Christian man"?!), it must be confidently defended against all disapproving frowns of "ethical" existences, though without claiming for it the *necessitas* of a divine decree, but only the *necessitas* of *freedom*.[26]

On any measure, this is a remarkable statement. Because friendship is in essence an expression of freedom, it is *sui generis*, depending only on its "own inherent quality." For this reason it is likely to be viewed with suspicion, especially in situations of oppressive political control. To flourish it must be "defended" against the "disapproving frowns of 'ethical' existences," that is, against those who understand life as defined by conformity ("obedience") to the relational requirements of the mandates of work, state, and family. Bonhoeffer does not disparage these latter spheres. He sees them as God-given, if often distorted by sin. The startling thing is his contention that human life is not fulfilled within these spheres *alone*. Indeed, it can be stifled by them. One can be a good parent, citizen, worker, even Christian, but not be a "complete man." Full human dignity, he hints, can only be completed in the context of free friendship.

This argument leads Bonhoeffer to the paradox of friendship as "the *necessitas* of *freedom*." It is not altogether clear what this means. Friendship, it seems, does not have the *necessitas* of a divine decree, in the way the other mandates do. Presumably that means one is not *required* by God to be or have friends of this kind. On the other hand, Bonhoeffer seems to suggest that Christian life is fulfilled in the sphere of freedom. So is friendship the freedom of the "'Christian man'?!" (exclamation and question marks) or not? We shall come back to that issue in the next

---

26. Ibid., 192–93.

section. And if friendship is a *necessitas*, what kind of necessity is it? There seems to be only one answer. Friendship is a necessary element of the *practical* realization of human potential, or in theological terms, for the living out of the *imago Dei*. Friendship puts humanity within our reach, so to speak. The American philosopher Walter Davis says that "the self is not a substance one unearths by peeling away layers until one gets to the core, but an integrity one struggles to bring into existence."[27] That's close to it. Friendship is the struggle to become ourselves with others. Its necessity is that we cannot fully become ourselves without the kind of other that Bonhoeffer calls friend. No Bonhoeffer as we know him without Bethge. No Bethge without Bonhoeffer. The friendship is intrinsic to the persons (i.e., necessary), yet there is no decree (*necessitas*) which mandates that these two should be to each other as they are.

FRIENDSHIP WITH GOD

How then does friendship relate to the life of faith in God? Bonhoeffer clearly regarded this as an important question. But time ran out before he could address it in any systematic way. We are left again with hints and pointers, not a finished argument. That the issue is not straightforward is evident in the ambivalence, even confusion, expressed in the great letter discussed above. Friendship is not *heilsnotwendig* (necessary for salvation).[28] One can be a Christian yet be "ignorant of this area of freedom." On the other hand, friendship is closely related to becoming truly human and therefore is "Christian in the widest sense."

The tension between friendship and faith has a long history. In scripture Abraham and Moses are called "friends of God" (2 Chr 20:7; Jas 2:23; Exod 33:11). The Gospel of Luke is addressed to the "most excellent Theophilus" (= "friend of God," Luke 1:3). Many commentators regard this as more than the name of an individual. The Gospel is intended for the "friends of God," that is, for the followers of Jesus.[29] The major text is Jesus' word to the disciples: "I do not call you servants any longer,

---

27. Walter A. Davis, *Inwardness and Existence: Subjectivity in/and Hegel, Heidegger, Marx, and Freud* (Madison: University of Wisconsin Press, 1989), 105. See further my foreword in Little, *Friendship: Being Ourselves with Others*, x–xi.

28. See Sabine Bobert-Stürtzel, "Liebt ein Freund mehr als ein Bruder?" in Gremmels and Huber, eds., *Theologie und Freundschaft*, 100.

29. See Mikeal C. Parsons, *Luke: Storyteller, Interpreter, Evangelist* (Peabody: Hendrickson, 2006), 55–56.

because the servant does not know what the master is doing; but I have called you friends, because I have made known to you everything that I have heard from my Father" (John 15:15; also 15:12–17). Thus there is solid, if limited, biblical ground for a positive affirmation of friendship in human dealings with God.

On the other hand, the love expressed in friendship (*philia*) seems to have characteristics that place it in tension with the love of God manifest in Jesus Christ (*agape*). Take Bonhoeffer's three main marks of the friend. *Singularity* in friendship narrows the field of love from the many to the few. But the love of God is universal and inclusive. Jesus' parable of the Good Samaritan, offered in response to a question about the reach of neighbor-love, leaves no doubt that this love is to be extended to *any* person in need, even one unknown to us (Luke 10:25–37). *Reciprocity* appears to leave us in the comfort zone of like-minded people who play a zero-sum game of give and take between themselves. If this is not narcissism, as Kierkegaard argued, at least it seems to turn on receiving as much as we give.[30] How can this be squared with the words of Jesus: "For if you love those who love you, what reward do you have" (Matt 5:46)? God's love for the world is not solely those who love in return, but for those who do not. *Agape* reaches to the enemy (Matt 5:43–44). And according to Bonhoeffer, *freedom* lies "outside the sphere of obedience." But this seems to fly in the face of Jesus' condition: "You are my friends if you do what I command you" (John 15:14). Costly discipleship rather than free self-fulfillment is the meaning of faith. "If any want to become my followers, let them deny themselves and take up their cross and follow me" (Mark 8:34).[31]

What are we to make of this? No doubt some friendships can be singular to the point of destructive exclusion of others, mutual to the point of calculating benefits, and free to the point of indulgent self-centeredness. Perhaps all friendships at some moments or in some respects are affected by these tendencies. But does this come anywhere near describing the best friendships that we know or at least aspire to?

---

30. "Christian love teaches love of all men. Just as decidedly as erotic love strains in the direction of the one and only beloved, just as decidedly and powerfully does Christian love press in the opposite direction" (Søren Kierkegaard, *Works of Love* [trans. Howard and Edna Hong; New York: Harper & Row, 1964], 58).

31. For discussion of the tension between friendship love and God's love, see Wadell, *Friendship and the Moral Life*, esp. chapters 4–5; and Gilbert C. Meilaender, *Friendship: A Study in Theological Ethics* (Notre Dame: University of Notre Dame Press, 1981).

Do we not feel it to be a distortion of true friendship, not its essence? Certainly such an account is remote from the nature and consequences of the Bonhoeffer/Bethge friendship. Take this description:

> You need a friend. . . . If you want to have a friend and to be a friend yourself, you must be able to *sacrifice*; . . . you must be able to *forgive*, . . . you must be able to *love* the friend, as he is, with all his weaknesses, *bear* and support him through your love; so you must be able to be *faithful*. . . . If you want to have a friend, then you must be able to *pray for* him, set his life with yours before the eyes of God and ask his help for your *friendship*, for the friend needs that. Only if your *friendship has its ground in God*, call it "friendship." You must be able to *trust* your friend, you must be able to entrust yourself completely to him, in happy and [in] difficult times. He will share in your happiness and your pain, he will rejoice with you and will help you carry the burden that is hard for you. One lives life with the other, but you both should live your lives in God; *then you are* friends.[32]

Here Bonhoeffer interprets friendship *theologically* as grounded and lived in God. The difference between friendship per se and the brother-/sisterhood relationship in Christ was never satisfactorily clarified by Bonhoeffer. In the prison letters, as we have seen, he does not wish to subsume friendship under specific Christian categories. For the most part, the description he gives there can easily apply to people without theological commitment. However, when the particular friends share faith in God as the deepest common ground of their humanity, as did Bethge and Bonhoeffer, inevitably their relationship will be interpreted within the narrative of the gospel, and hence in relation to the creative and redemptive action of God. These words, therefore, are *primarily* for those to whom faith in God and discipleship of Christ are important. Yet Bonhoeffer is clear—a *theological* reading of friendship remains a reading of *friendship*.

All true friendship, but especially friendship grounded in God, is *self-transcending*. Singular it may be, but not locked up within itself. Friendship requires that friends live with and for the other. In the con-

---

32. Quoted by Bobert-Stürtzel, "Liebt ein Freund mehr als ein Bruder?" in Gremmels and Huber, eds., *Theologie und Freundschaft*, 103 (my translation; italics original). The original is found in Dietrich Bonhoeffer, *Werke*, Vol. 10, 543–44. This is a piece written in 1928. It signals much of what was to come later in the prison letters. (I am grateful to my friend Ursel Sturm for her help with the German texts used in this essay.)

text of faith, friendship is set "before the eyes of God." Those eyes behold the singular, but also rest upon the whole created order. The truth of friendship—the celebration of shared love—when grounded in God is therefore opened beyond the limits of the particular relationship toward the universal cause of God's love for the world. The Bonhoeffer/Bethge friendship exemplifies this. However singular at the center, its edges now reach to the ends of the world. It is precisely the singular friend, Eberhard Bethge, who bears testimony that Dietrich Bonhoeffer's "life and work overstepped the private sphere and no longer belonged only to those close to him."[33] In the theological context, singularity in friendship is always *singularity in self-transcendence* toward the other without limit.

All true friendship, but especially friendship grounded in God, is a *giving away* of the self. Reciprocal it may be, but not calculating. The qualities of a friend listed here—sacrifice, forgiveness, love, faithfulness, prayer, trust, carrying of burdens—without exception require the *self-giving* of the friend for the good of the other. Within friendship this self-giving may well be reciprocal, but reciprocity is the consequence, not the motivation, of the giving. The resemblance of this description of a friend to the New Testament depiction of the life of the disciple, indeed, the life of Christ himself, is unmistakable.[34] But the point is that, with the exception of the mention of prayer, all the other characteristics belong naturally to *any* genuine friendship. In these particular words, Bonhoeffer may well be reading friendship through the lens of Christian discipleship. But the reverse is also true. Faith in God can be read through the lens of friendship. Is it an accident that Bonhoeffer gave his life in resisting violence against many (unknown) others who had no chance to reciprocate, and was supported in this by the singular and reciprocal Christian friendship with Bethge? In the theological context, the reciprocity of friendship is fulfilled in the *giving away of the self* for the good of the other. "For those who want to save their life will lose it, and those who lose their life for my sake will find it" (Matt 16:25).

All true friendship, but especially friendship grounded in God, is *bound by love*. Free it may be, but not with the liberty of an unfettered market economy that urges, "get what you want, not what you need." In his description, Bonhoeffer stresses the imperatives belonging to friend-

---

33. Bethge, *Dietrich Bonhoeffer*, xxi.

34. Following Bonhoeffer's outline, see, for example, Luke 10:25–37; Matt 18:21–22; Mark 12:30–31; John 15:13; John 13:34; 2 Thess 1:11; Jas 5:16; Gal 6:2.

ship. To be a friend, you *must* be able to love, *must* be able to forgive, *must* be able to be faithful, and so on. These "musts" are not rules imposed externally on the freedom of a friend; they are the conditions under which that peculiar human freedom which goes by the name of friendship can arise and flourish. Again the parallel with the New Testament is striking. Jesus' words "You are my friends if you do what I command you" are no arbitrary imposition of a heterogeneous authority. The commands describe the character of life that leads to human friendship with God. They depict the life of Christ and, by extension, the life of the disciple in relation to Christ.

To see friendship through the eyes of God, therefore, is not to see something that is otherwise not present. It is to see into the nature of friendship through the window of God (in whom friendship is grounded) *and* into the nature of God through the window of friendship (which echoes the life of God). For this reason, Bonhoeffer was prepared to call friendship (and other aspects of human communion) "holy." Friendship at its best anticipates in time the holiness and communion of the eschatological kingdom of God.

> If wills have joined together for the sake of their joining, if a community has been affirmed, irrespective of rational purposive tendencies, then the intentionality in these acts reaches to the limits of time, i.e., to the limits of history, to God: it is "from God to God." Here is the entire "holiness" of human life in community, the relation with God which is found in friendship as in marriage and the life of a people, and thus also the indissolubility of all these structures of life.[35]

Augustine regarded particular human friendship (*philia*) as a school in and through which God draws us toward a love that, like God's own (*agape*), is universal in scope and inclusive in depth. Friendship is a sign and a call—a sacrament we might say—of the kingdom that is to come in God's fulfillment of time. Bonhoeffer does not engage Augustine in this regard. But their visions of friendship in God and with God are close.[36]

---

35. Bonhoeffer, *Sanctorum Communio*, 62, also 67.

36. See Marie Aquinas McNamara, *Friendship in Saint Augustine* (Fribourg: The University Press, 1958), esp. chapter 4; also Meilaender, *Friendship*, 16–24.

FRIENDSHIP IN GOD

Bonhoeffer's reflections on a theology of friendship stop here. Theologically, this "priceless treasure" grounds in God and derives its qualities from God; lives in God and reflects the life which is God; and ends in God, in the universal kingdom of mutual love which is God's destiny for creation. All this is bold enough. Yet it is tantalizing to wonder if we can take it a step further. Does friendship give us a framework within which to interpret the nature of God? Can we risk the assertion that there is *in* God something akin to friendship, or even speak of friendship which *is* God?

In a recent essay, Christoph Schwöbel outlines what he calls "a theological ontology of communicative relations." In it he attempts to trace the theological implications of *conversation* as a foundational expression of being in relationship.[37] Given the central importance of conversation in Bonhoeffer's interpretation of friendship, this presents an intriguing possibility. We cannot follow Schwöbel in detail here. But it is worth noting his broad approach. The argument is an exegesis of the place the Word of God holds in the narrative of scripture, and it moves in four steps. The first three are as follows:

1. Christian theology has the character of conversation.

2. This theology roots in the Christian life, which is "based in the practice of faith as an ongoing conversation about God and with God."

3. The conversation with and about God in turn grounds in the fact that "God engages in conversation with his creation, from creation until the consummation of God's conversations with his creation in the Kingdom of God."[38]

All this harmonizes well enough with Bonhoeffer's theological interpretation of communicating friendship, but the fourth step in the argument presents the real challenge. Schwöbel works from Karl Rahner's famous theological axiom that the economic Trinity is the immanent

---

37. Christoph Schwöbel, "God as Conversation: Reflections on a Theological Ontology of Communicative Relations," in *Theology and Conversation: Towards a Relational Theology* (ed. Jacques Haers and P. De Mey; BETL 172; Leuven: Peeters, 2003), 43–67.

38. Schwöbel, "God as Conversation," 45.

Trinity and vice versa.[39] Briefly stated, this means that the being and action of God in relation to the world (the economic Trinity) are the *self-manifestation* of God's being and action in relation to Godself (the immanent Trinity). In other words, what God is in God's revelation is what God is in Godself. Does this axiom hold for a theology of conversation? Does the relationship between the triune God and creation, interpreted as conversation, apply also to the nature of God as God, that is, to the relationship between Father, Son and Holy Spirit? "Is God only *in* conversation, or *is* God also conversation?"[40] The whole thrust of Schwöbel's essay drives toward an affirmative answer: "God relates to humanity in the way in which God is eternally in relation. God is *in* conversation with creation, because God is *as* conversation."[41] In short, the differentiated identity and ultimate unity of the three persons (*treis hypostaseis*) in the Trinity is constituted by their *conversational* relations.

But what *kind* of conversation is this Trinitarian exchange? Schwöbel nowhere uses the idea of friendship to answer this question, but he comes close, particularly in his discussion of mutuality in inter-Trinitarian relations.[42] But why not? If, as Bonhoeffer maintains, friendship is a constitutive human relation rooted in the being of God; and if friendship, so understood, can be a valid model of God's fundamental dealings with the world; and if God in the incarnation enters into close personal relations with human beings and befriends them ("I have called you friends") by sharing openly with them ("everything that I have heard from my Father"); is it not possible, in keeping with Rahner's axiom, to affirm that friendship as a singular, reciprocal, free relationship, bound by love, illustrates something of the essential nature of God in God's own being? In other words, the everlasting community of love we call the Trinity is an everlasting *community of friendship*, "where love offered is love wholly received and wholly returned, where perfect mutuality of love between Father and Son is the Spirit of Love."[43]

There are obvious weaknesses in this line of thought. Janet Martin Soskice argues that while Christians rightly speak of love flowing between

---

39. Karl Rahner, *The Trinity* (trans. Joseph Donceel; Tunbridge Wells, UK: Burns & Oates, 1970), 22.

40. Schwöbel, "God as Conversation," 62.

41. Ibid., 63.

42. Schwöbel, "God as Conversation," 64–65.

43. Wadell, *Friendship and the Moral Life*, 122.

the three "persons" of the Trinity, it is unwise to imply that these three are friends to each other, for that "would be a sentiment dangerously near to tritheism." However, she is prepared to concede that one may be able to say "'the Trinity is friendship' much as one says 'God is love.'"[44] But what is friendship without friends who participate in it? What is conversation without conversation partners who speak to each other?

Trinitarian thinking swings precariously between an emphasis on the oneness of God, to the detriment of genuine differentiation of the "persons" in the Godhead (modalism), and the opposite, a stress on the differentiation of the "persons," which undermines the essential unity of God (tritheism). Friendship as a model clearly risks the second of these dangers. But it nicely avoids the first. There is no space to explore this further. Suffice it to say the idea invites thought. Friendship as Bonhoeffer describes it, used as a hermeneutical resource in trinitarian thinking, *might* do something to counter the dangers of modalism and subordinationism that lurk in even so great a discussion of the theme as Karl Barth's in the volume with which this essay began. That would be a significant contribution. But that is for another day.

Meantime, in a world of religious violence, I find myself deeply grateful for the support and love of friends, and am happy to learn what is to be learned of God from a theological exploration of the meaning of friendship. I wonder, would the German theologian Dietrich Bonhoeffer agree with the words of the Italian philosopher Gianni Vattimo? "In my view, this norm—charity—which is destined to remain even when faith and hope will no longer be necessary, when the kingdom of God will be fully realized, justifies completely the preference for a 'friendly' conception of God and of the sense of religion. If this is an excess of tenderness, then it is God who has given us an example of it."[45]

---

44. Soskice, "Friendship," 170.

45. Gianni Vattimo, *Belief* (trans. Luca D'Isanto and David Webb; Stanford: Stanford University Press, 1999), 98.

2

Out of Bounds

Christian Spirituality in a World of Differences[1]

Elizabeth Green

> Turning and turning in the widening gyre
> The falcon cannot hear the falconer;
> Things fall apart; the centre cannot hold;
> Mere anarchy is loosed upon the world,
> The blood-dimmed tide is loosed, and everywhere
> The ceremony of innocence is drowned....[2]

THUS FROM HIS OBSERVATION post in Ireland did William Butler Yeats describe with poetic, indeed, prophetic insight the dawn of the twentieth century—a century that saw the definitive demise of the center—the so-called universal subject. From time almost immemorial, the privileged white male had occupied the limelight; the show had gone on socially, economically, politically, and symbolically exclusively around him. Now, as the various emancipation movements of modernity began to bear their fruit, the center could no longer hold as colonized peoples, workers, and people of all colors jostled, with various degrees of success, for a place at center stage. When women, too, joined in the fray, the universal subject was unable to hide his own gendered

---

1. The central thesis of this essay was worked out, albeit in different form, in the Thomas Burns Memorial Lectures, which I was invited to give at the University of Otago, New Zealand, in 2002 with the title "The God Outside." I am grateful to the University of Otago for this opportunity, as well as for the generous hospitality I received throughout New Zealand on this occasion. An extended form of this essay has been published in Italian: *Il Dio sconfinato. Una teologia per donne e uomini* (Torino: Claudiana, 2007).

2. W. B. Yeats, "The Second Coming" (1919), included in *Michael Robartes and the Dancer* (Churchtown, Dundrum, Ireland: Cuala, 1920).

particularity, and the maleness of his supposed neutrality was unmasked. All this led General Secretary of the WCC, W. A. Visser't Hooft, to consider modernity in terms of the history of emancipation from the Father as absolute subject.[3] In fact, many and diverse thinkers have come to the conclusion that fatherhood itself is inscribed in the very fabric of Western thought and that the authority enjoyed by the privileged white male is grounded in the absolute authority of the Father God. As Mary Daly forcefully and famously stated, "if God is male, then the male is God."[4] It is hardly surprising, then, as Elisabeth Schüssler Fiorenza has admirably documented, that Christianity, in order to survive, should use the same language as patriarchy, thus legitimating a social and symbolic order revolving around the absolute male subject.[5] The question must be asked, however, whether the God to whom Christianity seeks to bear witness actually does occupy center stage. Maybe the falcon cannot hear the falconer because it has its ear cocked in the wrong direction. In other words, where is God?

OUT OF BOUNDS: MIRIAM AND JESUS

Let us start to answer that question by turning to an Exodus story that deals precisely with the location of divine authority. Not a great deal is known about Miriam. While parts of the tradition identify her as the sister of Moses and others identify her as a prophetess, the prophet Micah recognizes her as being sent by God, together with Moses and Aaron, to lead Israel out from Egypt (Mic 6:4). At a certain juncture in the story, however, Miriam and Aaron are fed up with Moses hogging the limelight and with the privileged, sacred, and paternal position he is accorded: "Has the Lord indeed spoken only through Moses? Has he not spoken through us also?" they complain (Num 12:2). Although both Aaron and Miriam voice their criticism, only Miriam is punished, stricken by leprosy and shut outside the camp for seven days. In her telling comment, Claudia Camp affirms that while male Aaron is clean whatever he does—

---

3. W. A. Visser't Hooft, *The Fatherhood of God in an Age of Emancipation* (Geneva: WCC, 1982), 97.

4. Mary Daly, *Beyond God the Father: Toward a Philosophy of Women's Liberation* (Boston: Beacon, 1973), 19.

5. Elisabeth Schüssler Fiorenza, *In Memory of Her* (London: SCM, 1983); and *Jesus: Miriam's Child, Sophia's Prophet* (New York: Continuum, 1994).

"his status is ascribed not achieved"[6]—Miriam's defilement with leprosy and her subsequent exclusion serve only to reveal her irrevocable female difference. What interests us about this story is that while the priestly world-view here represented consisted of a series of concentric circles, at the center of which stood the tent of meeting, the spatial imagery evoked in this episode is actually far more ambiguous. Occasionally, in fact, the text displaces the tent where God met with Israel from center-stage to outside the camp (Num 11:26–30; 12:4). Furthermore, Miriam is the only character who occupies all three locations—tent, camp, and outside the camp. Yet, if the tent of meeting is situated outside the camp, then Miriam actually shares these locations with Yahweh himself. This leads Claudia Camp to conclude: "There remains a textual dialectic about where to locate the presence of Yahweh, in the center or on/outside the limen, that is not far removed from a similar tension about where women belong in Israel." We are thus faced with the possibility that Miriam is identified "with the God whose presence drifts back and forth across the boundaries, calling them into question."[7]

Miriam cast out from the camp recalls a far more famous figure who likewise bore his punishment outside the city walls. As the letter to the Hebrews puts it, "So Jesus also suffered outside the gate," and continues: "Therefore let us go forth to him outside the camp" (Heb 13:13). Crucifixion was not only performed outside the walls of the city but was also the form of death reserved for those on the very edges of the social order, right at the bottom of the imperial hierarchy. Since Jesus launched a full-scale critique of the religious and political power of the center and cast in his lot with those on the outside, it is hardly surprising that he should be expelled from the city as threatening its very integrity. That Jesus did in fact follow the trajectory from center to margin, crossing boundaries and calling them into question, is also powerfully suggested by the hymn Paul quotes in his letter to the Philippians (2:6–11). Here we read that "Christ Jesus, though he was in the form of God, did not count equality with God a thing to be grasped, but emptied himself, taking the form of a servant, being born in human likeness. And being found in human form, he humbled himself and became obedient to death, even death on the cross." In this christological affirmation we find at least

---

6. Claudia V. Camp, *Wise, Strange and Holy: The Strange Woman and the Making of the Bible* (JSOTSup 320; Sheffield: Sheffield Academic, 2000), 231.

7. Camp, *Wise, Strange and Holy*, 251.

three boundaries crossed by Jesus. The first is that rather strong dividing line between the human and the divine. Despite the barriers that theology was subsequently to erect between God and humanity (symbolized, interestingly enough, as female), here we find spirit becoming body, the Word (as the Gospel of John puts it) becoming flesh. The second boundary to be transgressed is that between master and servant. Here Jesus embodies the servanthood ideal—the master who defines importance, power, and prestige not in terms of mastery and dominion but as service to one's fellow human being. The third boundary to be crossed is that between life and death. Here not only does the source of life enter into death, assuming its full force, but, as Paul underlines, it is the death of the cross, that is, the death shared by the disinherited and castoffs of humanity.

The story does not end there, for the text continues: "Therefore God has highly exalted him and bestowed on him the name which is above every other name, that at the name of Jesus every tongue shall bow, in heaven on earth and under the earth, and every tongue confess that Jesus Christ is Lord, to the glory of God the Father." One might well lament the imperial language in which this part of the text is couched. What I suggest, however, is that in Jesus God followed the trajectory foreshadowed by Miriam, abandoning the center, crossing boundaries, continually going out of bounds to die outside the camp so that no one can claim the center exclusively for oneself. In Jesus, God actually redefines Lordship so that with the Christ the whole of humanity—in all its shapes and sizes and its many and varied hues—is exalted and the whole stage occupied. What God effectively does in Jesus, then, is to step outside the patriarchal order so that Rosemary Ruether is able to read the Jesus-story in terms of the emptying or *kenosis* of patriarchy.[8] Indeed, if we look at the text closely, we find that the whole boundary-crossing dynamic is rooted in the fact that Jesus "emptied himself."

Such emptying has given churchmen and theologians down through the centuries much food for thought as they have discussed exactly what Jesus emptied himself of, and how much and to what degree, afraid, perhaps, that divinity itself might be slipping through their fingers! Unlike other religious traditions such as Buddhism, Christian theology makes little room for emptiness or vacuity. (A different tale would be told, of course, concerning Christian mysticism.) For example,

---

8. Rosemary Radford Ruether, *Sexism and God-Talk* (London: SCM, 1983).

when Jürgen Moltmann in his doctrine of creation suggestively builds on Isaac Luria's idea of *zimsum* or God's self-limitation, he is unable to free himself of the negative connotations of nothingness as a God-forsaken space whose annihilating character is already implied.[9] Yet, coming back to the Philippians text, we find that here we have not so much a metaphysical description of Godhood as a way of being in the world, which we are invited to emulate: "Do nothing from selfishness or conceit, but in humility count others better than yourselves. Let each of you look not only to his own interests but to the interests of others. Have this mind among yourselves, which you have in Christ Jesus, who though he was in the form of God . . ." (2:3–6). In other words, the self-emptying of Jesus is a model for our own self-emptying. Paul is not only talking about the trajectory followed by God in Jesus but also about the sort of trajectory we are invited to follow, which, it would seem, leads us out from the center and across boundaries and out of bounds to celebrate difference.

THE QUEST FOR LESS: MORE MARYS

What might this mean in terms of our spiritual practice? How can we as Christians help to build the *ecumene*, a world that is home to everybody and in which women and men of different faiths, of different colors, of different cultures, of different sexual orientations live together in peace and harmony and justice? What attitude might be helpful for us to cultivate? What model does God's self-emptying in Jesus imply? To answer these questions, let us seek aid from a well known gospel story: the story of the rich man who approaches Jesus with a question: "What must I do to inherit eternal life?" After having assured himself that the man knows and has indeed observed the commandments, Jesus informs him that he is lacking one thing: "Go, sell what you have, and give to the poor, and you will have treasure in heaven; and come, follow me" (Mark 10:21). Jesus' reply, "You lack one thing," is truly strange because this man lacked absolutely nothing. He was undoubtedly a respected member of both society and the religious community, living an upright life. Furthermore, he had everything in terms of economic security that money could buy "for he had great possessions." What did this man lack? He lacked a lack! His life was decidedly too full; he needed to make space in his life; he

---

9. Jürgen Moltmann, *God in Creation: An Ecological Doctrine of Creation* (trans. Margaret Kohl; London: SCM, 1985), 87.

needed to experience emptiness. As in Jesus' case, "emptying himself" is the premise on which the rest of his spiritual journey was to be based, and the first thing he needed to get rid of were his things, objects, possessions, in short, his wealth. While the scriptures certainly condemn the accumulation of wealth, always at the expense of others, here we are faced not so much with an ethical demand as an invitation to an attitude—that of letting go, of making space, of welcoming nothingness into our life. In fact, the rich man's possessions were not so much the problem as his grasping after them ("At this saying his countenance fell, and he went away sorrowful"), the reverse of Jesus' beginning his "pilgrimage" by not grasping after godhood. Christians such as Anthony de Mello who have lived alongside other spiritual traditions and interacted with them, stress the importance of such *not grasping*, in terms of letting go of precisely those things we hold most dear, be they possessions or affections or even convictions and ideas about God![10] Happiness ("eternal life") is not to be found by grasping after things but by precisely the opposite—letting go. The gospel paradox is this: plenty is created by lack!

According to the Buddhist tradition, the spiritual journey is embarked upon by giving one's own rooms a thorough house-cleaning. First of all, the rooms have to be emptied, and only then can they be furnished with what proves to be necessary. But emptiness is not created solely by ridding ourselves of attachments to houses or friends, which we erroneously assume will guarantee our happiness; we need to free ouselves of other things, too. "What must I do to inherit eternal life?" is a question put more than once to Jesus. The wealthy man is convinced that eternal life can be inherited by *doing*. There is no doubt that Christianity has placed great emphasis—ever since the first human creature was placed in the garden to tend it—on *doing*, creating, working, producing. "Works," in fact, have played a central rôle in Christian self-understanding, either as a way of assuring salvation (in Catholicism) or as proof of its assurance (in Protestantism). This insistence on humanity as *homo faber* has led to a critique of Christianity for having promoted in the West a world-view conducive to technical developments, with dire ecological consequences. Even now, as we are increasingly aware of the worldwide ecological disaster, some scientists think the crisis can be solved by *more*, not less, *doing*, the so-called technological fix. What, however, if we were

---

10. Anthony de Mello, *Call to Love: Meditations* (Anand, India: Gujarat Sahitya Prakash, 1991).

to free ourselves of our constant activity, of our need to fill our time (and our children's) with ceaseless activity? What if we were to heed the words of the psalmist: "Be still and know that I am God" (Ps 46:10)?

The Anglican theologian John Macquarrie likes to think of the creator God not so much as *doing* but as *being*, not so much as *creating* as *letting be*.[11] Indeed, as Moltmann has rightly stressed, after the six days of creation God "rested on the seventh day from all his work that he had done" (Gen 2:1). On the seventh day, the whole creation just *was*, existing in all its stillness before God. The Sabbath tradition, then, may help us workaholics find a way of balancing work with rest, activity with passivity. In fact, the Sabbath laws not only consider rest as an intrinsic part of God's creation, enabling women and men to live in harmony with the cosmos, but also as an antidote to a world (Egypt) built on economic exploitation. In the society that God is bringing into being, nobody is overworked so that a small minority may rest perpetually; the Sabbath laws apply to all social classes. Furthermore, they are extended to domestic animals and the land itself. What happens during the Sabbath year when the land is allowed to lie fallow? Does Israel starve? Not at all! Because the earth is allowed to rest, it actually becomes more fertile. Paradoxically, being still produces flourishing; doing nothing actually reveals itself to be highly productive. "Sitting quietly, doing nothing, spring comes and the grass grows." Although this is a Buddhist saying, it calls to mind a little parable of Jesus in Mark's Gospel in which a man plants a seed that sprouts and bears fruit despite the fact that the man does absolutely nothing to ensure its growth. On the contrary, "he sleeps and rises" and the seed grows "he knows not how" (Mark 4:27–28).

We are in the process of doing some thorough spring-cleaning. We have stopped grasping at our goods, and we are beginning to let go of our ceaseless activity. Instead of trying to fill or flee the void, we are actually making it our home. Yet we still need to empty ourselves of something else—the words which fill our lives, springing out at us from billboards, screaming at us from the television, cavorting across our computer screens, residing inside our very heads! It hardly needs to be said that Christianity is a religion of the Word. Yet instead of enfleshing that Word in our lives, we (and some more than others) have thought that the Word, rather than becoming body, should become other words in a not-so-

---

11. John Macquarrie, *Principles of Christian Theology* (Library of Philosophy and Theology; London: SCM, 1966), 225.

merry merry-go-round of ceaseless repetition. And if we just shut up? If making friends with emptiness means befriending silence? Whereas the Oriental tradition has much to say about silence (!), Christianity has definitely preferred to think in terms of listening. It's not hard to see how they are two sides of the same coin; one can hardly *hear* if one is talking all the time. For Judaism, the Decalogue itself is preceded by the divine imperative: "Hear, O Israel" (Deut 5:1), which might well be the most important commandment of all.

The story of Mary and Martha (Luke 10:38–42) illustrates these last two principles rather well. Martha is definitely very busy, fulfilling society's expectations of a woman's place: "distracted with much serving." She is also getting extremely frustrated and, rather than directing her frustration towards its source (Mary), she turns to Jesus: "Lord, do you not care that my sister has left me to serve alone? Tell her then to help me." Martha is busy doing and cannot abide the fact that Mary has freed herself of society's constraints and has *chosen* to do nothing. Mary, in fact, is doing nothing except sitting, listening, and remaining in silence. *She*, says Jesus, has chosen the "good portion." Mary, in fact, would make a good candidate for Virginia Woolf's "Society of Strangers," women who simply decide to opt out of male-centered society with its processions, possessions, power-games, and war. Not allowing one's own power to be stolen for ends ultimately hostile to a multicoloured humanity turns out to be life-saving in more ways than one; maybe the falcon cannot hear the falconer because it is talking too much! Christianity, then, has much to learn from Eastern practices of meditation in which one simply sits in silence, listens, and waits. For in silence God speaks, and out of silence the Word is born.

Had another Mary been debating, discussing, arguing politics or theology, engaging in "erudite conversation" or merely chattering away, she certainly would not have heard the angel. Despite visual representations of the Annunciation painted by artists down the centuries, Mary, of course, never actually sees the angel. The dialogic nature of the whole scene is emphasized so that her response depends first and foremost on her ability to hear: "Let it be to me according to your word" (Luke 1:38). If we think that such silent hearing will never get us anywhere, let us remember that the reception of the angelic voice proves to be extremely fertile and gives rise to a new embodied human life, which on entering the world changes it in concrete ways: "he has put down the mighty from their thrones and exalted those of low degree; he has filled the hungry with good things, and the rich he has sent empty away" (Luke 2:52–53).

BOUNDARY-CROSSING: JESUS ONCE MORE

"The centre cannot hold." In a globalized world, we (whoever "we" may be) can no longer seek to occupy center-stage, mutually excluding each other from the limelight. I am suggesting that by crossing the boundaries that shore up our own identities, by reaching out towards the other, by going out of bounds, we will learn to live in a world of differences. If we take as our model for such boundary-crossing the God outside embodied in Jesus, we see that it is rooted in the fact that he "emptied himself" (Phil 2:7), an emptying that can inform our own spiritual practice of non-attachment, of not doing, of silence. But where will all this lead us?

The gospel has absolutely no doubts, and replies: to death and to no ordinary death at that, but death on the cross. That Jesus' death is the heart of the story is obvious from all the gospels, born as they are out of the passion narrative. Right from the outset, the reader is alerted that in the end, Jesus will meet his death: "The Pharisees went out and immediately held counsel with the Herodians against him, how to destroy him" (Mark 3:6). Furthermore, whatever the Apostle Paul knows of the earthly life of Jesus, he chooses to ignore, deciding "to know nothing among you except Jesus Christ and him crucified" (1 Cor 2:2). The death of Jesus on the cross, then, is no mere accident or unfortunate side effect of his ministry but actually sums up or even recapitulates his own life-journey; Jesus proceeds from emptiness to emptiness suspended in the emptiness of his radical faith. Jesus' death outside the camp is none other than the logical consequence of a life spent crossing boundaries. To put it bluntly, in the course of his ministry Jesus stepped on too many toes, upset too many people, and rocked the boat a little too much. Before proceeding any further, we must remember, of course, that Jesus himself was a Jew born in and nourished by the Jewish tradition and the Jewish faith; we are not trying to oppose a Christian Jesus to Judaism but rather saying that over him Judaism itself was divided, and that according to the not-unbiased gospel accounts only some sectors (and then not in their entirety) of Judaism opposed him.

Having taken as our starting point the story of Miriam, we are not surprised to discover that one of the boundaries Jesus regularly crossed was that dividing pure from impure. In order to reach out to humanity,

Jesus ate with people considered sinners, touched and healed sick people regarded as impure, conversed with women, consorted with foreigners, and crossed numerous boundary lines, thereby threatening a social and religious order that depended on the strict maintenance of such boundaries for survival. Another boundary Jesus called into question was precisely that dividing the human from the divine. Jesus pointed people towards God; in him the divine power was so present that people were freed from their illnesses, anxieties, and guilt. At the heart of his ministry, Jesus did not place religion with all its trappings but rather the well-being of his fellow men and women. Jesus made himself neighbor to men and women of all walks of life, of different faiths and cultures, as, full of compassion, he lived out the great commandment to love God and his neighbor! In doing this, Jesus consistently crossed the boundary between master and servant, redefining importance and prestige in terms of servanthood. It's hardly surprising, then, that the crowds were "astonished at his teaching, for he taught them as one who had authority and not as their scribes" (Mark 1:22), while some of those self-same authorities "sought a way to destroy him" (Mark 11:18). In order to destroy him, however, the religious authorities needed the assistance of civil authority—Rome.

Much has been written on whether or not Jesus was a political revolutionary, perhaps a member of the Zealots, bent on overthrowing imperial power. To answer such a question is arduous precisely because of Jesus' own boundary-crossing techniques. According to Luke's account, Jesus is accused before Pilate of subverting the nation, of inciting people not to pay taxes and of declaring himself king (Luke 23:2). In the enigmatic language of the Fourth Gospel, Jesus declares himself both to be and not to be king, while his enemies tell Pilate, "If you release this man, you are not Caesar's friend; everyone who makes himself king sets himself against Caesar" (John 19:12). That political language could be used to condemn Jesus surely means that Jesus' message itself was unconfined and had worrying political implications. Reaching out to humanity, Jesus had crossed too many boundaries, called into question too many centers of power, and so was led to die outside the city gate.

Jesus' death as his last act of boundary crossing is the direct result of the divine Exodus towards a suffering humanity. Why was he able to be neighbor to a suffering and far-from-attractive humanity? How was he able to accompany and guide his followers in moments of difficulty, encouraging them to cross the boundaries that were often of their own making? How was he able to face the growing opposition his life and mission inevitably engendered? Perhaps the secret lies precisely in that initial *kenosis*, befriending emptiness in the three ways briefly touched upon above. It is not difficult to see that Jesus *refused to grasp* after wealth, family, hearth, and home, living out the radical faith he enjoined on his followers. However, it is precisely in the passion story where his non-attachment becomes evident. He is divested of his friends and followers who abandon him; shorn of his clothes, naked, and exposed, he is robbed of his sense of self; his vocation is ridiculed and spat upon; wounded and suffering, he is divested of his bodily integrity and finally reduced to nothing, abandoned even by God: "My God, my God, why hast thou forsaken me" (Matt 27:46, Mark 15:34)?

Or, let us consider his *not doing*. It is true that in the gospels we often find Jesus pressed for time, hurrying urgently from one place to the next. But then we discover that he has gone off into the mountains alone or is quietly resting in a boat. Once again, the passion narrative highlights this aspect of the Jesus-story. How we wish that he would react, *do* something to prevent his arrest in the garden. Yet, in the unfolding of the various scenes, Jesus appears completely passive, doing nothing, saying little. Finally, in fact, Jesus keeps his silence so that, infuriated, Pilate explodes, "You will not speak to me? Do you not know that I have power to release you and power to crucify you"(John 19:10)? Such was the image of passive docility Jesus evoked that he was soon described by the early church in the words of Isaiah: "as a sheep led to the slaughter is dumb, so he opens not his mouth" (Acts 8:32). It is precisely in the cross, then, that Jesus' own emptying—of his attachments, of his works, of his words, of divinity itself—comes to the fore.

A CROSS-CENTERED SPIRITUALITY

As the cross is both the direct result and the final instance of Jesus going out of bounds and, as such, boundary crossing was made possible by his initial self-emptying, *the cross is thus able to recapitalute and perfectly symbolize the essence of the Christian journey*. Jesus himself invites us to take up our cross, while Paul affirms: "But far be it from me to glory except in the cross of our Lord Jesus Christ, by which the world has been crucified to me, and I to the world" (Gal 6:18). Hardly what we had in mind! In fact, if we think of the evil the preaching of the cross has legitimized throughout history, a cross-centered spirituality may seem a strange proposal. Down through the centuries, in fact, the cross has been wielded by those at center stage precisely to keep others—women, peoples of color, workers, and so on—well away from the limelight. A certain "preaching of the cross" has helped to consolidate a world of differences as the idea of self-emptying has been proclaimed in order to keep some hands empty and others more than full. Rather than being a way of enhancing human possibilities, *kenosis* has been a way of precluding the majority from life's abundance: "The key to this ideological deformation is the socioreligious group's movement from powerlessness to power," declares Rosemary Radford Ruether. "When the religious spokespersons see themselves as primarily stabilizing the existing social order and justifying its power structure, then prophetic language . . . becomes a language to sacralize dominant authorities."[12] Ruether thus considers the notion of *kenosis* as a powerful critique of patriarchy and patriarchal notions of power and masculinity. British theologian, Daphne Hampson, agrees with Ruether on this point but believes that "the theme of self-emptying and self-abnegation is far from helpful" for women.[13] Indeed, it might seem ironic that after women have struggled for decades to have goods to call our own, to pursue our own activity, and to speak our own language, the idea of emptiness makes its way (admittedly rather shyly) onto the scene. Obviously something else must be going on here. But what? The answer, I suggest, lies in the resurrection.

Jesus' death on the cross is not the end of the story; the Philippian hymn continues: "God has highly exalted him." The cross, then, present at the beginning, in the middle, and at the end of the Jesus-story is much more than the crucifixion of a Jewish man carried out by the Romans two thousand years ago. The cross, as such, is always death *and* resurrection because, as Paul argues, had Christ not been raised from the dead, then our faith would be quite useless and would never have been connected to Jesus of Nazareth at all. In other words, had not that something which we call resurrection happened to Jesus, then his memory would have been consigned to oblivion together with those of the other religious visionaries or political outcasts crucified by Rome. According to Luke in the book of Acts, the proclamation of the resurrection is at the heart of

---

12. Ruether, *Sexism and God-Talk*, 28–29.

13. Daphne Hampson, *Theology and Feminism* (Signposts in Theology; Oxford: Blackwell, 1990), 155.

Peter's first speeches: "You crucified and killed him . . . But God raised him up" (2:24); "This Jesus God raised up" (2:32); "You killed the author of life, whom God raised from the dead" (3:15); "Jesus Christ of Nazareth whom you crucified, whom God raised from the dead" (4:10).

What I am suggesting, then, is that the cross, always understood as death *and* resurrection, is the quintessential cipher of that dynamic by which emptiness becomes abundance, losing one's life means gaining it, giving up something means getting more back, silence speaks, and doing nothing produces flourishing! The cross stands for that dynamic in which radical faith and the divine promise encounter each other, embrace, and are mutually fulfilled. In other words, the cross (always understood as death *and* resurrection) manages to overcome those dualisms that continually plague us. Death-resurrection, then, is the supreme instance of the divine way of being, to which the scriptures witness and of which both Hannah and Mary sing: "He has filled the hungry with good things, and the rich he has sent empty away" (Luke 1:53). Such a dynamic does not merely reverse the status quo so that the oppressor becomes the oppressed or vice versa but actually transforms it, opening it up to new possibilities. This is the dynamic at the heart of the life and teaching of Jesus and the path he invites us to take: "Unless a grain of wheat falls into the earth and dies, it remains alone; but if it dies it bears much fruit" (John 12:24). According to the logic of the gospel, life is gained not by grasping after it or by hanging on to it, but by letting it go. This means that "one who does not renounce all cannot be my disciple" (Luke 14:33). Similarly, a person becomes important not by virtue of the prestige and power he or she wields over others, but precisely by turning one's back on power and prestige to reach out and serve one's fellow human beings: "Whoever would be great among you must be your servant, and whoever would be first among you must be your slave" (Mark 10:44).

This same dynamic that overcomes and transforms apparent oppositions is enfleshed in the life of the Apostle Paul, who is able, for example, to transform weakness so that it becomes power and strength and to re-define external perishing so that it becomes inner renewal. Because, as we have seen (Gal 6:12), Paul's life rests solely on the cross of Christ, the resurrection principle is already active in him, changing death into life, not only for himself but also for those whom he encounters (2 Cor 4:12). While Paul knows, on the one hand, that the cross is scandalous and sheer folly, on the other hand, he is convinced that in it lies divine power and wisdom. The logic of the cross (death *and* resurrection, let us remember) means, therefore, that God has chosen the weak "to shame the strong ... what is low and despised in the world, even things that are not, to bring to nothing things that are" (1 Cor 1:27–28). In other words, God has chosen nothingness in order to bring forth abundance, scarcity to bring forth flourishing, absence from which to create plenty!

The verse from the Gospel of John we have already quoted continues: "He who loves his life loses it, and he who hates his life in this world will keep it for eternal life" (John 12:25). Once again, the same principle is stated, but this time in a dualistic scheme, which by opposing "this world" to "eternal life" actually betrays the meaning Jesus is trying to convey! It is not surprising, then, if down through the centuries the dynamic of the cross as I have outlined it here as the heart of a spiritual practice has been profoundly misunderstood. On the one hand (as I have mentioned), situations of suffering, exploitation, and gross inhumanity have been legitimized by preaching the cross of patient forbearance and suffering in this life together with the promise of resurrection in the life to come. On the other hand, prosperity and abundance in this life have been proclaimed as signs of God's blessing with no regard to emptiness, and no heed to the suffering produced by unjust social and economic systems which produce wealth for the few and poverty for the many. In the first instance, the cross is preached with a delayed, other-worldly resurrection, while in the second we have a this-worldly resurrection but no cross. As we can see, then, it is not easy to keep the polarity of cross and resurrection together without losing one of the terms. Not only did the wealthy man of the gospel story face this difficulty, but so did the disciples. When Jesus declares that "it is difficult for those who trust in riches to enter the kingdom of heaven," the disciples are amazed and wonder who will ever make it. Peter is concerned and seeks some sort of assurance from Jesus; after all, hadn't he and his fellow travelers given up homes and family to become disciples? At this juncture Jesus replies, "Truly, I say to you, there is no one who has left house or brothers or sisters or mother or father or children or lands, for my sake and the gospel, who will not receive a hundredfold now in this time, houses and brothers and sisters and mothers and children and lands, with persecutions and in the age to come eternal life" (Mark 10:29–30). The churches have often understood this saying as promising a reward, a prize for having given up so much, but I think that Jesus is simply stating in another form the dynamic intrinsic to the cross and to the spirituality it would engender. "Receiving a hundred-fold" is a direct consequence of having left everything, that is, of having embraced emptiness and made it our home. The one leads into the other, just like death and resurrection go together; the grain of corn produces much fruit only if it dies.

CONCLUSION: ONE MORE MARY

We are now in a position to sum up. I have suggested that if the world is to become *ecumene*, a true home to humanity with our many and various differences so that no one group of people can lay claim to center-stage ("the centre cannot hold"), a cross-centered spirituality is required. We have seen that the cross, always to be understood in terms of death *and* resurrection, is a result of Jesus' refusal to hold onto the center (divinity itself!) and his own journey towards humanity, which leads him out of bounds to die outside the city gate. The basis of this trajectory is *kenosis*, and it is precisely this emptiness that we are invited to befriend in our own boundary-crossing journey towards God, each other, and our own selves. Drawing on the episode of the encounter between Jesus and the rich man, I have suggested that such emptying means freeing ourselves of our attachments, be they goods or affections, of our ceaseless need always to be doing, and of the constant noise made by countless words. Only then will we be able to walk the path of radical trust and discover how absence produces abundance, rest produces flourishing, and silence produces words pregnant with meaning.

The gospels provide us with several stories to help us get the point that Jesus himself made with his own life. One of these is undoubtedly the parable of the good Samaritan, the story of an outsider who crossed the road which the religious-minded priest and scribe refused to cross in order to reach out to the wounded man. However, as we began this essay by claiming that the center cannot hold and that women and men of all colors, shapes, and sizes now occupy center stage and can and indeed must image forth a cross-centered spirituality, let us bring it to a close with another gospel variation on the same theme, centered this time on a woman. The story of the woman who anoints Jesus is found in all four gospels in different forms, but all have in common the following elements: a woman who anoints Jesus whilst he is at table; criticism leveled at the woman by one or some of the male followers of Jesus; and the defense of the woman by Jesus, with an interpretation of her action.

Once more we find the key elements of boundary-crossing, emptying, and body-centered action. Whilst scholars are unsure of exactly what place women could and did occupy at banquets, there is little doubt that the woman (whose gender makes her, just like the Samaritan, already out of bounds) crossed social and religious boundaries that should have excluded her from such a meal and rendered her action inappropriate. Having gathered her courage to cross the threshold, the woman proceeds to lavish some very body-centered attention on Jesus; no words are exchanged as she anoints his head or his feet, drying them with her hair. To do this, she, like the Samaritan, is very likely spending all her resources, emptying the jar of the expensive perfume it contained. Just as in John's version, the perfume fills the whole house, so this story is redolent with Christ-like meaning. Whilst the disciples' criticism centers on the perceived waste of such lavish generosity, Jesus reads the woman's action as foreshadowing his own death. In love and compassion, the woman in fact crosses boundaries to reach out to a man near to death, her self-emptying being mirrored in the pouring out of the priceless oil. It is hardly coincidental that John places this episode in which Mary anoints Jesus' feet and wipes them with her hair immediately before the episode in which Jesus himself (crossing the master-servant boundary) washes and dries his disciples' feet with the water he has poured out—clearly creating an interpretive link between the two events in terms of self-giving, sisterly and brotherly love, and the cross (death, let us remember, *and* resurrection). The gospels also link the woman's action to the Eucharist and thus to the cross; just as the bread is to be broken and the cup shared, according to Jesus, "in memory of me," so whenever the gospel, understood as death *and* resurrection, is proclaimed, so will the story of this woman be re-told "in memory of her."[14] Just as we began with the story of Miriam, so we end with the story of the woman who anointed Jesus, stories of two women who in different ways image forth the God who in Jesus goes out of bounds, offering us a way of discipleship in a world of differences.

---

14. Cf. of course, Schüssler Fiorenza, *In Memory of Her*.

3

The Resurrection of Christ and the New Earth

Jürgen Moltmann

CREATION IS RESURRECTION

IN THE CATHOLIC LITURGY for Easternight, the reading of the first creation story, in Genesis 1, is prescribed. This is a wonderful sign of a cosmic Christology: The world began with a resurrection out of the darkness of chaos to the light of a beautiful cosmos. "Already on the first day of creation the work of the new creation is flashing up—in the midst of the old creation. With this the creation has, from the beginning on, an eschatological character. We can perceive the creation to be a great and real promise of God."[1] With the creation "in the beginning," her future in God's kingdom is already inbuilt. All the creatures are real promises of their coming completion. Creation out of chaos is like a resurrection, and the resurrection of the dead out of the realm of death is like a new creation. God who awakens the dead is the same God who calls into being what is not (Rom 4:17). God, who raised Jesus from the dead, is the Creator of the new being of all creatures. Resurrection and creation belong together because the resurrection of the dead and the annihilation of death are not only the overcoming of sin and its evil consequences but also the completion of the original creation. Together, they are nothing less than the negation of the negative and the perfection of the positive.

---

1. Medard Kehl, Preface to *Schöpfung und Neuschöpfung. "Neuschöpfung" als theologische Kategorie im Werk Jürgen Moltmanns* by Pablo Carlos Sicouly (KKTS 76; Paderborn, Germany: Bonifatius, 2007), 14.

THE LIGHT OF EASTER

From the beginning, Christians saw in the light of Christ's Easter appearances the light of the morning of the first day of the new creation. They called the feast of the resurrection of Christ on Sunday the "eighth day" after the Sabbath and the "first day" of the new week. In this light of the new creation, Christ appears as the firstborn of creation (Col 1:15), reconciling with God all things in heaven and on earth (Col 1:20). This is the starting point of cosmic Christology, because in these dimensions we understand the resurrection of Christ not only as an "eschatological act of history" ("eine eschatologische Geschichtstat Gottes"), but also as the first act of the re-creation of this transient world to her lasting and true form—the eternal creation, "world without end."[2] Resurrection is not only the meaning of history but also the meaning of nature.

EASTER NARRATIVES OF THE DISCIPLES AND THE WOMEN

To understand the cosmic aspect of Christ's resurrection from the dead more proficiently, we must pause for a moment to reconsider the New Testament Easter narratives.[3] Jesus' disciples were frightened and fled when Jesus, in whom they had placed their entire messianic hope, died on the cross, powerless and abandoned by the God he had called "Abba, dear father" in Gethsemane. "But we had been hoping that he would liberate Israel," said the disciples on the way to Emmaus (Luke 24:21). Jesus' crucifixion by the Roman power was the greatest disappointment of their lives. So they betrayed, denied, and abandoned the one by whom they felt they had been betrayed and abandoned. His shameful death was the end of their messianic hope for Israel's future.

But the other disciples, the women who had also left everything behind and followed Jesus, remained loyal to their dying friend and "were also present, watching from a distance." They kept eye contact with Jesus, and as eyewitnesses they are called by name (Mark 15:40). For them, obviously, the observation of dying and death was not alien. They went to the grave of their friend and master when the Sabbath was over and

---

2. Jürgen Moltmann, "The Cosmic Christ," in *The Way of Jesus Christ: Christology in Messianic Dimension* (trans. Margaret Kohl; London: SCM, 1990), 274–312.

3. Ted Peters et al., eds., *Resurrection: Theological and Scientific Assessments* (Grand Rapids: Eerdmans, 2002); Thorwald Lorenzen, *Resurrection, Discipleship, Justice: Affirming the Resurrection of Jesus Christ Today* (Macon, GA: Smyth & Helwys, 2003).

found the grave empty and heard an angel say: "He is not here, he has been raised" (Mark 16:6). It was only at this point that they were deeply frightened and fled, trembling with amazement. Why? Birth and death are normal features of a finite life on earth. Jesus' resurrection from the dead shattered the regular order of things.[4]

Jesus was taken away from the living by his death, and he was taken away from the dead by his resurrection. His death was the end of the disciples' future hope, while his resurrection was the end of the women's trust in death as the end of life. The disappointment of the disciples' hope and the shock of the women who had seen where Jesus was buried were banished only by the appearances of the risen Jesus, who summoned them not to be afraid but to believe in the new being that he embodies (Mark 16:14; John 20:27).

This has consequences not only for the moral but also for the natural life of human beings. To live in the presence of the risen Christ is to experience the Spirit of resurrection giving "new life to our mortal bodies" (Rom 8:11) and inspiring us with hope for the "resurrection of the flesh." As we wait for this "redemption of our body," we hear the "groaning of the whole creation" together with us (Rom 8:22). The Spirit of resurrection is forming our solidarity of suffering and hope with all living things on earth. Living in the presence of the risen Christ opens our lives to cosmic dimensions.[5] For the life-giving Spirit is "poured out on all flesh" (Joel 2:26; Acts 2:2ff.): in Hebrew, *kol basar*, "all the living."

RESURRECTION: THE MEANING OF NATURE

By "nature" we understand the present condition of the distorted creation, which is replete with beautiful things but also with terrible disasters. Yet we call this nature God's creation because we trust in the faithfulness of its Creator and see how, with respect to God's aims, it can be improved. What has Christ to do with nature? Already Paul, some thirty-five years after Jesus' death, talks of Christ's mediation of all creation: "Yet for us there is one God, the Father, from whom are all things, and we exist for him; there is one Lord, Jesus Christ, through whom are all things, and we exist through him" (1 Cor 8:6). If all things exist "through Christ,"

---

4. Donald H. Juel, *A Master of Surprise: Mark Interpreted* (Minneapolis: Fortress, 1994), chapter 8.

5. Jürgen Moltmann, *The Source of Life: The Holy Spirit and the Theology of Life* (trans. Margaret Kohl; London: SCM; Minneapolis: Fortress, 1997).

then not only the redeemer of history but also the wisdom of the whole original creation is revealed in him. But that means nothing less than that the first Christians saw Christ in all natural things, and all natural things in Christ.[6] Consequently, the powers of nature were to be honored as little as the idols of human power, as the emperor or the capital. The sun, moon, and stars are good elements of creation, but they are not themselves gods. Under the rule of the risen Christ, people were liberated from the divinization of natural forces and from their demonization. Orientation to the forces of nature, which are themselves in need of redemption, is pointless. Christ reconciles the human not only to God but also to God's good creation so that humanity may enter again into the creation-community.

In practice this cosmic Christology means that the Christian communities in the multi-religious towns of the ancient world did not present themselves as composing only one of the many religious communities of a hitherto unknown deity, but as the community of the Creator and Redeemer of all things, and as one establishing peace and unity with nature. What they were bringing into the world was not a new religion but new life. They did not offer competition between religions, for their missionary task was to achieve the reconciliation of humankind and the peace of the cosmos. The Church sees itself as the beginning of the reconciled cosmos and as an anticipation of the new creation. Every church and cathedral is an image of the whole cosmos, for "the most High does not live in houses made by people; as the prophet says: 'Heaven is my throne, and earth my footstool'" (Acts 7:48; cf. Isa 66:1–2).

MATTER WITH A FUTURE

The first enlightenment of the eighteenth century recommended simple, mechanically conceived materialism, with Descartes (1596–1650) in his representation of the objective world in a purely geometrical manner as *res extensa*, and with La Mettrie (1709–1751) in his concept of *L'Homme machine* (1747). The nineteenth century, however, produced a new dialectical materialism. This approach tried to interrelate human subjectivity and the objectivity of nature in order to conceive of humankind in an appropriately natural way, and nature in an appropriately human way.

---

6. In the *Gospel of Thomas*, Jesus says: "I am the light set over all things. I am the universe; the universe proceeded from me and the universe returns to me. Split a piece of wood, and I am there. Pick up a stone and you will find me" (logion 77).

When young Karl Marx writes, "Motion is the first and supreme of the innate characteristics of matter, not only as mechanical and mathematical movement, but much more so as impulse, vital spirit, and anguish—to use Jakob Boehme's term—of matter,"[7] there are unmistakeable echoes of the Pauline image of creation's groaning and longing (Rom 8:19–23). Twentieth-century philosophers such as Ernst Bloch, in his "principle of Hope," process philosophy, and open-systems theories developed this idea of dialectical materialism further.[8] There can be no absolute subject/object dichotomy; the subject of recognition plays a decisive role on all levels, as quantum physics tells us. And matter is always process-matter, that is, matter in the process of transformation. Matter is not only given reality but at the same time open potentiality. Matter is subject to processes of continuing transformation with a determined past and an as-yet indeterminate future. All formed matter is matter with a future. But what kind of future?

The modern sciences interpret nature on the basis of anthropocentric interests. Nature must be subject to human research and domination. The nature of the earth will find its home in the human scientific-technical civilization, which governs, uses, and—hopefully—will also preserve it. Nowadays the symbols of nature, known traditionally as *signatura rerum*, are considered and used as information for human exploitation. In this paradigm, humankind stands over against nature, alienated from nature, and hostile to nature.[9]

Theology of the natural world has always read the "book of nature" theocentrically and interpreted it eschatologically. All created things point to their Creator: "The heavens sing the praise of the Eternal." They also point beyond themselves to the future of their redemption in their true form in God's coming kingdom. Human beings too are God's creatures. The immanence of God's Spirit in their souls is the reason for their permanent self-transcendence. "What we shall be has not yet been disclosed, but we know that when Christ appears, we shall be like

---

7. Karl Marx, *Die Frühschriften* (ed. S. Landshut; Stuttgart: Kröner, 1953), 330.

8. Ernst Bloch, *Das Materialismusproblem, seine Geschichte und Substanz* (Frankfurt: Suhrkamp, 1972); Ernst von Weizsäcker, ed., *Offene Systeme I: Beiträge zur Zeitstruktur von Information, Entropie und Evolution* (Stuttgart: Klett-Cotta, 1974).

9. We can find an outstanding starting point for a hermeneutics of nature in the "Bedeutungslehre" of the famous biologist Jakob von Uexküll. See *Streifzüge durch die Umwelten von Tieren und Menschen. Bedeutungslehre* (Hamburg: Rowchlt, 1956). In order to understand what we know, we need the step from science to hermeneutics.

him, because we shall see him as he is" (1 John 3:2). The result is an anticipatory community between human culture and the nature of the earth in the prospect of a common future in the new creation. People who long for the redemption of the mortal body will join in community with all creatures groaning under the burden of transience and longing for the coming glory of God. We shall therefore decipher the *signatura rerum* within the framework of an eschatological hermeneutics. This allows us to elicit the significance of nature in the light of its transcendent resurrection.

THE RESURRECTION OF NATURE

The young Karl Marx had this vision of the goal of world history: "Therefore *society* is the complete existential unity of humankind and nature, the authentic resurrection of nature, the achieved naturalism of humankind and the achieved humanism of nature."[10] He was able to conceive of nature as redeemed from its state of alienation only in terms of its resurrection in the world of humankind. He did not see this as the extended human domination of nature and its subjugation to human will, but rather as a mutual interpenetration of humankind and nature. Without a naturalization of humanity, no humanization of nature was possible. And this essential unity of humankind and nature was to appear in the "classless society," a society free from domination. Authentic "communism" was to overcome not only contradictions in human society but also contradictions between humans and nature—and even contradictions within nature itself.[11] Otherwise, the "resurrection of nature" would be meaningless. Nevertheless, young Marx underestimated the power of evil and the destiny of death. Like Ludwig Feuerbach, he was an idealist who denied evil and ignored death. He must have known, however, that every resurrection presupposes death. Therefore, a "humanism of nature" cannot be a "resurrection of nature." Every humanization of nature, as shown by the already failed Soviet experiment of communism and the now-failing global experiment of capitalism, leads not to a resurrection of nature but rather, in all probability, to the end of nature. The advancing crisis of the climate is a warning sign of our times.

---

10. Marx, *Die Frühschriften*, 237.
11. See ibid., 235: "This communism . . . is the mystery of history solved."

But if a resurrection of nature in human society is inconceivable, where can such a resurrection take place? Where can this corruptible and mortal world put on incorruption and immortality? Traditionally, we think of a realm beyond this world in heaven or in an Elysium or in a paradise regained. But this dream is closer to Plato than to Jesus Christ and the New Testament. The resurrection of the dead takes place on this earth and leads those who are given life to "a new earth, in which righteousness will be established" (2 Pet 3:13). The kingdom of God comes "on earth as it is in heaven." Resurrection and eternal life are God's promises for people on earth *and for God's beloved earth*.

THE PROMISE OF THE EARTH

There is a great change in spirituality and theology on the way today: We discover anew the spirituality of the body and of awakened and watchful senses; we discover again the religion of the earth, that is, the Sabbaths the earth shall celebrate for its creator; we discover that our heaven lies on earth, when righteousness shall dwell on a new earth (2 Pet 3:13). Inhabitants of heaven are angels, but we are children of the earth, "earthlings" from the beginning on. "The Christ-heaven lies on earth not in heaven, for Christ has come into flesh, and in flesh he will erect the heaven of God," said Christoph Blumhardt, contemporary of Nietzsche, spiritual father of Brunner and Barth, the religious-socialism of Leonhard Ragaz and some Pentecostal theologians today, and as "theologian of hope" (Barth), a predecessor of myself in Württemberg. For Blumhardt, the kingdom of God "lives with the earth." In simple terms, "I have no God in heaven, the angels have him there. I will pray down here; this is where I have to have God," and "finally God will be a God whom we may behold on earth."[12] Why do you want to go to heaven? The resurrection of the dead will happen on earth.

Young Dietrich Bonhoeffer took this up: "Only the one who loves God and the earth in one breath can hope for the kingdom of God." Christ doesn't lead people into the after-world of religious escapism, flight from the world, but gives them back to the earth as her faithful people. "Whoever loves God loves God as Lord of the earth; and who-

---

12. Leonhard Ragaz, "Der Kampf um das Reich Gottes," in *Blumhardt, Vater und Sohn—und weiter!* (Zurich: Rotapfel, 1922), chap. 4, sec. 1: "Das Reich Gottes für die Erde," 44–62.

ever loves the earth loves her as God's earth." Because—and this is the final reason—"God's kingdom is the realm of resurrection on earth."[13]

I would like to add: Far from leading human beings away from earth to heaven, Christian hope leads them to the kingdom of God which comes on earth. Human beings have come from the earth and belong on earth and do so both in time and eternity. If heaven opens for them, it is heaven on earth. On earth Christ was born, on earth stands the cross of Christ, and it is on earth that we may expect deliverance from evil. It is this transitory life that will be transformed into eternal life; it is this earthly life that will be raised to eternal life. The "life of the world to come," as the Nicene Creed says, is life on the new earth. I believe in the "resurrection of the flesh," not only of the human body but also the life of the whole groaning creation (Rom 8:19–25). Why? God the creator remains faithful to God's creation as the redeemer, too; God does "not forsake the works of his hands." God doesn't give anything up for lost and destroys nothing God has made, for God is God.

---

13. Dietrich Bonhoeffer, *Dein Reich komme: Das Gebet der Gemeinde um das Reich Gottes auf Erden* (Hamburg: Furche, 1958), 12.

4

Totus Homo

Augustine on Resurrection

Tarmo Toom

In 1995, Professor Thorwald Lorenzen published his magnum opus under the title, *Resurrection and Discipleship*. As a former student of this extraordinary teacher-theologian, I would like to add a footnote to one of the themes of his book—the holistic understanding of resurrection.[1]

I have opted for an exploration of the views of Augustine in order to show that even the convictions of a neoplatonic patristic theologian were drastically modified by the holistic Christian understanding of resurrection. Addressing the topic of resurrection, Augustine was compelled to consider "how our faith, instructed by God, praises the body"[2] and how it even taught the resurrection of the body. I will contend that for Augustine, resurrection means nothing less than the resurrection of *totus homo*, the resurrection of the whole human being, body and soul.

For Christians, the goodness of body or materiality is not only affirmed by God's verdict, "It was very good!" (Gen 1:31),[3] but is also

---

1. Thorwald Lorenzen, *Resurrection and Discipleship: Interpretive Models, Biblical Reflections, Theological Consequences* (Maryknoll, NY: Orbis, 1995), 266–95.

2. Augustine, *Sermo (Sermon)* 241.7.

3. Augustine, *De civitate Dei (The City of God)* 11.23; *Contra Fortunatum (Against Fortunatus)* 21; *Confessiones* 13.38.43; *De Genesi ad litteram (On Genesis Literally Interpreted)* 3.24.36; *De libero arbitrio (Free Will)* 3.13; *De natura boni (The Nature of the Good)* 12 and 34; *Soliloquia (Soliloquies)* 1.1.2. In *Ad Simplicianum (To Simplicianus)* 1.2.18, Augustine wrote: "God is the creator both of the body and of the soul. Neither of these is evil, and God hates neither."

reaffirmed by the incarnation of the Son of God.[4] The incarnation of the Son of God, in turn, constitutes the transcendental possibility for the bodily resurrection of the Son of God and consequently the bodily resurrection of human beings. The body of Christ was resurrected as the "first fruits of those who have died" (1 Cor 15:20). "The resurrection of the Lord's body is found to serve as the model (*exemplum*) for our outer man's resurrection."[5] Those "knowing the Scriptures [and] the power of God" (Mark 12:24) could in no way deny the resurrection of the body. Augustine bolstered his case with a traditional argument: just as God had created human bodies from nothing, God would recreate human bodies in resurrection, even if these were disintegrated. After all, "He who can create what was not, can he not restore that which already existed?"[6]

Augustine's theology of the resurrection of the body is not original. It is traditional. The apostles believed in the resurrection of the body, and so did post-apostolic theologians.[7] This means that even though the

---

4. Augustine, *De civitate Dei* 10.29; *Contra Faustum (Against Faustus)* 11.3, 7; *In Johannis evangelium tractatus (Tractates on the Gospel of John)* 23.5–6. "The assumption of human nature [i.e., body and soul] by the divine Word means that the human nature is infinitely valuable," according to M. R. Miles, *Augustine on the Body* (American Academy of Religion Dissertation Series 31; ed. H. G. Little; Ann Arbor, MI: Scholars, 1979), 95.

5. Augustine, *De Trinitate (The Trinity)* 4.1.6; cf. Acts 4:2, 17:31; 1 Cor 15:12, 20–23; Phil 3:20–21; Col 1:18; 1 Thess 4:14; 2 Tim 2:11; Augustine, *Contra Julianum opus imperfectum (Against Julian, an Unfinished Book)* 6.34.1; *Enarrationes in Psalmos (Explanations of the Psalms)* 40.5, 66.1; *Epistulae (Letters)* 55.2; 205.2.6; *Sermones* 22.10; 240.2; 241.1; 242.1; 242A.1–3; 361.10.10; Ps.-Justin, *De resurrectione* 9; Tertullian, *De resurrectione carnis (The Resurrection of the Flesh)* 38, 48, and 51. Miles, *Augustine on the Body*, 113, writes: "From the time of *Contra Faustum Manichaeum* and *Contra Felicem Manichaeum* (c. AD 398), the reference to Christ's body as *exemplum* of the *resurrectio carnis* increase, and show increasing significance in Augustine's thought."

6. Augustine, *Sermo* 361.12; cf. *De catechizandis rudibus (Catechizing the Uninstructed)* 25.46, 27.54; *Sermo* 242.1; 2 Macc 7:22–23; Rom 4:17–20; Athenagoras, *De resurrectione* 3 and 11; Ps.-Justin, *De resurrectione* 5; Tertullian, *De resurrectione carnis* 11.

7. Apart from the New Testament, Irenaeus, for example, confessed that Christians "hope for the salvation of the whole human being, that is, body and soul" (*Adversus haereses [Against Heresies]* 5.20.1). Contemporary Christians still acknowledge that "[f]or Christian faith resurrection means that human beings in their individuality and wholeness, body-soul-spirit, have a future beyond death" (*Confessing One Faith: An Ecumenical Explication of the Apostolic Faith as it is Confessed in the Nicene-Constantinopolitan Creed [381]*; Faith and Order Papers 153; [Geneva: WCC, 1991], 99).

belief in bodily resurrection was de-emphasized in the Middle Ages,[8] and neglected or ridiculed in modern times,[9] the contemporary revival of a holistic understanding of resurrection has nevertheless wonderful patristic precedents, including the teaching of Augustine.[10]

By way of introduction, I would like to make the point that to develop a theology of resurrection is to undertake an exegetical project. For a Christian theologian, the canonical Scriptures suggest the theological ideas and guide the process of making theological deductions. Theology involves exegesis, although it cannot be reduced to exegesis. The subtitle of Professor Lorenzen's major book—*Interpretive Models, Biblical Reflections, Theological Consequences*—suggests that what the Scriptures say has theological implications and that working out these theological implications is the proper task for a Christian theologian. Investigating an intricate anthropological issue, Augustine also affirmed the primacy of Scripture when he concluded, "But this too is something we are not permitted by the same text of Scripture to believe."[11] In sorting out references to the designations, "living breath" and "living soul," he asked rhetorically, "What is this ... but negligence in attending the Holy Scripture?"[12] And when Augustine was forced to entertain an unanswer-

---

8. In 1336, Pope Benedict XII stated that the souls of the just are rewarded by a direct vision of God immediately after death. It has been argued that this statement shifted attention away from the bodily resurrection. See Karl Rahner, "The Resurrection of the Body," in his *Theological Investigations*, Vol. 2 (trans. K.-H. Kruger; Baltimore: Helicon, 1963), 206.

9. See W. J. La Due, *The Trinity Guide to Eschatology* (New York: Continuum, 2004), 91.

10. This is by no means to assert that there existed something like a patristic consensus about the bodily resurrection or about resurrection in general. See the "models" constructed by B. E. Daley, "A Hope for Worms: Early Christian Hope," in *Resurrection: Theological and Scientific Assessments* (ed. Ted Peters, Robert J. Russell, and Michael Welker; Grand Rapids: Eerdmans, 2002), 136–64, and his classic *The Hope of the Early Church: A Handbook of Patristic Eschatology* (2d ed.; Peabody: Hendrickson, 2003). In one of his letters, Augustine expresses his frustration about the less-than-satisfactory state of the question of resurrection: "I confess that I have not yet read anywhere anything which I would esteem sufficiently established to deserve to be either learned or taught by human beings" (*Epistula* 148.5.16). Late in his life, he also admitted that "I have not discovered how to discuss this matter briefly and do justice to all the questions which are commonly raised about it" (*Enchiridion* 23.84). Resurrection remained a "mystery" (1 Cor 15:51).

11. Augustine, *De Genesi ad litteram* 6.7.12.

12. Augustine, *De civitate Dei* 13.24.

able question about bodily resurrection, he conceded, "I admit, we find no definite answer to this in the Scriptures."[13] Because doing theology meant then, and means now, to investigate the implications of the teachings of the Scriptures, Augustine admonished that "the divine word must be treated again and again with devout care."[14]

At this point, let us look at one characteristic example of Augustine's attentive reading of the Scriptures. When Augustine exegeted Matt 22:30, he argued that sexual differentiation remained intact after the bodily resurrection. The text says, "They shall not be given in marriage." "Scrutinizing, as usual, the iota of the word of the scripture," Augustine concluded that this verse assumed the existence of women after resurrection,[15] since in those times men married, but women were given in marriage.[16] Again, even though Rom 8:29 speaks about conforming to the image of the *Son* (*imaginis Filii*), Augustine did not take the Son's masculinity but rather his age—the ideal and mature thirties—to be that to which the just would be conformed in resurrection.[17] At the same time, the bishop of Hippo also contended that the function of gender-defining sexual organs would be altered, for there would be no lust, sex, childbirth, or marriage in the resurrected life.[18] Although a resurrected body will have all its sexual characteristics, it will be so for the sake of beauty. Sexual organs will be "accommodated not for the old uses, but to a new beauty."[19]

---

13. Augustine, *Sermo* 242.2.

14. Augustine, *De diversis quaestionibus* (*Different Questions*) 67.7.

15. H. I. Marrou, *The Resurrection and Saint Augustine's Theology of Human Values* (trans. M. Consolata; Villanova: Villanova University Press, 1966), 26.

16. Augustine, *De civitate Dei* 22.17.

17. Augustine, *De civitate Dei* 22.15–16; cf. *Sermo* 242.4. Similarly, Eph 4:13 employs a phrase "to perfect man" (*in virum perfectum*), but Augustine reads it gender-inclusively (*De civitate Dei* 22.18; cf. 20.21). Apparently, Augustine reacted to Jerome's conjecture that in the resurrection women would receive male bodies. See Jerome, *Commentarorium in Epistolam ad Ephesios* 5.29; F. Van Fleteren, "Augustine and the Resurrection," *Studies in Medieval Culture* 12 (1978): 13.

18. In *De bono conjugali* (*The Good of Marriage*) 2, Augustine explicitly states that intercourse is characteristic of mortal bodies only (cf. Ps.-Justin, *De resurrectione* 3; Tertullian, *De resurrectione carnis* 60–63). See M. R. Miles, "Sex and the City (of God): Is Sex Forfeited or Fulfilled in Augustine's Resurrection of Body?" *JAAR* 73 (June 2005): 307–27.

19. Augustine, *De civitate Dei* 22.17.

From the Scriptures, Augustine also learned about the resurrection of *totus homo*, the resurrection of the body and the soul.[20] Ancient Israelites considered a human being to be a psychosomatic unity, and Christians inherited their holistic anthropology from the people of Israel and Judah. But because of the increasing influence of Greek thought, Christians came to differentiate more emphatically between a person's soul (the intelligible reality) and body (the sensible reality). This is where Christian anthropology went beyond that of the Israelites. It gradually moved from an Israelite dichotomous anthropology to a Greek dualistic anthropology.[21] Consequently, while retaining the Israelite belief in the resurrection of the dead, Christians had to make a case not only for the resurrection of the dead (and the immortality of the soul) but also and especially for the resurrection of the body.[22]

The task just mentioned proved to be rather complicated, however, because the "pagan" philosophers of Augustine's day absolutely denied something so naïve and absurd as bodily resurrection.[23] Augustine grumbled, "These men, desiring to have something to condemn in Christian doctrine, attack the eternality of the body."[24] For instance, in the very beginning of his *Vita Plotini*, Porphyry announced the disposition of his teacher: "Plotinus seemed to feel ashamed of dwelling in a body."[25] Neoplatonists considered only the soul to be immortal, and

20. See Isaiah 26; Daniel 12. According to G. W. E. Nickelsburg, *Resurrection, Immortality, and Eternal Life: Intertestamental Judaism and Early Christianity* (expanded ed., Harvard Theological Studies 56; Cambridge: Harvard University Press, 2006), 216: "Following the lead of Daniel, resurrection of the body becomes a fixed *topos* in the tradition." See Wisdom 1-6; 2 Maccabees 7 and 12; Matthew 22; 1 Corinthians 15; Revelation 20.

21. Peter Lampe, "Paul's Concept of a Spiritual Body," in *Resurrection*, ed. Peters, Russell, and Welker, 104 and 114.

22. For instance, the Jewish apocalyptic text, 1 Enoch 102-4 (circa 100 BCE), which speaks about the resurrection of the righteous ones, does not mention the resurrection of their bodies.

23. Augustine, *De civitate Dei* 22.3-4, 25-7; *De fide et symbolo (Faith and the Creed)* 6.13, 10.24; *De Trinitate* 13.3.12.

24. Augustine, *De civitate Dei* 13.16.

25. Porphyry, *Vita Plotini* 1.1. Porphyry was a Neoplatonic philosopher who explicitly rebutted the Christian conviction of the resurrection of the body. For Augustine's accounts of his position, see *De civitate Dei* 10.29, 13.19, and *Sermo* 241.7, where he quotes a phrase from a lost work of Porphyry: "But every kind of body is to be shunned." Yet, Augustine still tried to reconcile the Christian belief in the resurrection of the body with Porphyry's psychology through the concept of *corpus spiritale* (*De*

for that reason only the soul deserved their full attention. Augustine assessed the situation:

> People have tried to work these things out by human reasoning, but it is the immortality of the soul alone that they have succeeded in getting to some notion of, and then only a few out of them, and with difficulty, and only if they have had plenty of brains and plenty of leisure and plenty of education in abstruse learning.[26]

Furthermore, because body was something one needed to get rid of, Neoplatonists found it ridiculous to consider death, that is, the separation of soul and body, a punishment. Oh, no! Bodily death, leaving behind any kind of body, was the liberation of the soul rather than its punishment! Because of such understandings of these things, Augustine could state, "Our faith . . . is totally different from any beliefs of the heathen in the resurrection of the dead."[27]

The belief in the resurrection of body/flesh[28] had always been part of the Christian *regula fidei*, and therefore Augustine asserted with full confidence, "The Church has believed most faithfully in the resurrection and immortality of the flesh, first in Christ and then in all those who are of the new age."[29] For a baptized Augustine, the idea of the "body putting on imperishability" (1 Cor 15:53) was no longer an oxymoron and philosophical nonsense. On the contrary, the resurrection of the body/flesh was a fundamental article of faith!

Nevertheless, it took some time before Augustine became a convinced proponent of the resurrection of the body. After his Neoplatonic conversion and arguably before his baptism, Augustine, just like the above-mentioned philosophers, considered the body a "prison" (*carcer*) and something which entangled the wings of the soul "by [its] sticky

---

civitate Dei 22.27; *De Genesi ad litteram* book 12). See G. Watson, "St. Augustine, the Platonists and the Resurrection Body: Augustine's Use of a Fragment from Porphyry," *ITQ* 50 (1983/1984) 221–32.

26. Augustine, *De Trinitate* 13.3.12; cf. *Sermo* 240.4–5. Curiously, Augustine himself wrote a treatise on the immortality of the soul (*De immortalitate animae*) but never a treatise on the resurrection of the body/flesh.

27. Augustine, *Sermo* 173.2.

28. Augustine pointed out that the word *body* meant "flesh," for "even after his resurrection the body of Christ is called flesh" (*Enchiridion* 23.91; cf. Tertullian, *De resurrectione carnis* 35).

29. Augustine, *De civitate Dei* 22.7; cf. *De fide et symbolo* 10.23; *In Johannis evangelium tractatus* 23.6; *Sermo* 241.1.

lime."[30] Yet when Augustine confessed the Creed of Milan at his baptism, he confessed his belief in "the resurrection of flesh (*in carnis resurrectionem*)."[31] Consequently while refuting various inadequate positions after becoming a Christian,[32] Augustine came to defend the truth of the resurrection of the flesh. His first argument for it can be found in *De animae quantitate* 76 (388 CE).

Because Augustine developed a *theological* anthropology, he had to consider the impact of the fall and sin on human nature. He deliberated that it was not the (material) body as such but the "*corruptible* body" which troubled the soul. The body which was "very good" (Gen 1:31) was corrupted by a willful turning away from God, by *aversio*. To be even clearer, Augustine further distinguished between a postlapsarian "flesh and blood" and the body which would be resurrected.[33] He had

30. Augustine, *Soliloquia* 1.14.24; cf. *Contra Academicos (Against the Academics)* 1.3.9. Later, in *Enarrationes in Psalmos* 142.8, Augustine explained that the word *prison* meant the corruption of the body rather than the body as such.

31. Cf. Augustine, *Sermo* 362.7.7. For the Creed of Milan, see J. N. D. Kelly, *Early Christian Creeds* (3d ed.; London: Longman, 1992), 173, and J. T. Lienhard, "Creed," in *Augustine through the Ages: An Encyclopedia* (ed. Allan D. Fitzgerald; Grand Rapids: Eerdmans, 1999), 255. Among other factors, the counter-philosophical, anti-Docetic, anti-Gnostic, and anti-Manichaean contexts may explain the preference of the provocative phrase, "resurrection of the *flesh*" (cf. the Apostolic Creed, the Creed of Milan) to that of the scriptural "resurrection of the *dead*" (cf. the Niceno-Constantinopolitan Creed, the Athanasian Creed). See J. G. Davies, "Factors Leading to the Emergence of Belief in the Resurrection of the Flesh," *JTS* 23 (1972): 448–55; *Creeds & Confessions of Faith in the Christian Tradition*, Vol. 1 (ed. J. Pelikan and V. Hotchkiss; New Haven: Yale University Press, 2003), 162–63, 669, 672, 676–77. Yet, the early Christian emendation of the word *dead* to the word *flesh* continues to cause complaints. For example, Balthasar observes that "Purists have removed the word 'body' [*Fleisch*] from the [German] creed as not sufficiently proper." See Hans Urs von Balthasar, *Credo: Meditations on the Apostles' Creed* (trans. D. Kipp; San Francisco: Ignatius, 2000), 95. However, there is still a further complication, as Bynum points out: "One cannot argue that refutation of Gnosticism or Docetism required bodily resurrection, for the question is exactly: why *not* Docetism?" See C. W. Bynum, *The Resurrection of the Body in Western Christianity, 200–1336* (Lectures on the History of Religions 15; New York: Columbia University Press, 1995), 27.

32. Augustine, *Contra Faustum Manichaeum* 20.22; *Sermo* 237.1 (Manicheism); *De civitate Dei* 22.4, 11-2, 26 (Neoplatonism), and *De civitate Dei* 14.5 (the difference between the two).

33. Augustine, *De agone Christiano (Christian Combat)* 32.34; *Enarrationes in Psalmos* 142.8; *Enchiridion* 23.91; *Epistula* 205.2.5, 16; *De civitate Dei* 13.16; *De fide et symbolo* 10.24; *De doctrina Christiana (Christian Instruction)* 1.19.18; 362.17.20-19.22. At times Augustine uses the words *flesh* and *body* interchangeably, but when he speaks about bodily resurrection, he usually insists on a distinction between the words *flesh*

to, because the Manichees were quick to point out that "Flesh and blood cannot inherit the kingdom of God, nor does the perishable inherit the imperishable" (1 Cor 15:50).[34] Augustine explained:

> To obtain blessedness ... we need not be rid of every kind of body, but only of the corruptible, irksome, painful, dying body; not of such bodies as the goodness of God made for the first human beings, but only of such as the punishment of sin has imposed upon us.[35]

In other words, the problem was not with matter but with sin. As Augustine explained, the body as such did not burden the soul, but the corruption of the body did,[36] just as the Scriptures said: "For a corruptible body burdens the soul" (Wis 9:15).

It is worth examining the reasons why Augustine affirmed the doctrine of the resurrection of the body as a necessary constituent of the resurrection of *totus homo*. His reasons may be more important than his particular conclusions.

First, bodily resurrection was necessary for preserving one's personal identity. Augustine employed a simple analogy to show that body was indeed part of what a person was: if someone tramples on your foot, you do not say, "You trample on my foot; but, you trample on me."[37] One's body is part of "me," the *ipse*, to whom the body belongs. In Luke 24:39 the resurrected Jesus too asks his disciples to touch his body in order that they might "see . . . that it is I myself." The body of the resurrected Christ had his transformed yet recognizable form . . . yes, he even had the scars of his wounds.[38] In the resurrection, Christian martyrs will also have their scars. Yet their scars "will not be a deformity, but a badge of honor."[39] For Augustine, such identity markers were important be-

---

(corrupted) and *body* (uncorrupted). See M. Alfeche, "The Rising of the Dead in the Works of Augustine (1 Cor 15:35–7)," *Augustiniana* 39 (1989): 72–84.

34. Augustine, *Contra Faustum Manichaeum* 11.3, 7, 16.29. For comparison, Tertullian wrote anti-Gnostically, "We are quite aware that this [i.e., 1 Cor 15:50] too is written; but ... our opponents place it in the front of the battle" (*De resurrectione carnis* 48).

35. Augustine, *De civitate Dei* 13.17.

36. Augustine, *De civitate Dei* 14.3.

37. Augustine, *Sermo* 361.14.14. Augustine called the "I" of an embodied soul *persona* (*Epistula* 137.11).

38. Augustine, *De civitate Dei* 22.15; *Retractationes (Reconsiderations)* 1.16; *Sermones* 242.3; 362.13.13.

39. Augustine, *De civitate Dei* 22.19. Bynum, *Resurrection of the Body*, 98, n.144,

cause they ensured the "continuity of the self as an individual person with an individual history."[40] Indeed, Augustine suggested that "it is in the Creator's plan that ... each individual shall preserve his own special features and a recognizable resemblance to his former self."[41] Precisely because the body provides the material and formal continuity of a person, Augustine insisted that the faithful would arise "in the same body (*in eodem corpore*)."[42]

Preserving personal identity through the continuity of the body, however, proved to be a tricky matter. Luke 21:18 offered a promise, "But not a hair of your head will perish." This promise laid a complicated burden of proof on those who defended bodily resurrection, because even the number of hairs (or alternatively, all the hair ever grown) seemed somehow important for the persevering of one's personal identity. The fact that "all bodies are to be restored whole and entire" invited "a challenge by people who are eager to pick a quarrel."[43] Because of the inquisitiveness of his lay congregants, as well as the problem of hair that falls out, Augustine also had to consider the problem of nail clippings, lost limbs, excess fat, and human bodies digested by cannibals.[44] These

---

quotes a rabbinic text from roughly the time of Augustine (*Sanhedrin* 91a–91b), which states explicitly that human beings are raised with their *defects* and then God will repair these later.

40. S. A. Harvey, *Scenting Salvation: Ancient Christianity and the Olfactory Imagination* (Berkeley: University of California Press, 2006), 233.

41. Augustine, *Enchiridion* 23.90.

42. Augustine, *De catechizandis rudibus* 27.54; cf. *De civitate Dei* 13.19; 22.12; Tertullian, *De resurrectione carnis* 52. Ps.-Justin asserts the sameness of the body very pointedly: "The resurrection is a resurrection of the flesh which died" (*De resurrectione* 10). However, if the resurrected body of Christ was the same, then why did Mary in the garden and the disciples on the road to Emmaus not recognize Jesus? Augustine reasoned that the resurrection was so unexpected that "they could not see him, even though they saw him" (*Sermo* 237.1). Mary and the disciples, who were Jews, believed in the general resurrection of the dead, but not in the resurrection of a single person, Jesus Christ, before the eschaton. Furthermore, because Jesus was accustomed to speaking in parables, they thought that his predictions about his resurrection referred to something else (Augustine, *In Johannis evangelium tractatus* 120.9; cf. John 20:9).

43. Augustine, *Sermo* 243.3.

44. Augustine, *De civitate Dei* 22.12, 19–20; *Enchiridion* 23.89; cf. 2 Macc 7:10–11; Athenagoras, *De resurrectione* 4–8; Ps.-Justin, *De resurrectione* 4; Tertullian, *De resurrectione carnis* 4. In *Sermo* 173.2, Augustine even interpreted the parable of lost sheep as a simile for the collection of dispersed limbs at the resurrection. At other times, Augustine dismissed the discussions about the exact nature of the resurrected body as irrelevant (*Sermo* 362.25.27; cf. 1 Cor 15:35–36).

awkward but sometimes rather entertaining arguments were usually brought forward against the idea of bodily resurrection, but Augustine revisited them in order to defend an important point: one's body was an essential part of one's personal identity.

Yet this affirmation of the bodily continuity of the person through resurrection had to be qualified. The resurrected body was not exactly the same body that a human being had during his or her lifetime. There would be a new act of God, which would alter the body so susceptible to sin to a body no longer able to sin (and die).[45] "We will all be changed" (1 Cor 15:51). The "perishable body" will put on "imperishability," and the "mortal body" "immortality" (1 Cor 15:53). The resurrected body "will be the same one, but it won't be the same one. It will be the very same one, because it will be this flesh; it won't be the same one, because it won't be mortal."[46] This means that the resurrected body will be not an "animal and earthly body" but rather a "spiritual body" (1 Cor 15:44). The "spiritual body," however, is neither pure spirit[47] nor a heavy[48] and corrupted lump of matter that feeds from other matter,[49] but a body in

---

45. Augusine, *De civitate Dei* 22.30.

46. Augustine, *Sermo* 154.17.

47. That is, in the resurrection, bodies will not be transformed into spirits but into spiritual *bodies* (*De civitate Dei* 13.20; *Enchiridion* 23.91; *Epistula* 205.2.10; *De fide et symbolo* 6.13; *Sermo* 242.11). However, some doubt about whether this will be the case is expressed in *Epistula* 148.5.16 (410 CE). Be this as it may, in *Sermo* 362.13.14, Augustine quotes Luke 24:39 to prove the above-mentioned point: "Look at my hands and my feet, see that it is myself . . . for a spirit does not have flesh and bones as you see that I have." Luke wrote these words to prove that the resurrected Jesus was not a mere spirit (Luke 24:37). For Augustine's handling of Luke 24:39, see M. Alfeche, "The Basis of Hope in the Resurrection of the Body according to Augustine," *Augustiniana* 36 (1986) 263–80.

48. Augustine responded to arguments about the natural weight of body, which were used to disprove bodily resurrection, in several of his writings, e.g., *De agone Christiano* 25.27; *De civitate Dei* 13.18; *Enchiridion* 23.91; *Sermones* 240.3; 242.5–10; 362.8.8.

49. Augustine studied the issue of whether the resurrected body still consumed food in *De civitate Dei* 13.22, 23; *Epistula* 102.6; *Sermones* 242.2, 12 and 362.11–122. He concluded that there was no *necessity* for the person with a resurrected body to eat, although just like angels and the resurrected Christ in Luke 24:43, the resurrected person had the *power* to do so if the person so willed. Here Augustine had an interesting proof text: Tobit 12:19: "Although you were watching me [i.e., the angel Raphael eating], I really did not eat or drink anything—but what you saw was a vision." The resurrected bodies will be sustained not by food but by a life-giving Spirit (Rom 8:10–11; 1 Cor 15:45). Nevertheless, the digestive systems will still be existent, but for the sake of completeness and beauty. See Augustine, *De civitate Dei* 22.19, 30; *Contra Julianum (Against Julian)* 5.5.22; *Enchiridion* 23.91; *Sermo* 243.4, 6; cf. Tertullian, *De resurrectione carnis* 61.

perfect subjection to the spirit.[50] Speaking about the "spiritual body," Augustine made sure that he was understood correctly: resurrected humans "will be spiritual not because they will cease to be bodies, but because they will be sustained by the quickening spirit."[51] His point was that in resurrection, human beings would not merely be resuscitated to their previous bodily conditions—as Lazarus was (John 11:44)—but their bodies would be transformed (Phil 3:21) into a qualitatively different mode of existence. For Augustine's mature theology of resurrection, the metaphor of the seed (1 Corinthians 15) did not adequately emphasize the discontinuity alongside the material/formal continuity. Mortal bodies rotted rather than developed organically into something new. The resurrected body, however, was free from these processes and developments rather than a victim of them. Accordingly, Augustine preferred the non-organic images of re-cast statues and re-built ships to that of the seed.[52] Thus for him, this means that resurrected human beings are body and soul minus corruption,[53] expressed in the epigramic statement: "The flesh that is now your embarrassment will afterward be your embellishment."[54]

Resurrection of the same body is not denied by Augustine, therefore, even to naturally deformed or accidentally mutilated persons. There should not be any despair, however, for their disfigured bodies will be amended and perfected.[55] "The bodies of the saints ... will rise free from any blemish or deformity, as they will be free from any corruption, burden, or impediment."[56] Augustine was not sure, though, whether the bodies of evil persons would be without "blemish or deformity."[57]

Augustine's second major reason for affirming the resurrection of the body was that it was a consequence of his anthropology. He believed

50. Augustine, *De civitate Dei* 13.20; *De continentia (Continence)* 19; *De fide et symbolo* 6.13.

51. Augustine, *De civitate Dei*, 13.22. The Scriptures too speak about the redemption *of* bodies rather than the redemption *from* bodies (Rom 7:24; 8:2; Augustine, *Sermo* 155.15).

52. Bynum, *Resurrection of the Body*, 72, 96, 101–2.

53. Augustine, *Sermones* 241.7; 242.4; 242A.3; 278.5; 362.15.18—16.19.

54. Augustine, *Sermo* 240.3.

55. Augustine, *Enchiridion* 23.86.

56. Augustine, *Enchiridion* 23.91; cf. *Sermo* 217.10; Isa 35:5–6; Ps.-Justin, *De resurrectione* 4.

57. Augustine, *Enchiridion* 23.92.

that a human being, *totus homo*, is neither the body alone nor the soul alone, but body *and* soul.[58] Once again, despite the fact that "there is a great difference between soul and body,"[59] a human being "is not a body alone or a soul alone; rather a human being is composed of both body and soul."[60] To quote H. I. Marrou (in an inclusive version),

> St. Augustine tries to express a single fundamental truth: human beings are at one and the same time soul *and* body, flesh *and* spirit; and if human beings are to be truly saved their salvation must embrace their whole being and therefore their bodies must also, by glorious resurrection, be taken up to eternity.[61]

For Augustine "the soul is not the whole human being" although the soul is "the better part of a human being," and "the body is not the whole human being" although the body is "the inferior part of a human being."[62] Taking a lead from Varro, Augustine writes, "What is a human being? . . . [T]here are two elements in human nature, body and soul, and . . . of these elements, the soul is the better and by far the more worthy. . . . The body is to a human being as the horse is to the horse rider."[63] The soul is

---

58. The bishop of Hippo definitely assumed that *totus homo* consisted of a body and soul, although the issue of *how* the body was related to the soul bothered him throughout his life. See John Rist, *Augustine: Ancient Thought Baptized* (Cambridge: Cambridge University Press, 1994), 97–104. Human beings have a single human nature, which combines the two radically different kinds of entities—a body and a soul. These radically different entities come together and constitute a single *persona*. See Peter Burnell, *The Augustinian Person* (Washington DC: Catholic University of America Press, 2005), 7, 41–44; Gerard J. P. O'Daly, *Augustine's Philosophy of Mind* (London: Duckworth, 1987), 43–45, 57–58.

59. Augustine, *In Johannis evangelium tractatus* 20.10.

60. Augustine, *De civitate Dei* 13.24; cf. 14.4; *Confessiones* 10.6.9; *Epistula* 3.4; *De Genesi adversus Manichaeos (On Genesis against the Manichees)* 2.7.9; *In Johannis evangelium tractatus* 19.15; *De moribus ecclesiae catholicae (The Way of Life of the Catholic Church)* 1.4.6; *Sermones* 128.9; 154.9; 277.3; *De Trinitate* 15.2.11. Cf. Athenagoras, *De resurrectione* 15 and 25; Ps.-Justin, *De resurrectione* 8; Tertullian, *De resurrectione carnis* 34. Platonic anthropology took a human being to consist of three elements—spirit, soul, and body (cf. 1 Thess 5:23), but Augustine acknowledged that people often spoke only about two, body and soul (*De diversis quaestionibus* 7; *Epistula* 3.4; *De fide et symbolo* 10.24; *Soliloquia* 1.21).

61. Marrou, *Resurrection*, 16.

62. Augustine, *De civitate Dei* 13.24; cf. *Epistula* 3.4; *De fide et symbolo* 10.24; *De immortalitate animae (The Immortality of the Soul)* 2.2; *De musica (Music)* 6.5.12-13; *Ad Simplicianum* 1.2.18.

63. Augustine, *De civitate Dei* 19.3.

"a certain kind of substance ... fitted to rule the body,"[64] and also a means between God and body.[65] It does not follow, however, that since the body is inferior to the soul, the body can simply be eliminated. A human being is a unity of body and soul, and none of the constituent elements can be eliminated without destroying the human being. As John Rist asserts, "Augustine became almost as hostile to 'spiritual' reductionism as he had been since his conversion to 'material' reductionism."[66] He wrote:

> I want the whole thing (*totum*) to be healed, because I am the whole thing. I don't want my flesh, as something foreign to me, to be separated from me for ever, but to be all healed with me for ever.[67]

Augustine affirmed the unity of the body and soul in the resurrection for both the unjust and the just. This was not a new development, as Nickelsburg points out: "Late resurrection texts [of the Bible] specify resurrection of the body as the means by which God will administer rewards and punishments."[68] On one hand, the death of an *unjust* person and the punishment of the body because of the sin of the soul[69] testify to the necessary unity of body and soul. The "death" of the immortal soul is its separation from God;[70] the death of the mortal body is its separation from the soul.[71] The death of both body *and* soul is truly the death of *totus homo*, because the soul as well as the body is cut off from its source of life.[72] Once again, for Augustine the first death of a human be-

---

64. Augustine, *De quantitate animae* 13.22; cf. *De Genesi ad litteram* 12.35.68.

65. Augustine, *Enarrationes in Psalmos* 145.5; *Epistula* 140.3; *De immortalitate animae* 24.

66. Rist, *Augustine*, 101.

67. Augustine, *Sermo* 30.4.

68. Nickelsburg, *Resurrection, Immortality, and Eternal Life*, 217.

69. Iniquity brings about the death of the soul, and the death of the soul brings about the punishment of the body (Augustine, *De civitate Dei* 13.13; 14.3; *Contra Julianum opus imperfectum* 6.31; *De Genesi ad litteram* 6.22.33; cf. 1 Cor 15:45). See M. Lamberigts, "Julian of Aeclanum and Augustine of Hippo on 1 Cor. 15," *Studia Patristica* 43 (2006) 155–72.

70. Augustine, *De civitate Dei* 13.15. For Greek metaphysicians, except for the Stoics and Epicureans, the death of the soul was inconceivable. Whatever the death of the soul means, it seems that Matt 10:28, which speaks about the destruction of "body and soul" in hell, assumes it.

71. Augustine, *Contra Julianum opus imperfectum* 6.31.2.

72. Augustine, *De civitate Dei* 13.2.

ing is when the soul is "without God and *without* the body"; the "second death" of a human being (Rev 20:6, 14), eternal death, is when the soul is "without God but *with* the body."[73] The "second death" cannot take place "before the soul and body are united so completely that they cannot by any means be separated."[74] The reason why the unity of soul and body matters in the "second death" is that a person needs a body to feel the eternal pain (Matt 25:41; Rev 20:10)![75] Earlier, Augustine had defined sensation as a "direct awareness in the soul of a bodily experience."[76] However, naked souls and dead bodies do not feel anything. Therefore, the bodies of the unjust will be resurrected because only in this way their punishment "affects their entire being."[77] The souls of the unjust will receive their bodies as "partner[s] in punishment."[78]

On the other hand, the resurrection of a *just* person also testifies to the necessary unity of body and soul. Happiness, the end universally sought,[79] is unthinkable without a body.[80] Therefore, after being separated from their bodies in death, the souls of the saints "do not desire to forget their bodies."[81] Just persons (ethics matter!) will receive their

---

73. Augustine, *De civitate Dei* 13.2.; cf. Athenagoras, *De resurrectione* 18–23; Tertullian, *De resurrectione carnis* 15–17, 56, and 60.

74. Augustine, *De civitate Dei* 13.2. In *De civitate Dei* 13.11, Augustine also asserts that the "second death" "consists not in the separation of soul and body but in the union of both in eternal punishment."

75. The opinion of patristic authors differed on the eternity of the punishment of the wicked. Critics of the notion of eternal punishment have wondered what kind of God such convictions assume: a God of vengeance or a God of love, a God of justice or a God of grace? These objections were not unknown to Augustine (*De civitate Dei* 21.17; *Enchiridion* 29.112). He also wondered whether it was morally acceptable that sins committed in time were punished eternally (*De civitate Dei* 21.11).

76. Augustine, *De quantitate animae (The Magnitude of the Soul)* 25.49 (388 CE); cf. *Epistula* 148.5.16 (410 CE).

77. Augustine, *Sermo* 362.20.23.

78. Augustine, *Epistula* 166.6 (*De origine animae*).

79. Augustine, *Contra Academicos* 1.2.5; *De civitate Dei* 14.25; *Confessiones* 10.21.31; *Sermo* 150.4; *De Trinitate* 13.8.

80. Augustine, *De Genesi ad litteram* 12.35.68–36.69. For the diametrically different opinion of the philosophers, see *Sermo* 241.6. Augustine eventually concluded that in order to have a vision of God equal to that of the angels, resurrected souls needed to have their resurrected bodies to see God (*De civitate Dei* 22.29). In *Epistula* 147.9.22, Augustine thought that "perhaps" this was the case; but in *Epistula* 92.2–5; *De Genesi ad litteram* 12.3.6–12.26, 30.58–31.59, he denied that this was the case.

81. Augustine, *De civitate Dei* 13.20; cf. 2 Cor 5:2–4.

Totus Homo

bodies as "partner[s] in glory."⁸² Augustine declared, "This faith of ours promises . . . that the whole human being, who consists of course of soul and body too, is going to be immortal, and therefore truly happy."⁸³ Since the body was punished because of the sin of the soul in the first place, the body will eventually also share in the blessedness of the soul. The unity of the body and the soul is again presupposed.

To recapitulate, at least for two good interrelated reasons—because preserving one's identity requires a body, and because human being is constituted as the unity of body and soul—Augustine affirmed the doctrine of the resurrection of the body and, consequently, the resurrection of *totus homo*.

Finally, we may ask how Augustine's holistic understanding of resurrection is to be understood, inclusively or exclusively? Does it mean the deliverance of the whole society and the entire created order or strictly (some) human beings only?⁸⁴

The Greek fathers understood the salvation/transformation of creation more inclusively than did Augustine. Arguably, the bishop of Hippo was the first church father to limit the ambiguous words, "whole creation," in Rom 8:22 to the tripartite human being—that is, to the human body and soul/spirit.⁸⁵ The bishop noted that Rom 8:22 did not say *totam creaturam* but *omnem creaturam*, and therefore he took the text to refer to human body, soul, and spirit and not to the whole creation including angels and animals. Alternatively, the word "creation" in Rom 8:21–23 could refer to unbelievers—but still to human beings—because it was distinguished from the "children of God" in 8:21 and 23.⁸⁶ Likewise, Augustine's text of John 12:32, supported by P⁶⁶, read *omnia* ("all things")

---

82. Augustine, *Epistula* 166.5.

83. Augustine, *De Trinitate* 13.3.12; cf. Athenagoras, *De resurrectione* 25. J. A. Mourant writes, "Faith . . . teaches us that the full realization of our eternal happiness rests upon the resurrection of the body." (Mourant, *Augustine on Immortality*; Saint Augustine Lecture Series, Saint Augustine and the Augustinian Tradition, 1968 [Villanova: Villanova University Press, 1969], 15).

84. It might be wise to reiterate Thomas E. Clarke's warning here: "It is always risky to seek in an ancient writer the answer to a question which he never explicitly put to himself; anachronism has made the history of scholarship a road weighed with ugly corpses (Clarke, "St. Augustine and Cosmic Redemption," *TS* 19 [1958] 133).

85. Augustine, *De diversis quaestionibus* 67; *De fide et symbolo* 10.23–24.

86. Augustine, *Expositio Epistulae ad Galatas (Commentary on the Letter to the Galatians)* 63.5–7.

rather than *omnes* ("everyone"): "I will draw all things to myself." Yet his commentary restricted this verse to the elect and explained it anthropologically: "He did not allude to the totality of human beings, but to a creature in its personal integrity, that is, to spirit, soul, and body."[87] Yes, we may agree that "it is a horrible distortion of Christian eschatology to act as if only humans mattered,"[88] but one has to admit that in his approach, the bishop of Hippo was anthropocentric and not cosmocentric. Henri Marrou points out that already in his *Soliloquia*, Augustine "ventured to sum up the whole program of a philosophy in the simple binominal: *de anima, de Deo*. He had no place, it seems, for a *peri kosmou*."[89]

This said, it is important to keep in mind that for Augustine, human beings and the *kosmos* were not mutually exclusive categories. Both were God's creation and awaited eschatological transfiguration rather than eradication. Augustine affirmed that when "this world passes away, this will not come about by the utter destruction of things, but by their transformation."[90] The "old" world will become a "new" world, but it will still be a world. Just as the "old" world will become a "new" world, the human "animal [animated] body" will be resurrected as a "spiritual body" (1 Cor 15:44). But it will still be a body. Augustine offered the supporting idea that human beings were "made on the same day as beasts," and therefore "it is permissible to opine" in a sense that "soars astronomically beyond human thought" that the whole creation shared in the likeness of God.[91] While human beings are *rational* animals, they are nevertheless part of a larger category of created "animals," which is "groaning" for redemption. Augustine's anthropocentric focus in no way negated the all-encompassing salvation of the whole creation. At the same time, he understood the deliverance

---

87. Augustine, *In Johannis evangelium tractatus* 52:11.

88. Luke Timothy Johnson, *The Creed: What Christians Belivie and Why It Matters* (New York: Doubleday, 2003), 294.

89. Marrou, *Resurrection*, 29–30.

90. Augustine, *De civitate Dei* 20.14. Augustine pointed out that 1 Cor 7:31 spoke about the passing away of the form (*figura*) rather than the nature of world. The whole creation will experience a similar transformation/purification from corruption, as will resurrected human bodies (*De civitate Dei* 20.16). In *Confessiones* 12.28.38, Augustine said about the creation, "So it returns to you, the One, according to the appointed capacity granted to each entity according to its genus." He continued, "It remains for it [i.e., the creation] to be converted to him by whom it was made" (13.4.5).

91. Augustine, *De Genesi ad litteram imp.* 16.55, 59,

of the rest of the creation as a new act of God rather than an automatic side effect of the resurrection of human beings.[92]

One final point: human beings are social beings, not only as citizens of the earthly city, but also as citizens of the heavenly city.[93] "Nothing [is] so social by nature as this race."[94] This constitution of human beings as relational beings is patterned after the image of the Trinity. The divine persons are identified "by way of relationship."[95] Just as the Trinitarian persons are identified by their relationships, human beings too find their identity through their relationships. This implies, in turn, that the redemption of *totus homo* must comprise the redemption of the relationships of individual persons with other living beings. And indeed, the fact that there is said to be a fellowship between the just and the angels indicates the existence of (redeemed) social relations in the world to come.[96]

---

92. Clarke, "St. Augustine and Cosmic Redemption," 138–41.

93. The very designation "*city* of God" (cf. Revelation 21) implies the existence of social interaction and interpersonal relationships in the eschatological kingdom.

94. Augustine, *De civitate Dei* 12.28.

95. Augustine, *De Trinitate* 7.3.11. According to Porphyry, *person* meant a "unique collection of properties" (*Isagogue* 7.20–26), which was defined through relations to other persons (i.e., to other "unique collection[s] of properties"). The "unique collection of properties" is that by which the person is constituted as distinct. See Lucian Turcescu, *Gregory of Nyssa and the Concept of Divine Persons* (American Academy of Religion Academy Series; Oxford: Oxford University Press, 2005), 57; Richard Sorabji, *Self: Ancient and Modern Insights about Individuality, Life, and Death* (Chicago: University of Chicago Press, 2006), 138–42. There are three sets of "collections of properties" in the Godhead, which consist of unique combinations of "particular characteristics": the Father is fully divine, eternal, and *unbegotten*; the Son is fully divine, eternal, and *begotten*; and the Holy Spirit is fully divine, eternal, and *proceeding*. These three sets of "collections of properties" distinguish between the three divine persons as Father, Son, and Holy Spirit.

96. Augustine, *De civitate Dei* 12.9; 14.28; *Confessiones* 9.3.6, 9.13.37 (human beings, Nebridius, and Monnica); *Epistula* 147.9.22 (angels, who also have spiritual bodies [*De Genesi ad litteram* 6.24]). Second Baruch 50 too indicates that the resurrected dead will be recognizable.

Part Two
Scriptural Expositions

5

Mission in Matthew

Relating to the Resurrected Christ

Isam E. Ballenger

Through writings, lectures, and sermons, Thorwald Lorenzen has pointed out the correlation between the reality of the resurrection of Jesus Christ and the mission of the church, the former becoming manifest through the latter. Christian mission comes under legitimate suspicion when its practice betrays the reality upon which it is based. Such betrayal occurs when mission goals and methods become an enterprise that is something other than what Lorenzen might describe as "participation in the passion of God for the world." Lorenzen provokes a critical evaluation of the church and its mission, insisting on continuity with the biblical witness and a resultant discipleship that confronts social-ethical issues with resurrection faith.

Continuity and discipleship are themes found in the Gospel according to Matthew. Both concepts find their substance through relationships, the prior and ultimate relationship being within God, evidenced through the sending (mission) of the Son and the Holy Spirit. This sending in the New Testament is seen in light of God's acts on behalf of Israel, that is, as continuity with and fulfillment of Old Testament experiences and expectations. Jesus' mountain sermon, recalling Sinai exhortations of Moses, teaches an ethical standard to disciples, who through word and deed give evidence of the kingdom of heaven that has come and is coming. Matthew concludes his Gospel with the mission commission: disciples are to make disciples, who follow the teachings of Jesus and relate to the presence of the resurrected Jesus Christ.

The essence and aim of the church's mission is relating to the resurrected Christ, indistinguishable in Matthew's Gospel from being disciples and making disciples. This position is here defended by considering the idea of "sending" in the Bible, beginning in the Old Testament and continuing to fulfillment in the sending of Jesus, who in turn calls and sends disciples, thus continuing, but also intensifying, the divine-human relationship. It is this relationship that is to be extended for the good of all creation, that is, the particular for the universal. The "new reality" of the resurrection and the relationship-creating realm it affirms become mode and message of the mission, giving equal importance to being disciples and making disciples. This "new reality," Lorenzen maintains, is one of peace, justice, and equality. He summons the modern disciple to bear the costs both of resisting violence, racism, environmental degradation, and militarism and of representing the poor and powerless. It is herein suggested that Lorenzen's thought resonates well with Matthew's Gospel. No writing surpasses this Gospel in its mission expectations and its dimensions of discipleship.

One should consult the works of other New Testament scholars for discussion regarding the authorship, date, and location of the first canonical Gospel. Here a few brief comments will suffice. I use the traditional designation of "Matthew" for the author. It is assumed that the assembly to whom this Gospel was originally written contained Jewish followers of Jesus, whom Matthew proclaims as the one sent from God, crucified and resurrected. The assembly also included an increasing number of Gentiles. The writer is likely a Jewish Christian, writing in Greek, probably between 80 and 90 CE, from a city containing a significant Diaspora Jewish population, perhaps Antioch in Syria. While dependent upon sources such as Mark's Gospel and material designated "Q," Matthew finds these accounts inadequate to convey his concerns and teachings to his intended audience. Thus he rearranges, expands, abridges, and clarifies his sources, omitting and substituting according to his Christology, ecclesiology, missiology, and understanding of history.[1]

There is in the biblical witness a plurality that evokes continual listening, learning, and appropriating, that is, a plurality that arises from and, at the same time, perpetuates the mission of the church. Liberation theologians find in Matthew's Gospel a "Christology from below," provid-

---

1. See Jack Dean Kingsbury, *Matthew* (Proclamation Commentaries; 2nd ed.; Philadelphia: Fortress, 1986), 20–26.

ing a biblical defense for their emphasis upon orthopraxis as contrasted with orthodoxy. For Matthew, the resurrection of the crucified Jesus is the "hinge of history," from which there emerge potential relationships on a universal scale. Resurrection implies the end to boundaries and the possibility of a mission that is geographically, ethnically, racially, and culturally inclusive. *Resurrection implies contemporaneity*, bringing the crucified-resurrected Jesus and his teachings to bear upon modern times and issues currently facing the human family. Resurrection affirms the humanity of Jesus, the life he lived, the truth he served, the powers he denied, the teachings he imparted. None other than the crucified Jesus appeared to the disciples on the mountain in Galilee (Matt 28:16–20).

Matthew's Gospel proclaims that the Son of Man and the Son of God are one, and that through this divine-human relationship the kingdom of heaven has drawn nigh (4:17). Relationship begets relationships; this is the essence and method of Christian mission in the first canonical Gospel. The foundational and creational relationship is within God. The consequences of this "movement" within God are universal and historical; thus the relationship is designated a "sending." The One sent is the One who sends. Matthew in his mission commission states that those who are sent, designated disciples, live in relationship with the sender, with Life as opposed to the powers of death. All nations become "holy land," and out of the people of all nations, disciples are to replicate themselves (28:16–20). Because this divine-human relationship is personal, intense, specific, and consequential, one finds in Matthew the note of exclusivity, a calling necessary to establish the kind of relationship that is both possible, though not routine, and exemplary, though not exhaustive. Elicited everywhere and offered freely, the acceptance and full realization of this relationship does not happen without a conscious and consequential response (16:24–27). The exclusive relationship of Father and Son and the exclusive relationship of teacher and disciple serve the inclusive relationship with the world, the actual serving the potential, the kingdom come seeking the kingdom to come, that is, the church relating to her living Lord and consequently to the world.

MISSION AS SENDING

The word *mission* appears neither in Matthew's Gospel nor in any other New Testament writing. It is derived from the Latin *mitto*. The Greek equivalents are ἀποστέλλειν ("to send forth"), occurring 137 times in the New Testament, and πέμπειν ("to send"), occurring seventy-nine times, thirty-three times in the Fourth Gospel. The theme of mission, therefore, is sending forth a messenger or messengers. The basic biblical idea of sending is first and foremost that which occurs in God, that is, the Father sends the Son and the Spirit is sent by the Father and the Son.[2] The events of the Bible are consequences of sendings that take place within the Deity: first creation (a sending forth, represented by the repetition of "And God said . . ." in Genesis 1:3, 6, 9, 14, 20, 24; note also the prologue of John's Gospel, Colossians 1:15–20, and the prologue of the Letter to the Hebrews); and thereafter God's relation to the creation as depicted in election, judgment, salvation, and consummation. Mission begins in God and continues in God (an eternal sending), expressed by the concept of *missio Dei*, a divine mission that precedes, transcends, enables, and accompanies the mission of the church. The particularity expressed by election serves the universalism expressed by the New Testament metaphor "God is love." In the words of Lucien Legrand, "The God of historical election of Israel is also the God of cosmic benedictions."[3] Scripture attests to such "cosmic benedictions," noting the mysterious, unrestrained, and consequential movement of God, and to historical election, noting the self-imposed limitations of God's sending, a particularism in relationships, expressed in the Old Testament by exodus and covenant, and in Matthew by discipleship. Matthew gives examples of "cosmic benedictions" in encounters in which Jesus is surprised by a man's faith (8:5–13) and attracted by a woman's wisdom (15:21–28). In both examples, faith appeared to be out of bounds. An unexplained relation to truth is in the background. It seems clear, however, that Matthew's primary intent is to instruct the young church in its mission of relating to the resurrected Christ, that is, both by being and making disciples who do the will of God, following not only the commission of the Gospel (28:16–20) but also the example of Jesus as presented in the Gospel.

Mission (sending) implies relationship (Sender, Sent, Spirit) intrinsic to both the origination and the destination of the sending. Relationship implied in the Trinity (Father, Son, Spirit), the initiating sending (*missio Dei*), differs in significance but not in kind from relationship implied in the mission of the church. In both a vital communion unites the sub-

---

2. Lucien Legrand, *Unity and Plurality* (trans. Robert R. Barr; Maryknoll, NY: Orbis, 1990), xiv.

3. Legrand, *Unity and Plurality: Mission in the Bible*, 14.

jects for creative ends. The sending within God yields the Son and the Holy Spirit. The church that is born of this sending lives in and through its source of life, that is, in and through its relationship to the Son and the Holy Spirit. Other than habit, deeper than tradition, beyond doctrinal correctness, the divine-human relationship must be vital, living, and contemporary, making the petitions of the model prayer an appeal with passion (Matt 6:9–13) and willful participation. To summarize, the sending within the church (of the church) arises out of consciousness of and participation in the Trinity, relating to the Father, Son, and Spirit as indicated in the initiation rite of baptism (Matt 28:19).

It is important to underscore the metaphorical and symbolic character of this use of "sending." It serves to express an inevitable consequence of the reality of God as proclaimed in the Bible. The acts of God as recorded in scripture imply internal and external divine relationships. God as Trinity implies relationship, God as covenant partner implies relationship, and God as love implies relationship. Relationship necessitates making a distinction, the presence of another, inclusiveness, a movement within the self and beyond the self, a movement that can be termed "sending." Mission then implies a sending (relationship) whose aim is to bring into relationship or to restore relationship. The essence and aim of mission are one (being and making disciples). Matthew indicates this by reporting that Jesus brings vertical and horizontal dimensions together in the greatest commandments (Matt 22:34–40). Love is essence and aim. Being a disciple (relating to Jesus Christ) and making disciples (relating to others) are inseparable, as implied in the great pronouncement of Matthew's Sermon on the Mount (5:13–16).

MATTHEW'S MISSION COMMISSION

Mission, the "being sent" that begins, ends, and permeates the gospel narratives, should first be understood in its qualitative dimension (essence/aim) that in turn gives direction and substance to its quantitative dimension (expansion). Church mission history reveals that the latter dimension has often prevailed to the lamentable detriment of the former, one reason being the interpretation of a crucial passage in Matthew's Gospel. Mission in Matthew is diminished through a misinterpretation of the so-called Great Commission (28:16–20), when the meaning of these significant verses at the end of the Gospel is reduced to winning converts or extending one's own church organization. By such mistaken meaning the text has been associated with superficial church growth, colonialism, and cultural imperialism.

At the first world missionary conference in Edinburgh in 1910, a debate ensued because of the way Matthew's Great Commission was being used. Approximately 1,200 delegates attended, but only eighteen of these came from "younger churches" and only seventeen non-white delegates were present. Neither Roman Catholic nor Orthodox churches participated. The chairman of the conference was an American Methodist layman, John R. Mott (1865–1955), who was to become very influential in Protestant missionary activity. As a student at Cornell University, Mott participated in the work of the YMCA, which had been founded in England in 1885 by William Taylor as a student mission organization. D. L. Moody led the U.S. movement and was instrumental both in establishing the Student Volunteer Movement (SVM) in 1887 and in organizing the World Student Christian Federation (WSCF) in 1895. Mott became a leader in the student movement. His name is associated with the slogan: "The Evangelization of the World in this Generation." The slogan invited much criticism but also generated extensive enthusiasm. Gustav Warneck, German professor and founder of the study of missiology as a scholarly discipline, supposed that Mott's motto implied a superficial preaching of the gospel as quickly as possible in as many places as possible to as many people as possible. Little thought was given to the task of "making disciples." Some accused Mott of naïve American triumphalism. The Edinburgh Conference dealt with the question: "How Missions?" It dealt with strategy at a time when enthusiasm was at a high level. Enthusiasm gained the upper hand. The "Great Commission" was the basis, and obedience was the demand. Warneck, representing typical German *Gründlichkeit* (thoroughness), saw in Mott and the movement a mission limited to proclamation by large numbers of zealous but unprepared evangelists who moved rapidly from place to place. Warneck pointed out that the popular use of the commission in Matthew's Gospel contained serious errors of biblical exposition and interpretation. He sought to moderate Mott's "evangelization machinery" because it was based on an improper eschatological view, that is, that the church should hasten to fulfill its global mission and thereby make possible the second coming of Christ. Warneck pointed out that the imperative of the commission is to "make disciples," which requires more time and effort than mere proclamation. He also faulted the mechanical mode of calculating results and measuring success.[4]

Subsequent to Edinburgh, international mission conferences dealt with pertinent issues facing the world church and challenging cooperation between sending and receiving bodies. Mission during the twentieth century generally followed the patterns established in the nineteenth century: the period Kenneth Scott Latourette called "the great century." It was a time of geographical expansion, creating a momentum that shunned criticism and discouraged change. No text was more frequently quoted than the commission at the end of Matthew's Gospel. In Protestant circles today, Christian mission receives no more forceful defense or avid promotion than that originating from this concluding passage in Matt 28:18–20. This commission has achieved such prominence as to become the basis for ecumenical cooperation among numerous conservative evangelical church denominations. Among these traditions, the designation "Great Commission Christians" implies a commitment to global evangelism, often with the resultant planting of churches and promotion of a fundamentalist approach to biblical interpretation.

The major emphasis of the commission has been placed in the command "to go," granting traditional English translations an unwarranted priority. But as Gustav Warneck had earlier argued, the actual imperative of the text is to "make disciples," a task that has been neglected in favor of an easier, albeit superficial, path. Placed in the context of Matthew's Gospel, this text has as much to do with being a teacher as it does with being an evangelist. Matthew clearly does not represent mission as something to be accomplished hastily and to be measured by statistics. Mission in this Gospel necessitates the cost of persevering in relating to Christ, and is thus inseparable from relating after the manner of Christ to others and to creation.

The sending of the Son as proclaimed in Matthew's Gospel would appear to be a failure, if measured in terms of how far Jesus' mission extended geographically or how many persons it gathered numerically. Jesus limited his ministry almost entirely to Galilee (Matt 11:1), and although one reads of the crowds who gathered around him, those accepting the demanding cost of discipleship remained few in number (8:19–22; 10:37–39). Matthew makes clear that the mission of Jesus

---

4. See Stephen Neill, *A History of Christian Missions* (Pelican History of the Church 6; Harmondsworth, UK: Penguin, 1964), 332.

was intentionally a limited mission (10:5; 15:24), that is, until after the crucifixion and resurrection. During the ministry of the historical Jesus, windows to foreigners were opened slightly, perhaps preparing Matthew's audience for the inclusive commission at the end of the Gospel and perhaps indicating the universal sending of God ("cosmic benedictions") in contrast to the particularity of discipleship. The post-resurrection commission indicates that the mission goal becomes more inclusive (to the nations) with respect to the question, whither mission? but remains exclusive with respect to the question, what mission? (make disciples). The resurrection makes possible relationships that are new and unprecedented, nevertheless relationships inextricably bound to the past. History is prologue; the present and future are fulfillment.

FULFILLMENT OF OLD TESTAMENT EXPECTATIONS

One of the chief purposes of Matthew's Gospel, according to Donald Senior, was to provide his community with a sense of continuity with the past and a vision for the future.[5] Matthew proclaimed fulfillment rather than abandonment of Old Testament expectations (1:1–17, 22–23; 2:5–6; 3:3; 5:17; 12:17–21; 17:3–12; 21:4–5). Prophetic hope was met through the historical event and subsequent testimony: that in the coming of Jesus, God is now with us (1:23); Jesus is the Son of God (3:17), sent by the Father (10:40). Relationship with God, building upon the past, became more intimate, demonstrated and personified by the Son of God, who, in relationship with his Father, does the will of God and clarifies the reign of God. Thereby the Son of God elicits a following, members of which, motivated by the divine-human relationship, also learn and do the will of God and fulfill the mission of Israel. As Israel was to be a light to the nations and bring salvation to the ends of the earth (Isa 49:6), the disciples of Jesus are to be the light of the world (Matt 5:14) and make disciples of all nations, baptizing and teaching (28:19–20).

The divine-human relationship cannot but be consequential. Both the intention for Israel and the history of Israel testify to a consequential relationship, the climax being the event to which the New Testament testifies. As portrayed in Matthew's Gospel, Jesus relates in a special way to his disciples. As a consequence, mission is inevitable; it is what dis-

---

5. Donald Senior, *The Gospel of Matthew* (Interpreting Biblical Texts; Nashville: Abingdon, 1997), 77.

ciples do; going forth is assumed, not commanded (28:19). Relationship produces deeds. Salt will be salt and light will be light (5:13–14), both metaphors suggesting fulfillment. The Law (Torah) was likened to salt in Jewish literature, and the light of Israel's peculiar relation to God was to extend to the nations (Isa 42:6; 49:6). The epitome of fulfillment and vision for the future are evident in the final commission of Matthew's Gospel (28:18–20). In this passage, disciples are and will be those called of God to live in and through the presence of the resurrected Christ, demonstrating and proclaiming the "new reality" that offers hope and peace for the world.

THE PARTICULAR RELATIONSHIP OF THE DISCIPLE

As with the election of Israel, the calling of the disciples can be attributed only to the grace and wisdom of God. Statements in Matthew regarding the disciples indicate that Jesus called them, and they followed him; that is, Jesus initiated the relationship, and the reader is given no indication of any special qualification. In fact, the information regarding the call of Matthew would tend to disqualify him as a suitable candidate for discipleship; he was "sitting at the tax collector's booth" (Matt 9:9). His surprise and moment of decision are depicted in Caravaggio's famous painting *The Call of Saint Matthew*, showing the tax collector pointing to himself with one hand, as if to say, "Who, me?" while with the other he clasps a coin. Jesus' call came to Matthew and the others as an act of grace, the only requirement being the response. The response, however, was an act, a leaving and moving, each more convincing than mere verbal assent. It was the beginning of a relationship of redemption, in which the summoned would learn to live with new perspectives and heightened awareness.

Granted, the initial response of each of the Twelve is not recorded, and we cannot assume that the Twelve were the only followers. Crowds followed Jesus, heard his teachings and saw his healings. Many may have responded with differing degrees of understanding and commitment. This is no less true today. Limits of communion may not be imposed upon the resurrected Christ; no one formula is given for relating to the kingdom Jesus introduced. Making judgments is an exercise in futility, as explained in the parable of the tares among the wheat (Matt 13:24–30) and the parable of the net (Matt 13:47–50). Nevertheless, the first disciples are prototypes for the church. It is this high standard that is set in Matthew's final mission commission. What Jesus did with the twelve disciples does not represent all that was taking place because of the sending within God, but this particular relationship does represent, according to Matthew, God's design for the church as a community of disciples, living with the reality of God's presence and the intention of doing the will of God.

If the disciples in Matthew's Gospel may be taken as examples of discipleship, models for the goal of mission, it must be acknowledged that their discipleship was exemplified neither by perfection nor by success. Their discipleship was exemplified by their relationship. Matthew does not hide their humanity. On the contrary, they are at times weak and hesitant (14:30–31; 28:17), and they display "little faith" (6:30; 8:26; 14:31; 16:8). What then makes them disciples whose mission is to replicate themselves? It is their relationship with Jesus. They remain devoted followers and receptive learners, relating appropriately to Jesus as their teacher, a relation that would change, but not end with his death. The resurrected Christ entrusts them with the mission, assuring them of a continuing, although changed, relationship. Their task is to duplicate themselves, relying upon the authority and the presence of the resurrected Christ (10:1, 5–8; 28:16–20). Eduard Schweizer notes that they are "fishers of men," but they are to "fish" with absolute consistency on behalf of God, not on behalf of any substituted allegiance (4:19).[6] Schweizer's admonition is equally appropriate when, considering the mission commission, the disciples are to be teachers; they are to teach with absolute consistency on behalf of God, not on behalf of any substituted allegiance.

THE MOUNTAIN TEACHING FOR DISCIPLES

The Sermon on the Mount in Matthew 5–7 is the first detailed proclamation of Jesus according to this Gospel. Later when Jesus, again on a mountain, commands the eleven disciples to teach subsequent disciples from all nations "all that I have commanded you," he is probably recalling the Sermon on the Mount.[7] For whom and when are these teachings valid? Some interpret the Sermon as appropriate only for the apostles.

---

6. Eduard Schweizer, *Jesus* (trans. David E. Green; Richmond, VA: John Knox, 1971), 41.

7. Ulrich Luz, *Matthew 1–7: A Commentary* (trans. James E. Crouch; Hermeneia; Minneapolis: Fortress, 2007), 176–77.

Others interpret the Sermon eschatologically, postponing appropriation of its radical teachings until the kingdom of God, for which one prays (6:10), comes in fullness. Only then will the earthly kingdoms and structures yield to the absolute sovereignty of God. But the attitude that Jesus seeks is not one that will come from kingdoms and structures, not one that is produced by legal requirements and restraints, not an attitude driven by "in order to." Luther's fear of "salvation by works" is here unfounded. The teachings are for those who have consciously entered into a new relationship and have an attitude of "because of," an ethic that seeks no reward but stems from an inevitable intention whose source is a relationship. Hans Weder considers that the attitude Jesus had in mind is one that springs from the heart. Precisely, it springs from a relationship. Weder says that only from the heart can such an attitude toward God's reign come, and whoever will bear and increase the fruits of love must work from this attitude.[8]

The presence of the crowds who hear Jesus on the mountain cannot be overlooked. Matthew says that the crowds were astonished at his teaching (7:28-29). The crowds may represent Israel and, eventually, the nations, the "sea" where the fishers of men and women will cast their nets. Matthew's church will pursue its mission among the crowds, and the crowds will be astonished at the words and deeds of the church. One cannot preclude the possibility that from the crowds came more disciples. Matthew does not dwell on the crowds, however; his message represents the patient teaching and erratic following as centered on the Twelve and, after the resurrection, the Eleven. These to whom Jesus specifically directed his demands for righteousness would indeed suffer persecution and martyrdom (5:10-11). To these intimate companions the mission is given to elicit from the crowds those who will observe the teachings and practice the presence of the resurrected Lord. Matthew turns his attention to a particular relationship that serves as the model for the church comprising those who will live according to the teaching of Jesus, those who will allow themselves to make God's presence relevant by relating to the reality of the kingdom of heaven. Disciples today, while often not faced with opposition such as Matthew foresaw, err if they dismiss application of the Sermon on the Mount to contemporary issues. In fact, such negligence forsakes the mission by denying relationship with the

---

8. Hans Weder, *Die "Rede der Reden": Eine Auslegung der Bergpredigt heute* (Zurich: Theologisher, 1985), 24.

resurrected Jesus and devaluing the kingdom of heaven. This suggests neither literalism nor legalism regarding observance of the Sermon, for these approaches to Jesus' teachings demonstrate indifference to the resurrection promise, "I am with you always." On the other hand, to have nothing to say about war, militarism, refugees, human rights and human needs, and the exploitation of the creation demonstrates dismissal of Jesus' teachings, a rejection of discipleship, and alienation from the relationship-creating kingdom of heaven.

A RELATIONSHIP-CREATING REALM

"In contemporary mission thinking no one would contemplate trying to grasp the *missio Dei* without a thorough reference to the rule or reign of God."[9] The kingdom of heaven, Matthew's typical expression (thirty-three times), may provoke negative connotations among contemporary readers because both the concept of "kingdom" and the idea of "heaven" so often carry foreign or distorted associations. One should think of "kingdom" neither as a visible empire nor as the organized church. Although the church should exemplify the reality of the kingdom, no human boundaries can be established for God's reign. "Kingdom of heaven" and its correlate, "kingdom of God," are symbolic phrases that have a long history and convey many meanings. One will not find conceptual consistency. As recorded in Psalm 72, God's reign liberates and protects people from oppressive allegiances, structures, powers, and relationships that usurp God's sovereignty.[10] In the coming of Jesus, God's saving presence constitutes a relationship-creating realm that asserts God's gracious sovereignty over human existence.

David Bosch observes that in Matthew's Gospel, the public ministry of Jesus begins with the proclamation, "Repent, the kingdom of heaven is near" (4:17), followed immediately by the calling of the first four disciples.[11] Relating to this kingdom necessitates a new direction, and yielding to this kingdom as a reality alters former perspectives and introduces realities heretofore hidden or obscured. The kingdom

---

9. J. Andrew Kirk, *What Is Mission? Theological Explorations* (Minneapolis: Fortress, 2000), 29.

10. Rudolf Schnackenburg, *The Gospel of Matthew* (trans. Robert R. Barr; Grand Rapids: Eerdmans, 2002), 41.

11. David J. Bosch, *Transforming Mission: Paradigm Shifts in Theology of Mission* (American Society of Missiology Series 16; Maryknoll, NY: Orbis, 1991), 36.

of heaven represents the realm of divine life and concerns, a realm of relationships, to which the disciple responds and in which the disciple lives. Since the kingdom announced by Jesus is a relationship rather than an idea, the disciple waits in expectancy for new experiences of the kingdom, for opportunities to express love, to appropriate forgiveness and justice, and to oppose powers of death. Such is mission in Matthew, both a representation and an invitation: a representation of the divine life and sovereignty (giving evidence that the kingdom has come, that is, being salt and light) and an invitation to relate to the power of life as opposed to the powers of death (making disciples, baptizing and teaching, praying for the kingdom to come).

RELATING TO THE RESURRECTED CHRIST

Being a disciple is what makes a disciple. This statement has a double meaning. First, it means that to be is to act. Matthew makes this clear in the Sermon on the Mount. Call it the Great Pronouncement: "You are the salt of the earth...You are the light of the world" (5:13–14). Who you are is determined by the one with whom you relate, and in this case the disciples relate to Jesus, becoming through this relation both "salt" and "light." Mission is in being because, as has already been argued, being a disciple means to be in a special relationship with Jesus. But mission is also in acting, this being the more common thought regarding the mission of the church. (See the section on "Matthew's Mission Commission" above.) The missioner goes, teaches, converts, plants churches, and the like. To act is to be, as portrayed in the closing words of the Gospel (in the Great Commission). For Matthew, being in relationship and acting in relationship are inseparable when the relationship is with God, a truth enunciated in the fifth petition of the model prayer (6:12), by the parable of the two sons (21:28–32), and by the parable of the sheep and the goats (25:31–46). A statement from the introduction bears repeating: The essence and aim of the church's mission is relating to the resurrected Christ, indistinguishable in Matthew from being disciples and making disciples. Problems of authenticity arise, on the one hand, when a confessed relationship yields no deeds likened to salt and light; or, on the other, when deeds, springing from a confessed relationship, serve self-interests, be they ecclesiastical, national, or cultural.

In an Easter sermon, my son, John Ballenger, a pastor in Baltimore, Maryland, questioned the lectionary readings that included the account of the empty tomb but not an account of an appearance of the risen Christ. If the experience of resurrection is the crux of it all, why is that not included in the Easter reading?

"Well, fear not," the pastor said. "Even if it's not in the lectionary, it's certainly hard to avoid on Easter Sunday morning in church! Among evangelicals in general, and certainly among Baptists, the question, 'Have you had a personal encounter with the risen savior?' constitutes one of the basic steps in the faith journey." Ballenger continues, "May I be frank? I have no earthly idea what that means." The alert congregant could reply that personal encounter with the risen savior sounds like another way of saying, "relating to the resurrected Christ." However, both expressions need to be rescued from thoughtless repetition by those who do no more than repeat an expected formula and have no expectation of the presence of Jesus influencing contemporary actions and decisions. What on earth does it mean? Ballenger, the pastor, continued his Easter message, making clear that he did have some understanding of the earthly meaning of the question. He concluded that the risen Jesus is not among the dead; rather, he is in the midst of life, to be encountered by remembering his words, his teachings, his priorities, and the trust that evidenced a unique relationship with God, whom he called Father.[12] To seek and to find him in the midst of life and to know him as a living word, *hic et nunc*, a word heard, perceived, and obeyed, is to relate to Jesus who said, "And surely I am with you always, to the very end of the age" (Matt 28:20b).

Matthew, with his Christology from below, permits no separation of the risen Christ from the historical Jesus, no subordination of the particular historical life lived by Jesus to an exaltation in heaven. Matthew has no account of an ascension but rather concludes his Gospel with the promise of presence always. Regardless of the dignities conferred on Jesus by the church in the post-Easter development of its Christology, it was always and everywhere speaking of Jesus, who was crucified.[13] Thorwald Lorenzen refuses to surrender the resurrection as "the foundational event of the Christian faith,"[14] but for him it is always

---

12. Sermon by John Ballenger, Woodbrook Baptist Church, Baltimore, Maryland, April 8, 2007.

13. Hugh Anderson, *Jesus and Christian Origins* (New York: Oxford University Press, 1964), 240.

14. Thorwald Lorenzen, *Resurrection, Discipleship, Justice: Affirming the Resurrection of Jesus Christ Today* (Macon, GA: Smyth & Helwys, 2003), 60.

the "resurrection of the crucified Christ." The exaltation of Christ cannot be understood apart from the humiliation of Jesus, and the resurrection cannot be sought in a kingdom other than that Jesus proclaimed and lived. When suggesting that mission in Matthew is relating to the resurrected Christ, the life-story of Jesus may not be neglected, for it is essential to faith as the specific locus of God's dealings with humankind. Jesus offers the disciple a subject with whom to relate, and resurrection, while confirming this subject's union with life, frees this subject from time- and place-limitations, thus preventing the disciple from objectifying and grasping the subject, from anchoring the subject either in times past or in traditional formulas.

The mission command to make disciples is elaborated by two participles, *baptizing* and *teaching*, followed by a promise. Baptism, not an act denoting completion but rather an act of initiation, symbolizes the relationship to Jesus Christ. The baptized becomes a listener and learner of all that Jesus has commanded. The phrase "in the name of" represents commitment, ownership, and protection (Ps 124:8). God the Father and Jesus the Son have been linked in that Jesus the Son does the Father's salvific will (Matt 3:15) and reveals the Father (11:25–27). Disciples of Jesus do the Father's will (12:46–50), and they indicate their commitment to a life of obedience by baptism. The Holy Spirit will assist them in relating to the resurrected Lord just as the Spirit assisted Jesus in his mission (3:15; 12:18–21).[15]

The Great Commission, forming both the conclusion and summation of Matthew's Gospel, indicates what relating to the resurrected Christ means. It has to do with an acceptance of authority, the result being a continuing sensitivity to the teachings of Jesus and an effort to apply these teachings to contemporary life. This authority differs from religious law, making possible a righteousness that surpasses that of the Pharisees and the teachers of the law (5:20). Christian discipleship is not a relationship with a religion or a book or an organization or with anything that can be objectified or possessed. This is not to disparage these important entities, only to emphasize that they cannot substitute for the essential relationship that they serve to facilitate. Discipleship is a relationship with the Word in the freedom of the Spirit, that is, a communion with God. This is not a static relationship; on the contrary, it is

---

15. Warren Carter, *Matthew and the Margins* (Bible & Liberation Series; Maryknoll, NY: Orbis, 2000), 552.

dynamic, demonstrating a relevance that cannot ignore the dehumanizing powers present in the world, not only in individuals, but also in institutions and in the cultures these institutions promote. Relating to the resurrected Christ is relating to the reality established by the resurrection, and that reality "is one of peace, justice, and nonviolence—that is, those values for which Jesus lived and died."[16]

---

16. Lorenzen, *Resurrection, Discipleship, Justice*, 167.

6

Creation Reclaimed

Resurrection and Responsibility in Mark 15:40—16:8

David J. Neville

THE CONVICTION THAT GOD raised from death the crucified Jesus entails attributing ultimate significance to the life of Jesus of Nazareth in its totality, especially those features of his mission and message that led ineluctably to his execution on a Roman cross. To confess that God raised Jesus from the cold clutch of death honors the vision of life for which Jesus died. Christian epistemology and ethics are grounded in an apprehension of the resurrection of Jesus as God's vindication of the peculiarity of Jesus' life-work, that is, his bifocal orientation toward God and needy neighbors (cf. Mark 12:28–34). In the resurrection, God validated Jesus' responsiveness both to God's impinging reign and to humanity's pathetic plight. The resurrection is therefore God's acceptance of responsibility for the kind and quality of life Jesus lived. In other words, resurrection is both God's imprimatur on the moral shape and content of Jesus' life and God's self-identification with Jesus' mission and message. As Thorwald Lorenzen avers, at stake in the life-orientation Jesus chose, in the message he proclaimed, and in the relationships he fostered was a particular—and particularly contested—conception of God.[1] Few have done more than Lorenzen to elucidate the reality, meaning, and significance of the resurrection of Jesus. His two major studies on this theme are biblically accountable, theologically constructive, passionately imaginative, and affirming of life in all its profundity and pathos.[2]

---

1. See, e.g., Thorwald Lorenzen, "The Meaning of the Death of Jesus Christ," *ABQ* 4 (March 1985): 3–34.

2. Thorwald Lorenzen, *Resurrection and Discipleship: Interpretive Models, Biblical*

Since Mark's Gospel emerged from out of the shadows of the other canonical gospels during the late-eighteenth and nineteenth centuries, there have been countless studies of its ending, quite apart from the host of commentaries on the Gospel as a whole. This study might best be characterized as a theologically attentive reading of Mark's epilogue on its own terms, with minimal concern for source- or tradition-analysis. Naturally I brought my own interests and concerns to this text, but few of these remained undisturbed as I attended to distinctive features of Mark's epilogue, which is too often read in light of the more elaborate endings of Mark's biblical counterparts. Overshadowed as Mark's epilogue is in terms of length and narrative detail by his own crucifixion narrative and cribbed as it is by comparison with the other gospel endings, it nevertheless contributes much to understanding the meaning and significance of Jesus' resurrection. For Mark, at least, the resurrection of Jesus is nothing less than God's reclamation of creation and reaffirmation of responsibility for the future of the created order.

THE EXTENT OF MARK'S EPILOGUE (MARK 15:40—16:8)

In an earlier study,[3] I accepted Mark 15:40–41 as part of Mark's crucifixion narrative, but there are good reasons to treat Mark's notice of women observing from a distance as part of his epilogue.[4] The two "consequences" of Jesus' death—the splitting of the temple curtain and the centurion's "confession"—are reminiscent of the beginning of Jesus' mission at the time of his immersion by John, when the heavens were split and a heavenly voice announced (to Jesus), "You are my son . . ." (Mark 1:10–11). Thus, splittings and affirmations, immersion and death bracket the public life of Jesus.[5]

Reflections, Theological Consequences (Maryknoll, NY: Orbis, 1995); *Resurrection, Discipleship, Justice: Affirming the Resurrection of Jesus Christ Today* (Macon, GA: Smyth & Helwys, 2003).

3. David Neville, "God's Presence and Power: Christology, Eschatology and 'Theodicy' in Mark's Crucifixion Narrative," in *Theodicy and Eschatology* (ed. Bruce Barber and David Neville; Adelaide: ATF Press, 2005), 19–41.

4. Cf. Paul L. Danove, *The End of Mark's Story: A Methodological Study* (Biblical Interpretation Series; Leiden: Brill, 1993), 132–66, whose analysis of Mark's plot structure leads him to designate Mark 11:1–15:41 as the climax of Mark's "second-tier macro-event," 1:16–16:8, with 15:42–16:8 as denouement. No detail in his analysis, however, necessitates viewing Mark 15:40–41 as the final "eighth-tier constituent" of 15:16–41.

5. In Mark 10:35–40, Jesus uses the language of immersion to symbolize suffering and death. Cf. Rom 6:3–4.

Not only are previously unmentioned women introduced and named at Mark 15:40-41, but the same women and another previously unknown personage, Joseph of Arimathea, feature prominently in the remainder of Mark's narrative. Treating Mark's Gospel as an "aural text," Bridget Gilfillan Upton identifies various rhetorical features in Mark 15:40-16:8 to justify holding this section together.[6] Noteworthy, too, is Norman Perrin's suggestion that Mark 15:40-16:8 is reminiscent of the anointing story of Mark 14:3-9, which begins Mark's passion narrative proper and also features a woman. According to Perrin, Mark 14:3-9 and 15:40-16:8 enclose Mark's passion narrative in much the same way as Mark 8:22-26 and 10:46-52 enclose the central section of the Gospel.[7] Building on this insight, Marie Noonan Sabin observes: "In fact, *the anointing of Jesus by women* forms an inclusio around the whole narrative of his passion and death. While the narrative of Jesus seems to be moving him toward total defeat, the ritual action of the women continues to claim him as God's *anointed*."[8]

Strict delimitations are probably impossible, however, because Mark wrote for the ear rather than (solely) for the eye. The least that can be affirmed is that Mark 15:40-41 belongs as much with what follows as with what precedes. Here, as elsewhere (Mark 1:14-15; 3:7-12; 8:22-26; 10:46-52), it is best to envisage Mark 15:40-41 as transitional.

Although the question of where Mark's epilogue begins is a matter of some dispute, whether it originally ended at Mark 16:8 is more contentious. Few contest that Mark 16:8 is the best-attested ending,[9] but dissatisfaction with this ending has led both to later endings being appended and to conjecture about how a fuller, more "theologically" satisfying ending was lost. This is not the place to address the hoary question

---

6. Bridget Gilfillan Upton, *Hearing Mark's Endings: Listening to Ancient Popular Texts through Speech Act Theory* (Biblical Interpretation Series 79; Leiden: Brill, 2006), 65-78. The repetition of the same women's names in Mark's epilogue, albeit varied, contrasts with the scarcity of named women elsewhere (Mark 6:3, 17, 19).

7. Norman Perrin, *The Resurrection according to Matthew, Mark, and Luke* (Philadelphia: Fortress Press, 1977), 29.

8. Marie Noonan Sabin, *Reopening the Word: Reading Mark as Theology in the Context of Early Judaism* (New York: Oxford University Press, 2002), 196.

9. For an accessible discussion of the various endings to Mark's Gospel in extant manuscripts, see Michael W. Holmes, "To Be Continued . . . : The Many Endings of the Gospel of Mark," *Bible Review* 17 (August 2001): 12-23, 48-50. Cf. Danove, *The End of Mark's Story*, 119-31.

of whether or not Mark 16:8 is the originally intended ending, which is probably unresolvable without manuscript evidence earlier than that currently available. So although a sizeable number of critics considers that Mark's original ending was lost and some accept the integrity of the longer ending that extends to Mark 16:20,[10] I accept Mark 16:8 as both the earliest recoverable and likely original ending.

RESURRECTION AS CREATION RECLAIMED: MARK'S TEXT IN TRANSLATION AND INTERPRETATION

It is possible to subdivide Mark's epilogue into three scenes: the introduction of three women among a larger group observing Jesus' final hours from a distance (15:40–41); the entombment of Jesus by Joseph of Arimathea (15:42–47); and the visit to the tomb by the previously mentioned women (16:1–8).[11] But a two-part structure divided by the Sabbath is equally, if not more, defensible: (1) the pre-Sabbath entombment of Jesus by Joseph, enclosed by two notices about observing women (15:40–47); and (2) the post-Sabbath visit to the tomb by the aforementioned women (16:1–8). The following structured and fairly literal translation adopts the latter option because the Sabbath motif, reminiscent of God's originating creativity (Gen 1:1–2:3; cf. Exod 20:8–11), governs the movement of the narrative. God's life-generating and life-affirming creativity forms the necessary theological horizon for Mark's affirmation of Jesus' resurrection. In the interval marked by "Sabbath," which is passed over in silence,[12] God's creative impulse is reactualized

---

10. Against Mark 16:8 as the author's intended ending, see N. Clayton Croy, *The Mutilation of Mark's Gospel* (Nashville: Abingdon, 2003). In defense of the originality of Mark 16:9–20, see William R. Farmer, *The Last Twelve Verses of Mark* (SNTSMS 25; Cambridge: Cambridge University Press, 1974); and Delbert Burkett, *Rethinking the Gospel Sources: From Proto-Mark to Mark* (New York: T. & T. Clark, 2004), 252–63.

11. See Perrin, *Resurrection*, 14–15, reflecting his insight that the three references to women reflect Mark's penchant for threefold repetition with minor variations (22).

12. One is reminded of the seventh and concluding proposition in Ludwig Wittgenstein, *Tractatus Logico-Philosophicus* (trans. D. F. Pears and B. F. McGuinness; International Library of Philosophy and Scientific Method; London: Routledge & Kegan Paul, 1961): "What we cannot speak about we must pass over in silence." For Wittgenstein, that which must be passed over in silence is not necessarily unreal or nonsensical. As he avers in proposition 6.522, "There are, indeed, things that cannot be put into words. They *make themselves manifest*. They are what is mystical." Respect for the mystery of God and God's creativity in relation to the world manifests in epistemological humility, appropriately displayed in Nancey Murphy, "The Resurrection

Creation Reclaimed

in raising the crucified Jesus, thereby renewing the divine commitment to humanity—albeit not without challenging everything that human beings take for granted.

Scene 1: Women Witnesses to the Death and Entombment of Jesus (15:40–47)[13]

[40]Now, there were also women observing from a distance, among whom were both Mariamme of Magdala and Mariamme, mother of the younger [or less-prominent] Jacob and Joses, and *Salome*, [41]who when he was in Galilee followed him and attended him, *and many others who had accompanied him into Jerusalem*. [42]And as evening closed in,[14] *because it was a day of preparation, that is, "pre-Sabbath,"* [43]Joseph, a prominent council-member from Arimathea who himself was also anticipating the reign of God, having arrived, *after mustering courage* went in before Pilate and requested the body of Jesus. [44]*But Pilate, astounded that he might already be dead, summoned the centurion and asked him if he had died much earlier.* [45]*And after learning from the centurion*, he granted the corpse to Joseph. [46] And *after purchasing linen*, taking him down *he wrapped [him]* in linen and laid him down in a tomb that had been hewn out of rock, and he rolled a stone in front of the entrance to the tomb. [47]But Mariamme of Magdala and Mariamme, *[mother] of Joses, observed where he had been placed*.

Scene 2: Encounter in the Tomb (16:1–8)

[1]And after the Sabbath *had intervened*, Mariamme of Magdala and Mariamme, [mother] of Jacob, *and Salome purchased* aromatic spices *in order to go and anoint him.* [2]*And very early* on Day 1

Body and Personal Identity: Possibilities and Limits of Eschatological Knowledge," in *Resurrection: Theological and Scientific Assessments* (ed. Ted Peters, Robert J. Russell, and Michael Welker; Grand Rapids: Eerdmans, 2002), 202–18.

13. Uniquely Markan details are italicized, and verse numbers appear in square brackets.

14. Literally, "when evening had already arrived" (cf. Mark 1:32; 4:35; 6:47; 14:17), in which case Joseph attends to Jesus' burial on the Sabbath, which is reminiscent of Jesus'"work" on the Sabbath on behalf of the infirm. Thus, one who was anticipating the reign of God proclaimed and made present by Jesus on behalf of the needy, participates in that reign by attending to the needy Jesus on the Sabbath. In what follows, however, Mark explicitly notes that the timing was *pre-Sabbath*.

> of seven days, they arrived at the tomb *after the sun had risen.* [3] *And they were saying to one another, "Who will roll the stone from the entrance to the tomb for us?"* [4]*And looking up they observed that the stone had been rolled back . . . for it was extremely large.*[15] [5]*And entering into the tomb they saw a young man seated to the right with a white flowing robe thrown around [himself], and they were alarmed.* [6]*But he says to them, "Don't be alarmed. You seek Jesus the Nazarene, the crucified One. He has been raised; he is not here. Look—the place where they placed him.* [7]*Instead, go say to his disciples, even Peter,* 'He goes ahead of you in(to) Galilee; there you will see him, as he said to you.'"[16] [8]*And emerging they fled from the tomb, trembling and awestruck; and they said nothing whatsoever to anyone, so fearful were they.*

So much has been written on Mark's enigmatic epilogue that one hesitates to say more. But as I have waited patiently on this text and in the process changed my mind on a decisive issue, seven points have impressed themselves upon me: (1) the displacement of Jesus, at the end of a narrative in which he is regularly the focus of attention; (2) the presence of new characters who play unexpected roles; (3) the absence of any reference to an *empty* tomb; (4) a striking yet not widely recognized allusion to the creation story that begins the Torah; (5) the strength of the reiterated promise in Mark 16:7; (6) Mark's insistence that the women said nothing to anyone; and (7) the significance of the way in which Jesus is referred to in Mark 16:6. It has gradually dawned on me that the inexplicable nature of the reality to which Mark witnessed by recounting the mysterious young man's testimony to three perplexed and frightened women led Mark to intimate, by alluding to the creation story, that the Creator was again at work effecting something of the same order of magnitude as creation itself. One may not be able to provide a strictly rational account of God's mysterious creativity, but one may "tune in" to that creativity through responsive faith and faithful responsibility, which has the capacity to rearrange reality. There is no faith-less route to the conviction that God created the world or raised Jesus from

---

15. Although this final explanatory clause might indicate that the size of the stone made it possible for the women to see from a distance that it had been rolled away, it is probably a delayed explanation for the women's consternation about who would roll the stone back for them.

16. Where I place the internal quotation marks reflects an interpretive choice. It is possible that what the young man instructs the women to say ends with the reference to Galilee, after which the remainder is commentary.

death; once reached, however, the conviction that God raised Jesus from death puts everything in a new light, including how we apprehend and understand reality.[17]

1. The Displacement of Jesus

Perhaps the most noticeable feature of Mark's epilogue is the relative absence of Jesus. Although his death provides the rationale for this culminating section, Jesus himself is not the focal point of the narrative. Indeed, his name occurs twice only, once in each scene: first, when Joseph asks Pilate for "the body of Jesus" (Mark 15:43); and second, when the young man in the tomb acknowledges that the women seek "Jesus the Nazarene, the crucified One" (16:6). As when John's death is recounted in retrospect (Mark 6:17-29),[18] this is one of the rare Markan episodes in which Jesus does not occupy center-stage. Although Mark 5:21-43 relates that Jesus restored an apparently dead girl and was thus death's master, death now displaces Jesus.[19] In Mark's epilogue, the *dramatis personae* change so that the spotlight shifts from Jesus to the impact on others of his death and the announcement of his resurrection, which

---

17. Cf. James D. G. Dunn, *Christianity in the Making*. Vol. 1, *Jesus Remembered* (Grand Rapids: Eerdmans, 2003), 877-78: "The resurrection of Jesus...did not permit itself to be explained in terms of current or previous analogies. On the contrary, the interpretation that God had raised Jesus from the dead became itself paradigmatic, that which defines rather than that which is defined. In interpreting what they saw as 'the resurrection of Jesus,' the first disciples were affirming that what had happened to Jesus afforded an insight into reality which was determinative for how reality itself should be seen."

18. Note the echo of Mark 6:29 in 15:46. Yet as Pheme Perkins points out, "Unlike the disciples of John the Baptist (6:29), Jesus' disciples do not appear to claim the body" (Perkins, "The Gospel of Mark: Introduction, Commentary, and Reflections," in *The New Interpreter's Bible*, vol. 8 [ed. Leander E. Keck et al.; Nashville: Abingdon, 1995], 725).

19. In this connection, Donald Juel rightly critiques interpretations of New Testament eschatology that seek to construct a buffer against the reality of death. See Donald H. Juel, "Christian Hope and the Denial of Death: Encountering New Testament Eschatology," in *The End of the World and the Ends of God: Science and Theology on Eschatology* (ed. John Polkinghorne and Michael Welker; Harrisburg, PA: Trinity, 2000), 174. Focusing on Mark 13:1—16:8, Juel offers a compelling reading in which death and finitude are given their due, but without making them absolutes incapable of reversal by God the Creator: "How to speak of resurrection requires artfulness. The mark of theological wisdom is knowing when and how to speak of such matters in a way that avoids an escape from the reality of death—and that prevents closing off the future to new possibilities for those who take strange solace in the finality of death" (Juel, "Christian Hope and the Denial of Death," 181).

Mark has the young man attest without verbal embroidery: ἠγέρθη ("he has been raised"). In literary terms, the risen Son (Mark 16:6) features little more than the risen sun (16:2). The event of Jesus' resurrection is subsumed under Mark's interpretive account of it.

2. New Characters with Unexpected Roles

Mark's Gospel ends with wholly new characters. Three previously unmentioned women are named and feature prominently in the final two scenes of the narrative. Mark 15:41 indicates that these women had been part of Jesus' retinue since his time in Galilee, yet to this point their presence has not been acknowledged. Moreover, Joseph of Arimathea appears without explanation of his concern for Jesus. Mark's description of Joseph as one who was "anticipating the reign of God" may suggest some earlier association with, even sympathy for, Jesus, but as with the women his role with respect to Jesus is reduced to post-mortem care.[20] In the absence of male disciples, the loyalty of these women disciples and the care displayed by Joseph are remarkable.[21]

Noteworthy, too, is the atypical nature of the respective roles of these characters. The women come to the tomb to fulfill a traditional role—to anoint a body for entombment—but as a result of their encounter in the tomb are given the role of witness to a reality-altering event. Although their gender counts against their testimony being taken seriously (cf. Luke 24:11),[22] within the context of good news concerning Jesus, their faithfulness qualifies them as witnesses to a new divine initiative. By contrast, Joseph's gender and social status make him the

---

20. Cf. Elizabeth Struthers Malbon, "The Jewish Leaders in the Gospel of Mark: A Literary Study of Marcan Characterization," *JBL* 108 (1989) 276: "This is the service John's disciples performed for him (6:29), but it is performed for Jesus by one who might well be expected to be his enemy."

21. Cf. Raymond E. Brown, *The Death of the Messiah: From Gethsemane to the Grave*, vol. 2 (New York: Doubleday, 1994), 1157-59, 1244-47, who was none too sure about either the loyalty of the women or the care of Joseph.

22. See also the near-contemporary advice of Josephus, *Judean Antiquities 1-4* (trans. Louis H. Feldman; Flavius Josephus: Translation and Commentary 3; Leiden: Brill, 2000), 219: "Let not one witness be trusted, but let there be three or, at the very least, two, whose credibility their previous way of life shall attest. Let the testimony of women not be accepted because of the levity and boldness of their gender." For a nuanced discussion of whether, in Jewish society, women's testimony was accepted in legal cases, in which a witness's credibility was most stringently assessed, see Carolyn Osiek, "The Women at the Tomb: What Are They Doing There?" *Ex Auditu* 9 (1993) 102-4.

ideal witness, but his role is closer to that which the women expected to play. Furthermore, almost every indication to this point in Mark's narrative suggests that a person in Joseph's situation would most naturally be an adversary of Jesus. Yet such expectations are overturned by the courage and care displayed by Joseph.[23] The question arises, what is it about *this* part of the Jesus-story that opens up new and unexpected roles for people? Perhaps the radically re-creative initiative of God with respect to the crucified Jesus is intimated in the unexpected roles played by Joseph and women disciples.

3. No Empty Tomb

Despite the scholarly habit of referring to Mark's closing scene as an "empty-tomb" tradition,[24] in Mark's epilogue the rock-tomb in which Jesus' body is placed is *never* empty.[25] Whenever the tomb is mentioned, someone is present within it. Joseph places the dead body of Jesus in the tomb, then rolls a stone across its entrance. When the women arrive two mornings later, the stone has been rolled back so that they are able to enter the tomb. On entering the unblocked rock-tomb, the women see a young man in white seated to the right, who directs their attention to the

---

23. Mark 15:43 emphasizes Joseph's courage, and despite Brown's judgment in *The Death of the Messiah* that Joseph's actions were "the absolute minimum one could do for the dead" (1246), it needs to be recognized that under the circumstances Joseph's actions ensured that despite the dishonorable nature of Jesus' death by crucifixion, he was at least buried honorably. In this respect, Joseph's honoring of the dishonored Jesus prefigures the announcement of Jesus' resurrection. Although I accept the historicity of Joseph's burial of Jesus, this is not the place to defend this perspective. See Dale C. Allison, *Resurrecting Jesus: The Earliest Christian Tradition and Its Interpreters* (New York: T. & T. Clark, 2005), 352–63.

24. Note the titles of two influential studies: John Dominic Crossan, "Empty Tomb and Absent Lord," in *The Passion in Mark: Studies on Mark 14–16* (ed. Werner Kelber; Philadelphia: Fortress, 1976), 135–52; and Adela Yarbro Collins, "The Empty Tomb and Resurrection according to Mark," in her book, *The Beginning of the Gospel: Probings of Mark in Context* (Minneapolis: Fortress, 1992), 119–48. Even when an author's semantics contains patent contradiction, rarely does this lead to revision, as in Morna Hooker, *Endings: Invitations to Discipleship* (Peabody: Hendrickson, 2003), 18: "The women find the tomb empty, and the young man sitting there tells them that Jesus has been raised."

25. Since this point was impressed upon me when translating Mark's epilogue, I have noted only one other scholar who has made the same observation. See Colin Brown, "The Jesus of Mark's Gospel," in *Jesus Then & Now: Images of Jesus in History and Christology* (ed. Marvin Meyer and Charles Hughes; Harrisburg, PA: Trinity, 2001), 42, who interprets Mark's epilogue in terms of the purification of the defiling power of death. Thus he sees Mark's epilogue as a triumphant climax.

place where Jesus had been placed. *The tomb is open but not empty.* Jesus is absent, but the tomb bristles with presence and promise, not hollow emptiness.²⁶

The presence of a young man in the tomb is mysterious. In the canonical Gospel of Mark, the noun ὁ νεανίσκος occurs only at 14:51 and 16:5. Some therefore suggest an association between the young man in the tomb and the enigmatic young man who lost his outer garment when Jesus was arrested (14:51–52). Were any association intended, however, it was probably to emphasize the contrast between them.²⁷ In this connection, what the young man of Mark 14:51–52 is wearing (and loses) is described as being the same as what Joseph purchases to cover the dead body of Jesus (ὁ σινδών).²⁸ The apparel of the young man of Mark 16:5–6 is detailed using the same term used by Jesus in Mark 12:38 to characterize the long flowing robes that haughty scribes wear (ἡ στολή). Moreover, since the adjective λευκός is used twice only by Mark (9:3; 16:5), the whiteness of this young man's robe is reminiscent of the brightness of Jesus' garments at the moment of his "metamorphosis" on the mountain. Furthermore, the women see the young man clothed in white *seated to the right*. This phrase may simply indicate the young man's location within the tomb, but it echoes the phrasing of Mark 12:36 (citing Ps 110:1) and 14:62, where the image of being seated to the right signifies shared or delegated authority.²⁹ In such a mystery-charged episode, perhaps it is not too far-fetched to suggest that the young man seated to the right and enveloped in white is, as we might say, sitting in for Jesus, whose resurrected presence can only be apprehended indi-

---

26. This paradoxical dynamic is similar to Mark's depiction of divine presence (and power) precisely when Jesus experiences God's absence on the cross. See Neville, "God's Presence and Power," 30–41.

27. See Perkins, "The Gospel of Mark," 729: "The flight of that young man [in Mark 14:51–52], like that of the disciples, means no return. The only possible connection between the two passages might lie in the contrast. By describing the angel as a 'young man' Mark reminds readers of the missing disciples."

28. According to Andrew T. Lincoln, "The Promise and the Failure: Mark 16:7, 8," *JBL* 108 (1989) 288 and 293, this suggests that the young man of Mark 14:51 was suitably dressed for following Jesus on the pathway that leads inevitably to death even though he pulled out of his "shroud" (and the pathway) when threatened. So too Howard M. Jackson, "Why the Youth Shed His Cloak and Fled Naked: The Meaning and Purpose of Mark 14:51–52," *JBL* 116 (1997) 273–89.

29. The use of ἐν in Mark 16:5 rather than ἐκ, as elsewhere in Mark, occurs often in the epistles, e.g., Rom 8:34, albeit not with the dative plural.

rectly within the ambiguities of a life of faith and discipleship, to which the disciples are re-summoned.

Andrew Lincoln contends that Mark was deliberately ambiguous in describing the young man to the right robed in white.[30] He points out that the young men of Mark 14:51 and 16:5 are each described in the same threefold way—as young, as wearing something, and with a description of what was worn. He also notes that in that period angels could be described as young men dressed in white.[31] While Lincoln is probably right about the ambiguity of the figure encountered by the women in the tomb, and while it is reasonable to conceive of the young man as an angelic figure, perhaps the ambiguity identified by Lincoln is not the most crucial feature of the young man's "identity." If, as Lincoln suggests, the description of how the young man of Mark 16:5 is attired is indicative of his role in the narrative, especially by comparison with the description of how the young man of Mark 14:51 was dressed prior to losing his garment, I venture to suggest that this latter young man takes on "scribal authority," speaking authoritatively on behalf of Jesus in the new situation created by the resurrection. The echo of scribal attire, albeit bleached of haughtiness, and the image of being seated to the right combine to emphasize the authoritativeness of the young man's utterance. This is especially the case if one interprets the young man in white as a liminal figure, an intermediary who conveys an authentic message on behalf of the divine. Matthew explicitly depicts an angelic figure at the tomb, but Mark's account remains restrained. Ultimately, the figure of the young man is less important than the message he conveys, which is that the crucified One, Jesus the Nazarene, has been raised and is even now fulfilling his promise to go before his disciples in(to) Galilee (Mark 14:28), where he will be seen.

4. Resurrection and Creation: A Scriptural Resonance

Mark's crucifixion narrative is replete with scriptural resonances, through which Mark affirms God's presence and power to fulfill the divine pur-

---

30. Lincoln, "The Promise and the Failure," 293.

31. Craig A. Evans, *Mark 8:27—16:20* (WBC 34B; Nashville: Thomas Nelson, 2001), 536, supplies more parallels to support the view that Mark intended his young man to be considered an angel. In *Mark: A Commentary* (Hermeneia; Minneapolis: Fortress, 2007), 795–96, Adela Yarbro Collins characterizes the young man as an interpreting angel.

pose in and through Jesus' suffering and death.³² But after Mark 15:39, or perhaps 15:40 (cf. Ps 38:11), there is apparently no further allusion to scripture. Deuteronomy 21:22–23 provides the background to Joseph's action in requesting Pilate to release the body of Jesus for entombment, but Mark does not allude to Deut 21:22–23.

After initially concluding that intertextual resonances with Jewish scripture are absent from Mark's epilogue,³³ I was tempted to explain this absence as a result of the *de novo* character of the resurrection of Jesus, which was so radically new that there were no scriptural resources with which to interpret it. But my initial conclusion was wrong, or so I now think. Mark's temporal notices explicitly draw attention to the pre-Sabbath "day of preparation," the Sabbath day of rest, which forms an interlude, and "Day 1 of seven days." In Jewish tradition, especially Exod 20:8–11, the Sabbath day of rest recalls the culmination of the creation story in Gen 1:1—2:3, when God rests after creating the cosmos and all that is in it. Accordingly, the "day of preparation" coincides with the sixth day on which humanity was created, and "Day 1 of seven days" coincides with the day on which God's creative activity began. In Mark's narrative, Jesus dies on the day corresponding to humanity's creation, and his resurrection is announced on the day corresponding to the beginning of creation. Not only the specific days mentioned but also their sequence are important—sixth day, seventh day, first day.

This particular reading is reinforced by two further observations. First, on this interpretation, Mark's Sabbath-structured ending recalls the opening word of his narrative, Ἀρχή, which itself echoes "the beginning" of Genesis.³⁴ And second, seemingly contradictory temporal notices in Mark 16:2 also hint at the first creation story in Genesis.³⁵ Taken

---

32. See Neville, "God's Presence and Power," 30–41, and various studies cited therein.

33. The same observation was made by John E. Alsup, *The Post-Resurrection Appearance Stories of the Gospel Tradition* (CTM 5; Stuttgart: Calwer, 1975), 90, n. 269. N. T. Wright, *The Resurrection of the Son of God* (Christian Origins and the Question of God 3; Minneapolis: Fortress, 2003), 599–602, makes this point about the resurrection narratives in all four canonical gospels.

34. See Marie Noonan Sabin, *Reopening the Word* (Oxford: Oxford University Press, 2002), 34–37.

35. Yarbro Collins, *Mark*, 795, regards the temporal indicators in Mark 16:2 as "a typically Markan two-step progression, in which the second phrase qualifies the first …" Perhaps.

literally, the opening phrase in Mark 16:2 implies a pre-dawn period (cf. 1:35), whereas the final phrase explicitly indicates post-sunrise. If Mark 16:2 alludes to the first of the seven days of creation, which is made more likely by Mark's use of the cardinal rather than ordinal numeral in the phrase "Day 1—as opposed to 'the first'—of seven days,"[36] the temporal tension in this verse reinforces an association with the first day of creation by suggesting the *appearance of light out of darkness*. As Sergio Briglia notes with respect to Mark 16:2, "Marcos acumula tres indicaciones temporales: primer día de la semana; madrugada; salida de sol. Es el momento trascendente del anuncio de una nueva creación, un nuevo primer día en el paso de las tinieblas a la luz, es decir, de la muerte a la vida."[37]

The resurrection of Jesus is an act of divine recreation, which Mark intimates by alluding to the creation story that opens the Torah. This new act of divine creativity is also a return to the first day of creation, hence an act of reclamation and restoration. God's Sabbath-rest is interrupted to reclaim and to restore not only the crucified Jesus but the entire created order. A new—and renewing—passage from darkness to light, from death to life is begun in the resurrection of Jesus, in which God reaffirms responsibility for the future of creation as a whole.

Mark's return to the creation story to convey something of the overwhelming reality of the resurrection of Jesus has ontological, epistemological, and ethical implications. By alluding to the creation story, Mark affirms that Jesus' resurrection is not an event whose cause can be ascertained and/or assessed by the human mind alone. Like God's original creation, God's raising of Jesus from death can only be apprehended and affirmed in faith because it belongs to a transcendent order of reality. But this reality can be "known" and experienced via responsive faith and faithful responsibility. Faith in response to divine initiative is

---

36. See Susan Miller, *Women in Mark's Gospel* (JSNTSup 259; London: T. & T. Clark, 2004), 189.

37. Sergio Briglia, "Evangelio según San Marcos," in *Comentario Bíblico Latinoamericano: Nuevo Testamento* (ed. Armando J. Levoratti in collaboration with Elsa Tamez and Pablo Richard; Estella, Spain: Verbo Divino, 2003), 466: "Mark accumulates three temporal indicators: first day of the week; pre-dawn; the dawn of the sun. It is a transcendent moment of the annunciation of a new creation, a new first day in the passage from darkness to light, that is to say, from death to life" (my translation). Cf. Miller, *Women in Mark's Gospel*, 189: "The women go to the tomb at daybreak as light emerges from darkness, echoing God's action of creating light out of darkness in Gen 1.3–4."

a mode of access to an order of reality that can only be apprehended or experienced relationally.[38] In turn, responsive faith facilitates faithful responsibility, which seeks to enter more fully into the reality opened up by God's creative work through working in ways that are analogous to, and hence reflective of, God's restorative initiatives. Perhaps surprisingly, Mark's epilogue is yet another biblical resource for Christian ecological responsibility—as a means of witnessing to God's evident determination in raising Jesus to reclaim and to restore creation. And in so far as Mark interrelates resurrection and creation, the resurrection of Jesus signals God's reaffirmation of the ontology or metaphysic of *shalom* implicit in the creation story at the genesis of the biblical metanarrative.

5. Promise Reiterated

Unlike the other gospel writers, Mark recounts no appearance of the risen Jesus, only a reminder of the promise of one![39] Mark 16:7 recalls Mark 14:27–28, the point at which Jesus not only warns his disciples that all of them will "stumble" (σκανδαλίζομαι) but also reassures them that after his resurrection he will go before (προάγω) them in(to) Galilee.[40] Apart from occurrences in Mark 14:28 and 16:7, the transitive form of προάγω occurs in this Gospel only at Mark 10:32, where Jesus' "going ahead" on the way to Jerusalem provokes amazement and fear on the part of those following.[41] Jesus' warning about all the disciples stumbling proved true, and Mark expects the reiteration of his promise by an authoritative interpreter to carry conviction. Peter is almost certainly sin-

---

38. On the significance of the resurrection of Jesus for a Christian understanding of reality (ontology) and a correlative epistemology, see Lorenzen, *Resurrection and Discipleship*, 189–235, and *Resurrection, Discipleship, Justice*, 43–63.

39. Some have argued that Mark 16:7 refers not to an encounter with the risen Jesus but to the *parousia*. Representatives include Willi Marxsen, *Mark the Evangelist: Studies in the Redaction History of the Gospel* (trans. James Boyce et al.; Nashville: Abingdon, 1969), 75–95, following Ernst Lohmeyer; and Perrin, *Resurrection*, 17–40. However, Lincoln, "The Promise and the Failure," 285, provides compelling reasons for understanding Mark 16:7 as a reference to a post-resurrection encounter with the risen Jesus. So also Yarbro Collins, *Mark*, 797.

40. Evans, *Mark 8:27—16:20*, 401–2 and 537–38, follows Bas van Iersel in exegeting εἰς τὴν Γαλιλαίαν in Mark 14:28 and 16:7 as "in Galilee" rather than "into Galilee." Mark's usage permits this but does not preclude both senses. "In Galilee" emphasizes continued discipleship in the wake of the risen Jesus.

41. See R. T. France, *The Gospel of Mark* (NIGCT; Grand Rapids: Eerdmans, 2002), 577.

gled out because of his three-fold disowning of Jesus (Mark 14:66–72), also forecast by Jesus at the time of his warning about stumbling and his promise to lead them again in(to) Galilee. In narrative terms, the coming to fulfillment of Jesus' warnings to his disciples as a group and specifically to Peter creates confidence in the fulfillment of his promise. So, although only reiterated by the young man in the open tomb, one who has entered faithfully into Mark's story-world cannot but accept the inevitable fulfillment of Jesus' promise.

The meaning of *Galilee* in Mark's epilogue remains puzzling. As Sharon Ringe notes, "Galilee is the only place mentioned in this Gospel in connection with post-Easter hopes."[42] Some consider that Galilee is symbolic of the Gentile mission or the birthplace of such a mission, others that it indicates the locale of Mark's community or Mark's support for Galilean as opposed to Jerusalem interests. For Ringe, Mark's enigmatic ending sends hearers and readers back to the beginning of the Gospel, thereby facilitating a re-encounter with both the Jesus of historical memory and the Christ proclaimed in the post-Easter community.[43] In short, the end of Mark's Gospel is the beginning of the church's completion of the story begun by Jesus. This observation, now commonplace, is important, but more may be said.

Galilee appears twice in Mark's epilogue, once in each scene. In Mark 15:40–41, Galilee is the locus of Jesus' mission and call to mission, where people respond in faith and both follow and accompany him. That following and accompaniment might well lead to Jerusalem, the locus of Jesus' passion and death, but Galilee itself is associated with the mission of the living Jesus. Thus, when the promise of Mark 14:28 is reiterated in 16:7, this affirms the continuation of the mission of the living Jesus in response to, and as a result of, the impinging reign of God manifested decisively in the resurrection. Both before and after Jesus' crucifixion, Galilee is where the living Jesus leads those willing to follow and accompany him. The geographical movement from Galilee to Jerusalem and back again parallels Jesus' movement from life to death and back again. Yet that movement does not occur in isolation, only in relation to persons responsive to Jesus' call to discipleship/mission and therefore

---

42. Sharon H. Ringe, "The Church and the Resurrection: Another Look at the Ending of Mark," 242, in *Literary Encounters with the Reign of God* (ed. Sharon H. Ringe and H. C. Paul Kim; New York: T. & T. Clark, 2004), 235–46.

43. Ringe, "The Church and the Resurrection," 243–44.

responsible for shaping their lives in conformity with a thick, full-bodied understanding of God's resurrection of the crucified One.

6. *The Women Tell No One*

It is often asserted that the women who came to the tomb must (eventually) have told the disciples (or someone else) what the white-robed young man told them to tell them. This seems reasonable, since it is a matter of historical record that these three women were not the only ones who came to believe that God had raised Jesus from death. But this flatly contradicts the forceful assertion with which Mark's narrative concludes: καὶ οὐδενὶ οὐδὲν εἶπαν ἐφοβοῦντο γάρ. Two considerations allegedly mitigate the forcefulness of Mark's use of a double, compounding negative in his culminating clause: first, Jesus' emphatic instruction in Mark 1:44 that a cured man inform no one also makes use of the double negative construction, but seems to have the opposite effect; and second, the women's fear can be interpreted positively as an appropriate response of religious awe.

The use of double negatives is a common Markan syntactical construction,[44] and Mark 1:44 and 16:8 are similar enough to lead some to suggest that 1:44 is the key to understanding 16:8. As Dale Allison surmises, "Just as 1:44 means 'Say nothing to anyone (except the priest),' so 16:8 may well mean the women 'said nothing to anyone (except his disciples).'"[45] Possibly; but the double negative in Mark 1:44 gives emphasis to Jesus' negative command, which is disobeyed, whereas the double negative in Mark 16:8 gives emphasis to the women's disobedience to a positive command. The function of the double negative construction remains the same—emphasis—but what is emphasized differs, with the result that the similar syntactic construction underscores a similar narrative progression. In Mark 1:44 the emphatically negative command by Jesus is disobeyed, and in Mark 16:8 the positive command by the young man speaking on Jesus' behalf is emphatically disobeyed!

There is a scholarly tradition that interprets the response of the women in Mark 16:8 in positive terms, along the lines of "numinous awe."[46] Some within this tradition contend that if the women's response is

---

44. Vincent Taylor, *The Gospel according to St. Mark* (2d ed.; London: Macmillan, 1966), 46.

45. Allison, *Resurrecting Jesus*, 304.

46. See, e.g., J. Lee Magness, *Sense and Absence: Structure and Suspension in the Ending of Mark's Gospel* (SemeiaSt; Atlanta: Scholars, 1986), 87–105; Joan L. Mitchell,

understood positively, this implies that the women must be understood to have obeyed the young man's instruction. In Mark 16:8a, the term ἡ ἔκστασις may well signify ecstatic awe in response to an epiphany of some kind. It cannot be accidental that its only other occurrence in the narrative is at Mark 5:42, following Jesus' restoration of the apparently dead daughter of Jairus. Ecstatic awe in response to the restoration of life is entirely appropriate. On the other hand, everything else about Mark 16:8 suggests that however positively one might want to consider the women's awestruck state, their fearful flight from the tomb resulted in silence, not testimony. In fact, Mark 16:8b clearly identifies their phobic reaction as the reason for saying nothing whatsoever to anyone, and their flight is eerily reminiscent of the flight of the male disciples in the Garden of Gethsemane.

So, it would seem that Mark intended to terminate his "good-news announcement" concerning Jesus by recording that despite the women's loyalty they also failed in their discipleship and witness.[47] How, then, did he envisage that faith in the risen Jesus took hold among his disciples? If, as seems plausible, Mark's understanding of the good news concerning Jesus was indebted to Paul, it is not a so-called "empty-tomb" (or even "non–empty-tomb") tradition that he considers the principal witness to the risen Jesus but direct vision-encounters with the risen one.[48] If the witness of the young, white-robed man in the rock-tomb can be trusted—and Mark gives no indication that it should not be—then whether or not the women pass on the message given to them has no bearing on the coming to fulfillment of Jesus' promise in Mark 14:28. As for Paul (1 Cor 15:3–8), so also for Mark, faith is restored or generated by vision-encounters with the risen Jesus, which are likely alluded to by the young man's affirmation, "There [in Galilee] you will *see* him."[49] For Mark, the

---

Beyond Fear and Silence: A Feminist-Literary Reading of Mark (New York: Continuum, 2001), 66–75; Noonan Sabin, *Reopening the Word*, 192–214.

47. See Lincoln, "The Promise and the Failure," 285–87; Miller, *Women in Mark's Gospel*, 178–85.

48. I refer to "vision-encounters" rather than "visionary encounters" so as not to prejudice the interpretation of such experiences, which played a significant role in early Christianity. See Allison, *Resurrecting Jesus*, 238–39.

49. In arguing that Mark *presupposes* vision-encounters such as Paul refers to in 1 Cor 15:3–8, I remain unconvinced by Crossan that Mark's redactional concerns, especially an alleged animus against early Christian leaders such as those named by Paul, necessitated suppressing "resurrectional apparitions of Jesus" by the creation of an "empty tomb" story. See John Dominic Crossan, "Historical Jesus as Risen Lord," in *The Jesus Controversy: Perspectives in Conflict* by John Dominic Crossan, Luke Timothy

"noetic" apprehension of the risen Jesus is no less the result of divine initiative than the divinely established reality apprehended; the reality and truth of the resurrected Jesus transcend both the inherent ambiguity of life and inevitable human failure but nevertheless reach into people's lives with transformative impact.

7. Jesus, the Crucified Nazarene

Mark affirms the resurrection of Jesus, the crucified Nazarene (cf. Acts 2:22–24; 4:10). While "Messiah" and "Son of God" are Mark's principal confessional titles, neither features after the conclusion to his crucifixion narrative (15:39). Mark may be like Paul in giving priority to vision-encounters with the risen Jesus; but unlike Paul, whose discussion of resurrection in 1 Corinthians 15 affirms the resurrection of *Christ*,[50] Mark affirms that it is precisely *Jesus the crucified Nazarene* who is to be encountered in Galilee.

On four occasions during the course of Mark's narrative, Jesus is described as "the Nazarene" (1:24; 10:47; 14:67; 16:6). Since in Mark 1:9 Jesus is described as coming from Nazareth, which is not explicitly mentioned again, "the Nazarene" may simply identify Jesus as one who came from Nazareth.[51] Yet this description is not the most natural way to designate one who came from Nazareth.[52] As a result, perhaps one

---

Johnson, and Werner H. Kelber (The Rockwell Lecture Series; Harrisburg, PA: Trinity, 1999), 1–47.

50. I do not contend that Paul divorced the risen Christ from the historical Jesus—only that by comparison with Paul, Mark stresses the continuity between the crucified and risen Jesus. In 1 Corinthians 15, Paul uses the name Jesus twice (vv. 31 and 57) but only as part of a confessional title.

51. See Evans, *Mark 8:27—16:20*, 132: "The substantival adjective ὁ Ναζαρηνός, 'the Nazarene', functions as a description of a person from Nazareth." See also Michael O. Wise, "Nazarene," in *Dictionary of Jesus and the Gospels* (ed. Joel B. Green, Scot McKnight, and I. Howard Marshall; Downers Grove, IL: InterVarsity, 1992), 571–74, who argues that both ὁ Ναζαρηνός and ὁ Ναζωραῖος should probably be understood as "the man from Nazareth." Yet he accepts that "any solution must be considered tentative" (574).

52. See Matt 21:11; John 1:45; Acts 10:38. Since Luke 4:34 is the only certain parallel to Mark's almost-exclusive use of ὁ Ναζαρηνός (Luke 24:19 is textually uncertain), this strengthens the case for allowing that ὁ Ναζαρηνός may mean more for Mark than simply "of Nazareth." Perhaps he wished to associate this man from Nazareth with that earlier figure from Israel's early history who was a nazirite (consecrated to God) and a strong deliverer of Israel (Judg 13:2–7). Mark 1:7 and 3:27 underscore the strength of Jesus.

should give this descriptor titular force, as Edwin Broadhead does in his formalist analysis of Markan titles.[53] By noting both the distribution of "the Nazarene" image or title within Mark's Gospel and the various patterns of association connected to it, Broadhead shows it to be integral to Mark's polyvalent and paradoxical characterization of Jesus. Nevertheless, in Mark 16:6, this image of Jesus the Nazarene is conjoined with an unprecedented title, "the crucified One." According to Broadhead,

> Here, at the climax of the narrative, Jesus is identified for the first and only time by the title which interprets all titles. While the prism of his story has many facets and angles, it has but one focal point. In this way the varied imagery of Jesus the Nazarene is gathered under the hermeneutic of the cross. At the same time the image of the cross is filled out by the full story of Jesus' life and ministry.[54]

Crucially, Mark avoids a confessional title in his epilogue, thereby emphasizing continuity between Jesus the crucified Nazarene and the one who has been raised. Precisely the historical person who experienced crucifixion at the hands of Roman soldiers is the one now absent because raised. No doubt Mark's post-resurrection perspective explains the application to Jesus of such confessional titles as Messiah and Son of God, but it is *not* as Messiah and Son of God that Mark recounts the announcement of his "having been raised-ness." This indicates that *for Mark* the resurrection is not to be reduced to an interpretation solely about the abiding significance of Jesus and his way, even if the real meaning and meaningful reality of the resurrection can only be realized by faithfully following Jesus and his way.

HERMENEUTICAL POSTSCRIPT

As narrative testimony set within the liminal space between life and death—or, in this case, death and life—Mark's epilogue affirms divine responsibility for raising the crucified Nazarene, thereby returning to the first day of creation to reclaim the world so as to elicit faith and to invite those who respond faithfully to live in the being-renewed world

---

53. Edwin K. Broadhead, *Naming Jesus: Titular Christology in the Gospel of Mark* (JSNTSup 175; Sheffield: Sheffield Academic, 1999).

54. Broadhead, *Naming Jesus*, 39.

in a new way. As such, Mark 15:40—16:8 "names God," in the Ricoeurian sense of confessing "the trace of God in the event" it recounts.[55] As one of many varied forms of "naming God" within scripture, however, Mark's enigmatic ending both elucidates and eludes; it has the quality of a "limit expression," which with respect to the identity and character of God both reveals and conceals.[56]

For Paul Ricoeur, the archetypal limit expression is the "disclosure" of the divine name in Exod 3:13–15, which protects divine identity no less than it discloses it. The NT echo of this archetypal limit expression, according to Ricoeur, is the reign of God attested in the parables of Jesus. But in so far as the reign of God signifies divine action in the world for the purpose of human deliverance, the same can be said for the witness of Mark's epilogue. Albeit different in form from Jesus' parables, Mark's account of the young man's testimony to the "having been raised-ness" of the crucified Jesus also bespeaks redemptive divine action in the world. Ricoeur was inclined to view the resurrection narratives as falling on the side of the manifestation of the divine name, echoing the exodus narrative, but to regard Jesus' parables of the reign of God as falling on the side of the withdrawal of the divine name, corresponding to the pre-exodus episode of the burning bush in Exodus 3.[57] Mark's epilogue, however, evokes as much of the dialectical interplay between disclosure and concealment characteristic of limit expressions as any of Jesus' parables of the reign of God. Indeed, in as much as Jesus' parables often depict reversal, Mark's epilogue depicts the ultimate reversal—the resurrection of the crucified Jesus, by which God's being was bound in ontological solidarity to the moral shape of Jesus' life and in which God signalled creation's recovery.

---

55. See the essay, "Naming God," in Paul Ricoeur, *Figuring the Sacred: Religion, Narrative, and Imagination* (trans. David Pellauer; ed. Mark Wallace; Minneapolis: Fortress, 1995), 217–35. I here acknowledge my indebtedness to David Hunter (of blessed memory) for insight into this aspect of Ricoeur's hermeneutical project. See David M. Hunter, "Signs of Life: A Johannine Soteriology by way of the Narrative Hermeneutics of Paul Ricoeur" (PhD diss., Charles Sturt University, 2006).

56. See Ricoeur, "Naming God," 228–30, and the similar discussion of "limit expressions" at the end of his discussion of "The Self in the Mirror of the Scriptures," trans. David Pellauer, in *The Whole and Divided Self* (ed. David Aune and John McCarthy; New York: Crossroad, 1997), 201–20.

57. Ricoeur, "The Self in the Mirror of the Scriptures," 218–19.

As a result, Mark's epilogue places a question mark against every world-view—theistic or atheistic, pre-scientific or scientific, "conservative" or "liberal"—because it testifies to possibilities and hope that do not emerge from natural potentialities. Following in the wake of the earliest Christian witnesses to the resurrection of Jesus (cf. 1 Corinthians 15; Acts 1:21–22; 2:32) and alongside other early Christian writers, Mark unsettled the ontological and epistemic paradigms of his day. The reality to which Mark's epilogue points stands beyond natural potentiality and human expectation, continuing to beckon persons to live out a new vision of life in which human existence is impressed by and responsive to God's creative initiatives. The resurrection of the crucified Jesus is God's declaration of responsibility for the world's future, which in turn is both the basis of and summons to human responsibility to live and act in analogical conformity with this life-transforming event.

7

The Raising of Lazarus in John 11
Sign-Reading via Paul Ricoeur's Narrative Hermeneutics

David M. Hunter

EDITORS' INTRODUCTION

This chapter is an edited section of David Hunter's doctoral dissertation, "Signs of Life: A Johannine Soteriology by way of the Narrative Hermeneutics of Paul Ricoeur,"[1] *in which he demonstrated how the Johannine* σημεῖα *accounts (or sign stories) contribute positively to the soteriology of the Fourth Gospel. Especially important for his argument is Ricoeur's pair of concepts, "configuration" and "refiguration," within his narrative hermeneutics and theory of identity. In chapter 5 of "Signs of Life," Hunter discussed two aspects of configuration associated with Johannine soteriology, the memory of the exodus from Egypt and the resurrection of Jesus foreshadowed in the raising of Lazarus. The first part of the chapter discussed the memory of the exodus as the background for the term* σημεῖον *within the context of* YHWH's *acts of deliverance. This association grants an enhanced soteriological dimension to the sign stories in the Fourth Gospel. But for the purposes of this collection in honor of Hunter's friend and mentor, whose three research higher degrees focused on the Fourth Gospel, only the second part of the chapter dealing with the narrative account of the raising of*

---

1. David M. Hunter, "Signs of Life: A Johannine Soteriology by way of the Narrative Hermeneutics of Paul Ricoeur" (PhD diss., Charles Sturt University, 2006, (submitted posthumously). John Painter was principal supervisor and Thorwald Lorenzen was co-supervisor. Copies are held in the libraries of St Mark's National Theological Centre (Canberra) and Whitley College (Melbourne). For an overview, see David Hunter and Jeanette Mathews, "Signs of Life," in *"Into the World You Love": Encountering God in Everyday Life* (ed. Graeme Garrett; Adelaide: ATF Press, 2007), 78–92.

Lazarus is reproduced in edited form, even though Hunter's fuller discussion interrelates both aspects of configuration. In Hunter's argument, the raising of Lazarus in John 11 serves to focus attention on the climactic sign story within the Gospel, which prefigures the resurrection of Jesus, especially in the claim of Jesus in John 11:25: "I am the resurrection and the life." For Hunter, then, to consider the configuration of John 11 facilitates an exploration of a sign story intimately related to the central Johannine soteriological term—"life."

• • •

CONSIDERATION OF THE STORY of the raising of Lazarus in John 11 shows what may be gained from applying Paul Ricoeur's narrative hermeneutics to biblical texts. This account links a formal miracle story described as a σημεῖον (11:47; 12:18) with dialogues between Jesus and his disciples (11:7–16) and Lazarus' sisters (11:21–27, 32–33) and also with a crucial turning point in the narrative itself—the decision to arrest Jesus (11:53, 57). The composite character of John 11 implies that diverse components exist in close proximity to each other. This produces a tension of structure, themes, and story, but the formal, theological, and dramatic aspects of John 11 are closely integrated, making the tension productive.

John 11 is well suited to a re-reading via Ricoeur's narrative hermeneutics. The raising of Lazarus is in several ways the culmination of the account of the ministry of Jesus in the Fourth Gospel. Of particular interest is the sense in which John 11 brings the distinctive Johannine σημεῖα accounts to a close and climax (see John 2:1–11; 4:46–54; 5:1–9a; 6:1–14, 16–21; 9:1–9; 11:1–44). To this point, the σημεῖα accounts are of the genre of healings (4:46–54; 5:1–9; 9:1–11) or nature miracles (6:16–21), especially nature miracles of abundant provision (2:1–11; 6:1–14 [cf. 21:1–14]). Such accounts are familiar from the Synoptic Gospels. Stories of raisings from the dead are also found in Matthew, Mark, and Luke–Acts. However, the account of the raising of Lazarus is heightened by its emphasis on the lapse of time between Lazarus' death and his raising by Jesus (11:5–6, 38–40). This element is justified in terms of the theological agenda of the Gospel as "for God's glory" (11:4). Thus in the Fourth Gospel, this account plays the role of a narrative as well as a theological bridge. While conflict has been associated with the previous σημεῖα accounts, this account in John 11 links the ministry of Jesus to the decision to arrest and execute him. At a theological level, Jesus' life is linked to his passion and, importantly, to his validation through glorification. Jesus' raising of Lazarus leads to his own death, but in this context Jesus asserts, "I am the resurrection and the life" (11:25). Jesus himself becomes the subject of the account. As a consequence, it is not only power over death that is demonstrated but also the combination of the obedience of Jesus to the one who sends him and the faithfulness of the sending God, as deliverer, to Jesus. This theological high point in the Johannine narrative is remembered as a foundation element for the faith and hope of the reading community.

TENSIONS WITHIN THE RAISING-OF-LAZARUS ACCOUNT

The raising of Lazarus is likely a constructed account, created (or, in Ricoeur's terms, configured) by the evangelist. It stands at some distance from the chronology of the Synoptic Gospels, which relate the temple event and the subsequent parable-telling as precipitating Jesus' arrest (Mark 11:1—12:12; Matt 21:1–46; Luke 19:28—20:19). In contrast, the temple event in the Fourth Gospel occurs at the beginning of Jesus' ministry (John 2:13–22).

The deliberate placement of the temple episode within the Fourth Gospel is paralleled by a deliberate sense of organisation within John 11. Various forms, themes, and events are incorporated into the narrative. The evangelist weaves a unity from a number of tensions, and an analysis of these tensions best expresses the point of the configuration process.

Formal Tensions in John 11

Despite the complexity of the text, it is relatively easy to isolate a simple miracle-story form. The raising-of-Lazarus account contains elements typical of the miracle stories of the Synoptic Gospels,[2] for example, a description of the gravity of the situation (11:3, 14), the difficulty associated with the healing, that is, the length of time since death (11:17, 39b), an important word or command (11:33b), a demonstration of efficacy (11:44), and the impression created on those present (11:45–46).

Taking John 11 to be the evangelist's construction rather than an eyewitness or historical account, there remains a twofold question of

---

2. See Rudolf Bultmann, *History of the Synoptic Tradition* (rev. ed.; trans. John Marsh; Oxford: Blackwell, 1963), 218–28.

tradition-history: first, the possible dependence of this miracle story on a particular synoptic tradition; and second, the possibility that the raising-of-Lazarus account relies on some other background tradition.

The relationship between the raising of Lazarus and other raising accounts in the Synoptic Gospels has been discussed extensively. John Meier, who cautiously accepts that a historical event in the life of Jesus lies behind the raising-of-Lazarus account, argues that the phenomenon of Jesus raising someone from death is attested by four distinct sources: the raising of Jairus' daughter in Mark 5:21–43 (paralleled in Matt 9:18–26 and Luke 8:40–56); the raising of a widow's son at Nain in the special Lukan tradition (Luke 7:1–17); the raising of Lazarus in John 11; and the saying about the works of the Messiah, including raising the dead, in Matt 11:5.[3]

The names Lazarus, Mary, and Martha raise the question of possible connections between John 11 and both Luke 10:38–42 (Jesus' visit to the house of Mary and Martha) and Luke 16:19–31 (the parable of Lazarus and the rich man). Many discount any "cross-fertilization" between the Gospels of John and Luke, but Michael Labahn suggests that the name, Lazarus, derives from Luke 16, thereby indicating an ethical interpretation of the Johannine account, with the love of Jesus for Lazarus directed especially toward the poor, suffering, and marginalised, that is, the Johannine community.[4]

According to Meier, personal names and place names are unusual in the miracle stories of the Gospel tradition, Bartimaeus being the only other named beneficiary of a miracle (Mark 10:46–52) and Jairus the only other named petitioner (Mark 5:21–43). Meier correctly points out that names are also unusual in the miracle stories of the Gospel of John.[5] In the naming of characters in John 11, Meier suggests we have a phenomenon that goes against the grain and is thus more likely to be original. Names play a complex role within the Fourth Gospel, however, including the relative prominence of characters who are not named (the mother of Jesus and the beloved disciple) and some named characters

---

3. John P. Meier, *A Marginal Jew: Rethinking the Historical Jesus*, Vol. 2, *Mentor, Message, and Miracles* (New York: Doubleday, 1994), 777–837. Each account is said to derive from earlier but different traditions.

4. Michael Labahn, *Jesus als Lebensspender: Untersuchungen zu einer Geschichte der johanneischen Tradition anhand ihrer Wundergeschichten* (BZNW 98; Berlin: de Gruyter, 1999), 451–57, esp. 456.

5. Meier, *A Marginal Jew*, 2:821–22.

(Nicodemus, Thomas, and Nathanael) who play a minor role, if any, in the Synoptic tradition. The use of personal names should not be seen to indicate historical tradition in the Fourth Gospel.

Meier's argument for the likely originality of the place name Bethany is also tenuous. Within the Fourth Gospel, Bethany is the name of two different places some 100 kilometres apart but mentioned closely together at the end of John 10 and the beginning of John 11. Bethany across the Jordan (John 10:40; cf. 1:28) is where John was baptizing and the place to which Jesus has withdrawn, and Bethany in the neighborhood of Jerusalem is the context of the raising of Lazarus (belatedly clarified in 11:18). Thus the message to Jesus that Lazarus was ill was sent from Bethany near Jerusalem to Bethany across the Jordan. Raymond Brown notes the difficulties of Jesus' itinerary in John 10–12, indicating that the placement of the miracle story does not sit easily with the narrative flow in these chapters.[6] The association of Martha and Mary with Bethany (11:1) is found only in John; the village of Martha and Mary is unnamed in Luke 10:38. Nevertheless, the village is well known in the Synoptic Gospels as the home of Simon the Leper (Mark 14:3; Matt 26:6), a place where Jesus lodged (Matt 21:17; Mark 11:11–12), and the location of the ascension (Luke 24:50). These associations with Bethany near Jerusalem are absent in the Fourth Gospel.

One's decision about whether or not John 11 is reliant on a synoptic tradition is largely bound up with what one holds about the relation between the Synoptic and Johannine traditions. While there are links, there is no obvious literary source in the Synoptic tradition for the raising-of-Lazarus account. What then of proposals that the extra-canonical *Secret (Gospel of) Mark* contains an early form of the raising-of-Lazarus account;[7] or that both John and Mark borrowed from a pre-gospel

---

6. Raymond E. Brown, *The Gospel according to John (I–XII)* (AB 29; New York: Doubleday, 1966), 428.

7. The account of Jesus raising a young man from the dead is found within a letter allegedly by Clement of Alexandria (c. 150–215 CE) to a certain Theodore documenting a version of Mark not publicly known. The first documentation of the text is found in Morton Smith, *Clement of Alexandria and a Secret Gospel of Mark* (Cambridge: Harvard University Press, 1973). For the view that *Secret Mark* recounts an early version of the raising of Lazarus account, see Labahn, *Jesus als Lebensspender*, 442–49, and John Dominic Crossan, *The Historical Jesus: The Life of a Mediterranean Jewish Peasant* (New York: HarperCollins, 1991), 326–32 and 441. Meier, *A Marginal Jew*, 1.120–22, critiques Crossan's position and lists exegetes who regard *Secret Mark* as dependent on the canonical Gospels. Foremost among these is Raymond E. Brown, "The Relation of 'The Secret Gospel of Mark' to the Fourth Gospel," *CBQ* 36 (1974) 466–85.

collection of miracle stories (see especially the parallels between Mark 6–8 and John 6);[8] or that the fourth evangelist was influenced by Jewish traditions associated with Moses, Elijah, and Elisha, especially since the sea and feeding miracles have Mosaic overtones and the healings echo certain aspects of miracle stories associated with Elijah and Elisha? Put briefly, the story of the raising of Lazarus seems not to depend on any known tradition. The basic miracle story form is familiar, however, and stories of raisings from the dead are found in each canonical Gospel. The significance of the related account in *Secret Mark* is dependent on the unresolved question of direction of influence. The possibility of a pre-Johannine and/or pre-Markan collection of miracle stories is consistent with the general phenomenon of collections of Jesus-material but does not impact directly on formal tensions in John 11. Similarly, the possible background of either Moses or Elijah traditions does not establish any clear origins of the text.

In addition to the miracle story, John 11 features three main dialogues involving Jesus (and the disciples, Martha, and Mary) and concludes with the decision to arrest Jesus. Rudolf Bultmann identified key elements of the dialogues as coming from alleged revelation-discourses (11:9–10, 25–26), but he also saw the theology of the evangelist in evidence (11:4, 7–10, 16, 20–32, 40–42).[9] This combination of source material is indicative, for Bultmann, of the superseding of the theology of his proposed σημεῖα source.[10] The raising of Lazarus is reduced to a symbol of the revelation given to Martha.[11] At the same time, Bultmann, who had a positive view of the faith of Martha, proposed John 11:28–44 as "an antitype" to 11:17–27 (the dialogue with Martha) in the sense that the former passage provides a "description . . . of the primitive faith of those who need the external miracle in order to recognise Jesus as the revealer."[12]

---

8. See, for example, Paul J. Achtemeier, "Toward the Isolation of Pre-Markan Miracle Catenae," *JBL* 89 (1970) 265–91, and "The Origin and Function of the Pre-Marcan Miracle Catenae," *JBL* 91 (1972): 198–221; both of these essays are reprinted in Achtemeier, *Jesus and the Miracle Tradition* (Eugene, OR: Cascade Books, 2008).

9. Rudolf Bultmann, *The Gospel of John: A Commentary* (trans. G. R. Beasley-Murray, R. W. N. Hoare, and J. K. Riches; Philadelphia: Westminster, 1971), 395 n. 4.

10. Ibid., 395.

11. Ibid., 402.

12. Ibid., 405. This dual view of the Lazarus account corresponds to Bultmann's overall approach to the signs as strictly unnecessary, yet a "concession to human weakness" (696).

On the other hand, Labahn restates the argument that "the narrative importance of the miracle stories is not meant to be corrected in favor of other text genres."[13] He counters the argument that the fourth evangelist promotes the words of Jesus as a better path to faith, compared to the σημεῖα of Jesus. He proposes that the σημεῖα accounts lead into the christological controversies of John 5–11, as predicted in John 1:9–11. At the same time, the σημεῖα accounts have a soteriological content that addresses the concrete situation of the Fourth Gospel's first readers. Thus, discussion of formal tensions leads to the question of theological tension in John 11.

Theological Tension in John 11

Bultmann's discussion of δόξα in the Fourth Gospel is illustrated by the coming together of diverse theological elements in John 11.[14] The term δόξα is used throughout the ministry of Jesus in two senses—to refer either to Jesus' miracle-working or his crucifixion. The first of his signs displayed his glory (John 2:11). The concept of "the hour" of Jesus is introduced in the same sign story (2:4). This "hour" is the time of Jesus' death (7:30; 8:20; 12:23; 13:1), but is also designated a time of glorifying (17:1–5). These two senses of glorification are brought together in the story of the raising of Lazarus. It is the greatest of Jesus' signs and thus leads to the glory of God (11:4a). Yet it is also the beginning of the passion and the path to his own death, which becomes the glorifying of the Son of God (11:4b; also 17:1–5). As Bultmann notes: "the miraculous action of Jesus will bring him to the cross; that is, however, it will lead to his ultimate glorification. The position of the story makes that clear, and from now on the mention of Jesus' δοξασθῆναι has this meaning in view: 12.16, 23, 28; 13.31ff; 17.1,4f."[15]

Labahn's treatment of theological tension in John 11 leads to a discussion of the soteriological function of this action of Jesus. He suggests that the selection of the miracle accounts recorded in the Fourth Gospel (hinted at in 20:30–31) occurs because they show Jesus meeting

---

13. Michael Labahn, "Between Tradition and Literary Art: Observations on the Use of the Miracle Tradition by the Fourth Evangelist," *Biblica* 80 (1999) 188, and *Jesus als Lebensspender, passim*.

14. Bultmann, *Gospel of John*, 397–98.

15. Ibid.

a need.¹⁶ In other words, the σημεῖα accounts address the difficult concrete situation of first-century readers: "Die Abfassung des Evangeliums ist gleichsam einer Selbstwahrnehmung der Gemeinschaft, für die das Werk primär intendiert ist, durch einen Exponenten aus ihrem historischen, sozialen und gemeinschaftlichen Kontext."¹⁷ In this sense, the sign stories give content to the Johannine understanding of what it is to have eternal life.

At the same time, Labahn also emphasizes the role of the σημεῖα accounts in John 5–11 in the christological controversy with authorities.¹⁸ This confrontation culminates in the situation whereby the final σημεῖον (the raising of Lazarus) both leads to the arrest of Jesus and links the two main parts of the Fourth Gospel. For Labahn,

> Although all the miracles (except John 2,1–11; 4,46–54) performed by Jesus lead to conflict between the revealer and the world, the last miracle, the raising of Lazarus by Jesus, is the most important reason for killing Jesus and therefore is the immediate cause of the passion and resurrection of Jesus. On the other hand, the raising of Lazarus is an anticipation of the resurrection of Jesus ... With the mention of Thomas in 11,16 and in the resurrection chapter, John 20, we find another signal for this line of connection that leads from chapter 11 to 20, 24–29.¹⁹

However, no link between the soteriological content of the σημεῖα, the effect on witnesses to the raising of Lazarus, and the arrest of Jesus is mentioned.

Thus, Labahn defends the positive contribution of the σημεῖα accounts and gives both christological and soteriological weight to the Johannine miracle-story traditions, but the connection between these proposals is lacking. The proximity of the raising of Lazarus to the arrest of Jesus is a matter of narrative art, that is, a literary device in the construction of the Fourth Gospel. Further, although the σημεῖα may lead to a change in the world-view of those who witness them, this has

---

16. Labahn, *Jesus als Lebensspender*, 473–74.

17. Labahn, *Jesus als Lebensspender*, 469: "The writing of the Gospel is, at the same time, a self-perception of the community for whom the work is primarily intended, through an author from its historical, social and communitarian context" (Hunter's translation).

18. Labahn, "Between Tradition and Literary Art," 180–82, 196.

19. Ibid., 180–81.

no association with the arrest of Jesus. In this sense, Labahn ignores the dramatic tension in the account.

Dramatic Tension in John 11

The key to the dramatic tension in John 11 is the response of witnesses to the σημεῖον as recorded in 11:45–46. There is the response of belief, but there is also the reporting of the event to the authorities. Bultmann emphasizes the denunciation of Jesus to the authorities rather than the mass belief and the actions of the authorities.[20] This focus attends to the paradoxical outcome of the account: "It is precisely unbelief that unwittingly and unintentionally must precipitate the δοξασθῆναι of Jesus as v. 51 [the interpretation of the comments of Caiaphas] will make yet more clear."[21] Yet it is evident that the popular believing response to the σημεῖον is also the key to moves by the authorities against Jesus (11:47–48).

Paula Fredriksen's work on the arrest and death of Jesus underscores the popular response to Jesus.[22] Interested in the fact that Jesus was executed by the Romans using the method of crucifixion, generally reserved for political criminals, Fredriksen argues that Jesus was not arrested for his temple action. She critiques both the view that Jesus cleanses or purifies the temple and the apocalyptic/eschatological interpretation of the temple action. Her arguments support the Johannine chronology that Jesus was not arrested until some time after the temple action. She suggests, rather, that Jesus was arrested when he gained popular support some years later.[23]

Pilate knew who Jesus was because of the pattern (in the Fourth Gospel) of Jesus coming to the city for festivals, performing an action of some kind, then returning to Galilee.[24] On the third Passover festival mentioned in the Fourth Gospel, Jesus approaches Jerusalem having come to the notice of the authorities (11:55). Given that the priestly hierarchy was often deposed by Roman authorities after popular uprisings,

---

20. Bultmann, *Gospel of John*, 409–10.

21. Ibid., 410.

22. Paula Fredriksen, *Jesus of Nazareth, King of the Jews: A Jewish Life and the Emergence of Christianity* (New York: Knopf, 1999).

23. Fredriksen, *Jesus of Nazareth*, 234.

24. Ibid., 255.

Fredriksen suggests that Pilate was able to move against Jesus with their support.[25]

What is the role of the raising of Lazarus in such a scenario? Apart from noting that Jesus had a reputation for healings at festivals (Matt 21:14; cf. John 5:1–9), Fredriksen gives no credence to such an event preceding or provoking the popular response.[26] However, she acknowledges that in the Fourth Gospel the raising of Lazarus clearly precipitates Jesus' entry into Jerusalem (12:9–11, 17–19), accompanied by the popular acclaim that Fredriksen believes brought Pilate and the authorities to their decision.[27] In summary, Fredriksen favors the Johannine chronology that has Jesus visiting the temple over several years, but she regards the "dramatic signs" of the Fourth Gospel as unable to bear historical scrutiny.[28]

Both Meier and John Dominic Crossan take more seriously the import and subversiveness of Jesus' healing ministry. Meier accepts a historical tradition behind the Lazarus account but holds that the link between the raising of Lazarus and the arrest of Jesus is Johannine and therefore not historical.[29] On the other hand, Crossan speaks with enthusiasm of the meaning of healing, with healing and table fellowship being crucial to the "birth" of Christianity.[30] For Crossan, the early Christian community was well placed both to heal "illness" and to cure "disease."[31] Crossan emphasizes the theological dimension of accepting miracle accounts:

> it is very significant which events a faith interprets as miracle and which it does not, because that reveals what manner of God one worships. Finally even for believers and even within a theological framework, faith in an epiphanic God is not the same as faith in an episodic God. The former is a permanent divine presence pe-

---

25. Ibid., 253–54.
26. Ibid., 218–20.
27. Ibid., 250–55.
28. Ibid., 220.
29. Meier, *A Marginal Jew*, 2:831.
30. Crossan, *Historical Jesus*, 303–53; and Crossan, *The Birth of Christianity: Discovering What Happened in the Years Immediately After the Execution of Jesus* (New York: HarperCollins, 1998), esp. 293–304.
31. This terminological distinction is taken from the field of medical anthropology. See John J. Pilch, *Healing in the New Testament: Insights from Medical and Mediterranean Anthropology* (Minneapolis: Fortress, 1999).

riodically observed *by* believers. The latter is an absent presence periodically intervening *for* believers.³²

Jesus' healings reveal God, more specifically, a God who resists "discrimination, exploitation, and oppression."³³ In other words, the healing ministry of Jesus has theological and political potency. Nevertheless, Crossan does not link the healing ministry of Jesus to his arrest.

The decision to arrest Jesus because of his popularity has some plausibility for historians such as Fredriksen, who balks, however, at the difficulty of incorporating a miracle story into such a scenario. Nevertheless, that miracle stories provide the framework for the Johannine account of Jesus' ministry requires that they be included in any analysis.

To sum up, the raising-of-Lazarus account in John 11 exhibits tensions on three levels: formal, theological, and dramatic. These tensions result, respectively, from the use of obscure sources and traditions, the theological interpretation of the event within the Fourth Gospel, and the Johannine account of the decision to arrest Jesus. The text of John 11 is, in Ricoeur's terms, configured; it deliberately brings together various components (the miracle tradition, σημεῖον terminology, dialogues, the "I am" statement of Jesus, accounts of popular response to Jesus, and political consequences). For Ricoeur, however, configuration is a positive process, whereby each element of the narrative relates to the other in a manner akin to the functioning of metaphor. To this point, therefore, only half the task is done. It remains to assess the text on its own terms, by moving from an analysis of the text's prehistory to the meaning and significance of the configuration of these various elements.

THE NARRATIVE UNITY OF THE RAISING-OF-LAZARUS ACCOUNT

Given the tensions in John 11, what may be proposed regarding the unity of the account? In particular, what implications arise from the use of a miracle-story form termed a σημεῖον?³⁴

---

32. Crossan, *Birth of Christianity*, 304.

33. Ibid.

34. For a proposal regarding the soteriological role of the σημεῖα accounts based on extensive exegesis, see Labahn, *Jesus als Lebensspender*, esp. 495–502.

In Ricoeur's approach to Scripture as outlined in "The Self in the Mirror of the Scriptures,"[35] he identifies four characteristics of Scripture: written discourse, canon, polyphony, and limit expressions. To this point in the analysis of John 11, the emphasis has been on written discourse and polyphony. The many voices that make up biblical texts are well demonstrated by tensions in John 11. Different traditions have been brought together into the one narrative. From this point on, however, the focus is on how these individual elements qualify each other in the discourse.

The reading of John 11 as a limit expression will also come into focus. The centrality of death in this chapter is a fundamental pastoral and theological challenge. The death and raising of Lazarus is linked with the death and resurrection of Jesus as recounted later in the Fourth Gospel. In the sense that death and resurrection raise the question of the absence and presence of God, death is a limit experience and its discussion is a limit expression. In John 11 this discussion is set within the specific context of whether God is present with Jesus and the masses or with the Jewish authorities and Roman Empire.

What follows reads John 11 with respect for the genre of a Johannine σημεῖον account. This re-reading is part of a narrative hermeneutical, rather than historical, agenda. The σημεῖα accounts are remembered and written as witnesses to readers. In other words, the focus is on the way the σημεῖον account in John 11 functions in the Fourth Gospel rather than on the actions and identity of the historical Jesus.

This narrative is a witness intended to evoke attestation, or in the words of John 20:31, ταῦτα δὲ γέγραπται ἵνα πιστεύ[σ]ητε. The text leads to faith and faith leads to action. This dynamic is particularly apparent in John 11 in the phenomenon of mass belief. Exegetes have tended to play down this aspect of the account, but the following re-reading notes not only the mass response of belief to the raising of Lazarus, but also the political implications of this response. Emphasis on the character of God as deliverer, associated with the term σημεῖον in Jewish memory of the exodus event, provokes threatened authorities into the decision to arrest and execute Jesus. Belief in the liberating work of Jesus has its consequences, one of which may be to provoke persecution.

---

35. Paul Ricoeur, "The Self in the Mirror of the Scriptures," trans. David Pellauer, in *The Whole and Divided Self: The Bible and Theological Anthropology* (ed. David E. Aune and John McCarthy; New York: Crossroad, 1997), 210–20.

Parable and Metaphor in Reading John 11

Ricoeur's approach to metaphor and narrative was originally articulated in relation to the parables of the Synoptic Gospels but is also applicable to the Johannine σημεῖα. In Ricoeur's discussion of parables in the Synoptic Gospels, the key relationship is between the parable and the Kingdom of God. This relationship flows both ways, so that the parable informs the notion of the Kingdom of God while the parable is legitimated by association with the way of God in the world.[36] Similarly, in the Fourth Gospel the Prologue provides the interpretive key for every σημεῖον account, in particular, the promise of (eternal) life. Jesus is both Revealer and inaugurator of this soteriological promise, and his ministry has the same function.

Eduard Schweizer's engagement with the language of the Fourth Gospel is instructive in this connection.[37] In reading the parables of the Synoptic Gospels, Schweizer proposes that they exhibit a number of characteristics: the initial use of everyday language and activities (with which the hearer could identify); a startling or extravagant element that disrupts the anticipated picture that is developing; and a continuing dynamic and goal that has the potential to invigorate the hearer.[38]

Schweizer notes how the Johannine "I am" sayings exhibit the same characteristics as the Synoptic parables. Jesus uses everyday language and imagery that draws in the hearer, yet the images also contain a disruptive dimension: "[T]heir wording makes no sense, if one remains within the limits of the earthly world: a 'spring of water welling up to eternal life' (4:14), a bread 'that endures to eternal life' (6:27), a shepherd who 'lays down his life' and 'has power to take it up again' (10:17–18), a vine in

---

36. See Paul Ricoeur, "The Bible and the Imagination," in his *Figuring the Sacred: Religion, Narrative, and Imagination* (ed. Mark I. Wallace and trans. David Pellauer; Minneapolis: Fortress, 1995), 165–66.

37. See Eduard Schweizer, *"Ego eimi...": Die religionsgeschichtliche Herkunft und theologische Bedeutung der johanneischen Bildreden, zugleich ein Beitrag zur Quellenfrage des vierten Evangeliums* (2nd ed.; Göttingen: Vandenhoeck & Ruprecht, 1965; 1st edition, 1939), and, more recently, *Jesus, The Parable of God* (PTMS 37; Allison Park, PA: Pickwick, 1994); and "What About the Johannine 'Parables'?" in *Exploring the Gospel of John: In Honor of D. Moody Smith* (ed. R. Alan Culpepper and C. Clifton Black; Louisville: Westminster John Knox, 1996), 208–19.

38. See Schweizer, *Jesus, the Parable of God*, 19–34. His example is the parable of the leaven (Luke 13:21).

which people can 'abide' and that is identical with 'love' (15:4, 9). These things do not exist except in a world 'beyond.'"³⁹

Schweizer observes, however, that these Johannine "I am" sayings differ from the Synoptic parables in two ways. First, the link to the Kingdom of God is missing; the language of the Fourth Gospel has a different focus, namely, Jesus. Second, the use of adjectives to qualify the imagery (*good* shepherd, *true* vine) extends the function of the saying beyond the metaphorical: "the so-called parables in John were . . . normal qualifications in the category of direct and defining language."⁴⁰ He proposes that the post-Easter language and theology of the Fourth Gospel effectively inverted the manner in which the language functions. Jesus became the starting point for the imagery rather than its goal. For example, "Since 'vine' is a traditional picture for Israel, we could say that it is a well-known metaphor . . . Yet, the point that the Johannine Jesus makes is that he is the true vine. Therefore, the question that John 15:1 answers seems to be: Who is the *true* vine? Who is the genuine Israel? The answer, by implication, is: only Jesus, the Son of Man solely."⁴¹

These insights can be applied to the "I am" saying of John 11:25, but also to the whole narrative of John 11. In brief, the raising of Lazarus is an account from everyday life. It relates an everyday experience of death and the pain of grief. It is the death of Lazarus that brings Jesus to Bethany, and it is the grief of Martha (11:21) that provokes the central statement, "I am the resurrection and the life" (11:25). This "I am" statement is the startling element in the story. The literal sense of the text disintegrates. At this level, Jesus cannot be the resurrection and the life because he, too, loses his life. And Lazarus is not raised to immortality. But Jesus can be the resurrection and the life, the "life-giver," if through his death he validates every life lived in faithful response to God's call.

There is also an intensification of the miracle itself. It has been noted that there is an intertwining of a basic miracle story with a reflective interpretation, particularly in the central exchange between Jesus and the mourners (11:20–37). Further, the text reaches beyond reality in the final exchange between Martha and Jesus: "Lord, already there is a stench because he has been dead four days" (John 11:39). Surely it is too late to do anything. As the parable of the leaven provokes the ques-

---

39. Schweizer, "What about the Johannine Parables?" 213.
40. Ibid., 209.
41. Ibid., 215.

tion, "Can leaven work through such a huge mass of flour?" so also the reader of John 11 asks, "Can Jesus do anything at this late stage? Is not the situation beyond hope?" This questioning inquires into the continuing dynamic of the text. In the case of John 11, the account takes the hearer to the edge of experience and beyond, which parallels Ricoeur's notion of limit expressions.

Ricoeur's theory of metaphor underpins his notion of narrative. In brief, metaphor is characterized by being creative (rather than illustrative) and provocative (rather than definitive). The relationship between the two aspects of any metaphor, for Ricoeur, is one of tension, whereby the reader is spurred to imagine the subject in a new way. Metaphors function through their semantic innovation or dissonance. This metaphorical dynamic is worked out for Ricoeur's narrative hermeneutics in the idea of plot: "With narrative, the semantic innovation lies in the inventing of another work of synthesis—a plot. By means of the plot, goals, causes and chance are brought together within the temporal unity of a whole and complete action. It is this synthesis of the heterogeneous that brings narrative close to metaphor."[42]

In the context of John 11, Ricoeur's approach to narrative configuration takes seriously the various elements (formal, theological, dramatic) and how they relate to each other. Plot brings together disparate components. The metaphorical character of this coming together means that the components impact upon each other. The resultant narrative is a productive expression of many voices. Further, this narrative shares characteristics of parables, particularly in the sense that the account transcends certain limits. In the Fourth Gospel, the ministry of Jesus is summed up in the promise of eternal life (20:31). In John 11 the possibility of hope is a particular expression of soteriology, with the intention of inspiring faith. Thus, exegesis utilising Ricoeur's narrative-hermeneutical approach attempts to identify "itineraries of meaning," which readers are invited to continue in their lives.[43]

Re-reading John 11 via Ricoeur's Narrative Hermeneutics

Exegesis of John 11 often focuses on the "I am" saying (11:25) and the pivotal role of John 11–12 in the narrative. However, two additional ele-

---

42. Paul Ricoeur, *Time and Narrative*, Vol. 1 (trans. Kathleen McLaughlin and David Pellauer; Chicago: University of Chicago Press, 1984), ix.

43. Ricoeur, "The Bible and the Imagination," 149.

ments may be constructively emphasized: (1) the enduring dynamic of transformation; and (2) the role of popular belief in Jesus.

In terms of the dynamic of transformation, many changes occur at this point in the Fourth Gospel: the transition from public to private ministry; the change from glorification through σημεῖα to glorification through the cross; the development of Martha's faith; and the movement from general hostility to the specific decision to arrest Jesus. However, these changes are based on the transformation of Lazarus from death to life. Labahn comments: "Wäre allein die theologische Aussage der Redepassage entscheidend, so scheint es, daß die erzählte Auferweckung überflüssig ist. Daß sie ein integraler Bestandteil der vorliegenden Gesamtkomposition ist, macht jedoch bereits 11,4 deutlich. Der von diesem Vers ausgehende erzählerische Spannungsbogen wird erst durch das Herausrufen des Lazarus aus seinem Grab zum Ziel gebracht."[44]

With respect to literary structure, Dorothy Lee has proposed a chiastic arrangement of John 11:1–12:11, which remains centered on the actual raising of Lazarus.[45] Francis Moloney, who generally reads the Johannine text as downplaying faith on the basis of signs, also sees the glorification promised in John 11:4 as fulfilled in the raising of Lazarus.[46] Further, when considering the framework of the chapter, it is the threat to Jesus and his glorification in the moment of his death that is the subject of the first dialogue with the disciples. Notably, Jesus focuses his mission on the raising of Lazarus (11:11, 14, 15) rather than on any revelation independent of that. In the final discussion of the chapter (11:45–57), the subject is the decision to have Jesus put to death on the basis of his sign-working. In other words, the framework of the chapter is related to the σημεῖον account rather than the discourse of Jesus. Thus, the raising of Lazarus remains the key image of transformation.

---

44. Labahn, *Jesus als Lebensspender*, 379: "If the theological statement of the discourse passage alone were to be seen as decisive, it would appear that the narrated account of the raising [of Lazarus] is superfluous. That the account is an integral component of the overall composition at hand is already made clear by 11:4. The increasing narrative tension, which has its starting point in this verse, is brought to its climax in the call to Lazarus to come out of his grave" (Hunter's translation).

45. Dorothy A. Lee, *The Symbolic Narratives of the Fourth Gospel: The Interplay of Form and Meaning* (JSNTSup 95; Sheffield, England: JSOT Press, 1994), 192.

46. Francis J. Moloney, *The Gospel of John* (SP 4; Collegeville, MN: Liturgical, 1998), 332–33.

The popular belief of the crowd based on the raising of Lazarus mediates between that moment and the decision to arrest and execute Jesus. Texts describing the condemnation of Jesus always speak of the popular belief in Jesus on the basis of the raising of Lazarus and the other σημεῖα accounts. For example:

- 11:45 notes the believing response of those who witnessed the raising of Lazarus;
- 11:48 foresees the result of Jesus' "many signs" (11:47), namely, that "everyone will believe in him, and [as a consequence of this popular belief] the Romans will come and destroy both our holy place and our nation";
- 11:52 speaks of a mass gathering, which balances the gathering of the unbelieving authorities (11:47), "so as to gather into one the dispersed children of God"; and
- 11:55–57 refers to the great interest in Jesus and his confrontation with the authorities amongst the many people on pilgrimage.

The Gospel of John is often seen to critique popular faith (see 2:23–25; 4:48; 6:26–27). But faith is a difficulty for many in the Fourth Gospel, not only crowds. Those who approach Jesus are rebuffed (2:3–4; 4:46b–48). Inquirers such as Nathanael and Nicodemus are pushed beyond what they thought was appropriate recognition (1:49–51; 3:1ff). Martha confesses on the basis of Jesus' climactic revelation (11:27), yet she seems to have lost her hope outside the tomb (11:39b). The beloved disciple appears to be the most insightful of all, but it is unclear what he actually believes at the empty tomb (20:9). Thomas is humbled for his unbelief (20:24–29). In this context, true faith needs a miracle (account). As it is said, "these things are written that you may believe" (20:31).[47]

While John 11 may be read in terms of literary strategies (e.g., the development of a theology of glory) or imagery in tension (e.g., the life-giver condemned to death), an assessment of narrative flow—the way the story is told—maintains the importance of the raising of Lazarus

---

47. Commenting on John 11:45 in *The Quest for the Messiah: The History, Literature and Theology of the Johannine Community* (2nd ed.; Nashville: Abingdon, 1993), 373, n.23, John Painter notes the "problematic" quality of faith based on sign-seeing in several Johannine texts. As he points out, however, "authentic faith was not a reality during Jesus' ministry, but the Gospel was written for a new situation when such faith had become possible" (387–88).

and popular response to it. Jewish people who believe and bear witness to the transforming moment from death to life in the raising of Lazarus (12:17) suddenly become a threat to the Jewish authorities. In Johannine terms, they have seen the life-giving work of Jesus and bear witness to an itinerary of hope.[48] Moloney is right to see in Jesus' defense of Mary's anointing of him (12:7) the link between the raising of Lazarus and Jesus' impending death.[49] In terms of the configuration of John 11, the transforming dynamic of the raising-of-Lazarus account is embedded in the account of the death and glorification of Jesus.

Ricoeur parallels the terms "embedding," "intertextuality," and "metaphorization" as descriptions of the process whereby "one text in referring to another text both displaces this other text and receives from it an extension of meaning."[50] The role of the raising of Lazarus as a narrative and theological bridge for the Fourth Gospel is in evidence at this point. The life-giver, Jesus himself, is to lose his life. Yet he will be glorified in his execution. In this sense, Jesus himself becomes the object of the σημεῖον account and thus of the life-giving character of God (cf. John 5:21). The Johannine soteriology articulated in the σημεῖα accounts both informs and forms the faith of readers. In this re-reading of John 11, we have moved far from the notion of σημεῖον as simply authenticating the authority of Jesus.

The question of the role of σημεῖον terminology remains, however. Since the term is associated with the memory of the exodus,[51] what does the description of the raising of Lazarus as a σημεῖον contribute to the account? Three brief aspects of the potential contribution may be noted in the particular context of John 11.

---

48. With respect to the Synoptic Gospels, Ricoeur speaks of "the narrative-parable ... [as] an itinerary of meaning, a signifying dynamism, which transforms a narrative structure into a metaphorical process, in the direction of an enigma expression, the kingdom of God, an expression that orients the whole process of transgression beyond the narrative framework, while at the same time receiving in return a content of provisory meaning from the narrative structure" (Ricoeur, "The Bible and the Imagination," 147).

49. Moloney, *Gospel of John*, 349.

50. Ricoeur, "The Bible and the Imagination," 148.

51. Editors' note: In the first half of chapter 5 of "Signs of Life," Hunter explored the Jewish background to the term σημεῖον, establishing a link to the liberating action of God associated with the exodus event.

The memory of the exodus in Jewish Scripture and later writings is, in part, an affirmation of the constancy of the character of God as deliverer. Yahweh is recalled in terms of the self-defining act of bringing the people of Israel out of slavery in Egypt. This memory gives particular content to scriptural soteriology. Yahweh hears the cry of those who suffer. Similarly, the theology of the Fourth Gospel emphasizes both the character of God as the one who sends Jesus and the ministry of Jesus as a faithful expression of the character of God (e.g., 5:17). In turn, the Johannine σημεῖα accounts give particular content to the soteriology promised by the Fourth Gospel. In these accounts of abundance and healing, Jesus acts for the salvation of those who cry out. In John 11 the anguish of the sisters of Lazarus initiates the account (11:3), and the faithfulness of Jesus to his calling (in full knowledge of the danger) brings the chapter to its dramatic conclusion (11:7–16, 53, 57). Notably, Jesus himself also gives a loud cry as part of his prayer (11:43), giving some basis to the notion that he, Jesus, is becoming the object of God's liberation in this account.

The Johannine σημεῖα accounts are all actions of Jesus. Many exegetes associate Jesus' signs with the authentication of Moses and messenger christology. However, it is Moses as intercessor rather than as emissary that informs the Servant Songs of Deutero-Isaiah, which in turn are echoed in the Fourth Gospel. This type of redemptive figure is more relevant to the Fourth Gospel than the one who confronts Pharaoh in Exodus 4 and 7, although of course the former is developed as part of the exodus memory. Similarly, in the Fourth Gospel the redemptive role of Jesus is emphasized (e.g., John 11:49–52). Any simple authentication gives way to his roles of life-giver, intercessor, and inspiration.

Finally, it is notable that the miracle story of the raising of Lazarus in John 11 stands between the particular soteriology of the exodus memory and the anticipation of the resurrection of Jesus. Given that the literary unit, John 11–12, culminates in citations from Isaiah in John 12:37–41, the hope of a new exodus in Isaiah may be expected to inform the understanding of the resurrection. The exodus memory, especially in Deutero-Isaiah, is given a universal focus. The character of Yahweh is to act also for the salvation of the nations. Similarly in the Fourth Gospel, salvation is for the whole world. The promise of salvation is both personalized in Jesus and given an eschatological momentum by the "I am" saying (11:25–26). The Johannine community thus recalls in the configuration of the raising of Lazarus in John 11 not only a miracle story tradition but also a σημεῖον of God's constant character as deliverer and a living hope of salvation.

CONCLUSION

By following avenues of reading opened up by a consideration of Ricoeur's later narrative hermeneutics, a key aspect of the configuration of a Johannine σημεῖον account has been addressed. The evangelist links the raising of Lazarus to the end of Jesus' public ministry, his arrest and crucifixion, and his vindication in glorification. This climactic σημεῖον in John 11 functions as a narrative bridge to the passion account of the Fourth Gospel and articulates the central Johannine soteriological promise of hope—that of life overcoming death.

In the account of the raising of Lazarus, the central role of transformation suggests that Jesus' life-giving to Lazarus leads to losing his own life. Further, the Johannine community is able to read the narrative account as the inauguration of the victory of life, faith, and hope (cf. 16:33). Through a σημεῖον account, a world-view can be transformed from being based on the past experience of persecution to being based on an eschatological hope. With that centre of transformation restated and clarified, the narrative may speak beyond the real reader of the Johannine community and beyond the anonymous reader to a contemporary reader who is invited to continue the itinerary of hope.

8

Paul and Embodied Resurrection

Rethinking 1 Corinthians 15

Keith D. Dyer

THE HISTORY OF INTERPRETATION of Paul's extended reflection on the nature of resurrection in 1 Corinthians 15 is fraught with polarized positions and assumptions. Is Paul asserting the resurrection of the body over against the immortality of the soul? Do the Corinthian "opponents" of Paul deny resurrection as such, or do they have an over-realized understanding of it? Does Paul assume the existence of the empty tomb, or does he make no reference to it because he does not know about it or think it relevant? Are we imposing post-Cartesian polarities of matter and non-matter on an ancient text and perhaps conflating them with what we think are the Platonic polarities of body and soul?[1] Is Paul himself more influenced by Jewish or Hellenistic thought, and do his "opponents" assume a Stoic or Epicurean framework?[2] Do we remain beholden to outworn cultural stereotypes such as the classic Jewish-Greek and Hebrew-Hellenistic dichotomies? Or are we wrestling with more

---

1. Dale B. Martin, *The Corinthian Body* (New Haven: Yale University Press, 1995), brilliantly deconstructs these polarities and the assumptions often made about them.

2. Graham Tomlin, "Christians and Epicureans in 1 Corinthians," *JSNT* 68 (1997) 51–72, argues that Epicurean thought influenced some of the more well-to-do Corinthians such that the problem they had "with the idea of resurrection is not that it has already taken place, but that given the corruptibility of the body, it just cannot happen" (61). Yet these same Corinthians "seem to have believed in the resurrection of Jesus (15.4, 12)" (note 49). Michelle V. Lee, *Paul, the Stoics, and the Body of Christ* (SNTSMS 137; Cambridge: Cambridge University Press, 2006), presents a persuasive argument for the influence of Stoic thought on Paul's use of "body" language.

recent dualisms, finding in this text an uncomfortable affirmation of an apocalyptic scenario involving the rapture heavenwards of the faithful?[3]

As the earliest written defence of the resurrection of Jesus Christ, 1 Corinthians 15 has borne the weight of providing evidence for resolving many of these questions and the debates that surround them. Concerns as diverse as whether Christian martyrs consumed by lions could still participate fully in bodily resurrection, whether Christians should be cremated,[4] and what combination of flesh-body-soul-spirit-mind-heart constitutes the raised "body" have all prompted close analysis of Paul's most comprehensive reflections on the topic. For some, Paul's claim to have encountered the risen Christ (1 Cor 15:8) together with the Emmaus-road account in Luke 24:13–35 provide the basis for the most reasonable and credible understanding of resurrection—one with no need for empty tombs or the touching of fleshy bodies. For others, the testimony of Paul confirms the Gospel accounts in every detail. It is not possible here to address all these issues, but in response to the questions posed by the honoree of this volume,[5] I attempt to describe (yet again) a plausible and helpful context for Paul's remarks, to summarize the apparent intent of the passage, given that context, and briefly to reflect on

---

3. I appreciate the attempt to rescue us from a docetic "heavenism" in N. T. Wright, *The Resurrection of the Son of God* (Christian Origins and the Question of God 3; Minneapolis: Fortress, 2003), 470, where he writes of the book of Revelation offering "an integrated vision of a new creation in which 'heaven' and 'earth', the twin halves of created reality, are at last united," but I am less persuaded by his continuing emphasis on "physicality" in connection with 1 Corinthians 15, where the word doesn't occur, despite the insistence of some translators. His suggestion of the term "transphysical" is more promising (477). It may be unfair to lay this charge against Wright, but ironically, the more we stress the "physicality" of the raising of Jesus Christ and of the future resurrection, the more docetic we seem to become about the present "physicality" of creation, and the less it seems to figure in God's work of transformation.

4. See, for example, Rodney J. Decker, "Is it Better to Bury or to Burn? A Biblical Perspective on Cremation and Christianity in Western Culture," The William R. Rice Lectures, Detroit Baptist Theological Seminary, March 2006, 1–45; online at http://www.NTResources.com/documents/CremationLecturesHO5.pdf/. Decker concludes his informative article with: "Let the living (i.e., those who are genuine, regenerate followers of Jesus) *bury* their dead, for it *is* better to bury than to burn" (italics original).

5. It has been my privilege to co-teach an intensive unit at Whitley College called "Resurrection, Justice and Discipleship" with Professor Thorwald Lorenzen every second year since 1997. 1 Corinthians 15 is always a central text, and Thorwald is relentless both in challenging misreadings of Paul and in his pursuit of what the implications of the text might be—especially for those so often marginalized by the dominant discourses of Church and State.

some possible implications of all this for some contemporary debates about "resurrection."[6]

I should confess at the outset my own "reading site": I have grown weary of the dominant discourse that surrounds this chapter, at least in my own evangelical tradition. Paul is often interpreted as defending the physical, bodily resurrection of both Jesus (as the firstfruits) and the faithful (at the *parousia*, 15:23),[7] against those Corinthians who either deny resurrection altogether or think it has already happened or believe only in the immortality of the soul. Apart from the apparent confusion over what the Corinthians seem to have believed, this interpretation is problematical because it objectifies "resurrection" principally as a *past* historical event and a promised *future* hope, but leaves the *present* world in something of an ethical "black hole." It has become obvious over recent decades that attempts to fill this "black hole" with doctrines of personal sanctification, charismatic renewal, and/or seeker-sensitive church growth are not moving us appreciably closer to Paul's goal (*telos*) "that God might be all in all" (15:28). Our planet longs for human participation with the power of God in transforming all that is corrupt and perishable and in renewing all creation—that is, for an understanding of "resurrection" that addresses more than private, individual bodies— and I here join the growing chorus that understands 1 Corinthians 15 more explicitly in these ways.[8] More specifically, I argue that modern-

---

6. By this I mean the wider *ekklēsial*, popular, and scholarly debates. There have also been a growing number of formal, public debates in this area: Paul Copan, ed., *Will the Real Jesus Please Stand Up? A Debate between William Lane Craig and John Dominic Crossan* (Grand Rapids: Baker, 1998); Paul Copan and Ronald K. Tacelli, eds., *Jesus' Resurrection: Fact or Figment? A Debate between William Lane Craig and Gerd Lüdemann* (Downers Grove, IL: InterVarsity, 2000); John Ankerberg, *Resurrected? An Atheist and Theist Dialogue, Gary R. Habermas and Antony G. N. Flew* (Lanham, MD: Rowman & Littlefield, 2005); Robert B. Stewart, ed., *The Resurrection of Jesus: John Dominic Crossan and N. T. Wright in Dialogue* (Minneapolis: Fortress, 2006); and Marcus J. Borg and N. T. Wright, *The Meaning of Jesus: Two Visions* (New York: HarperCollins, 1999). Most of these debates highlight the polarities outlined above, and the debaters pass each other by like ships in the night. The latter two (Crossan-Wright and Borg-Wright) are more helpful in attempting to wrestle with assumptions.

7. I shall follow the convention of using italicized transliterations of Greek terms when speaking generally, and use a Greek font when drawing special attention to particular texts or words.

8. There are many who could be named in this connection. For me it has been the likes of Moltmann and Lorenzen who have been most significant in shaping my thinking.

ist, privatized interpretations have seriously neglected Paul's emphases on (and assumptions about) the corporate, relational, and ethical nature of resurrection, often ignoring the continuity in Paul's mind between firstfruits and *parousia*.

CLARIFYING THE WORDS

The Everyday Language of Being Raised

We live in an age when the denial or affirmation of "The Resurrection" has become a touchstone of orthodoxy for many Christians. Unfortunately, the content of the affirmations (or denials) often seems less important than a particular form of words ("bodily resurrection," "raised in very flesh and very bone," "physical resurrection")—words that often have more to do with our context in high modernism, or with combating the perceived threat of post-modernism, than in the testimony of the biblical accounts or of the Christian community since. The rejoinder often made is that in Paul's understanding, to deny "The Resurrection" is to deny the validity of Christian life and faith (15:17–19), a claim that underscores the importance of the issue but does not help to understand what the content of "The Resurrection" is—either for Paul or for us. The shrill voices of both biblical and scientific fundamentalisms often come together at this point, though with opposing conclusions: either Jesus and ultimately we, his followers, are raised in "very flesh and very bone" (as described by Grey's *Anatomy* rather than the slippery metaphors of the Fourth Gospel, for example), or the whole edifice of Christian faith collapses.

Unfortunately, this focus on the noun, "resurrection," and what is taken to be its self-evident meaning has obscured the very ordinary and simple verbal language that Paul and other early traditions use to describe how God has affirmed the crucified Christ. This reification of the noun "resurrection" ("reification" in the approximate sense of objectifying and ossifying a particular meaning over time) can lead to a reduction in meaning—a limitation to concepts and thought-forms of a particular context that may well have been important and true in their time but no longer adequately convey the transforming power and intent of the God who raised Jesus.

Such a process begins already when the earlier verbs give way to a noun. We see this in the raising stories (or later "resurrection traditions") of the New Testament. In the earlier letters and narratives, the verb forms of "being raised" (*egeirō*) and of "standing again" (*anistēmi*) predominate but eventually give way to the noun "resurrection" (*anastasis*).[9] Paul seemingly resists the move towards the increasing use of *anastasis* when speaking of what God has done for the crucified Christ, much preferring the use of the everyday passive verb "was raised" (*ēgerthēn*). But 1 Corinthians 15 is the very place where he explicitly brings these two semantic (and somatic!) domains together: affirming that Jesus Christ "was raised" (*ēgerthēn*) and that this event is inseparably linked with the "resurrection of the corpses" (*anastasis tōn nekrōn*). This is an astonishing move whereby Paul insists that what happened to Jesus also happens to all who follow him and are "in Christ." I argue below that this simple but profound equation—Christ's destiny is ours if we live his way; we are Christ's body—is Paul's main point in this chapter and provides the underlying thread and structure to the whole section.

Paul's preference for the passive form of *egeirō* is surely significant: Jesus Christ does not gatecrash the council of the gods like some Greek superhero forcing his way into divine company. Jesus *was raised* by God—always stated in the passive voice by Paul, with the early exception of 1 Thess 4:14 (ἀνέστη, *anestē*). For Paul, the raising of Jesus was *theo*logical in power, in motive and intent, and *christ*ological in content. Whatever else we may understand by the term "resurrection," it is God's "Yes!" to Jesus (2 Cor 1:17–20), and our concerns to support whatever the current orthodoxy dictates about the nature of "resurrection" should not lead us to minimize this dimension of God's affirmation, vindication, and exaltation of Jesus—call it what you will—God's "Yes!" to Jesus.

---

9. Remarkably, given the dominance of the verb *egeirō* (144 times in the New Testament), the noun form (*egersis*) occurs only once in the New Testament (Matt 27:53), and there on the lips of Jesus' opponents. By my reckoning, the everyday verb *egeirō* is used forty-one times in Paul (twenty-five times of the raising of Jesus), nineteen in Mark (twice of Jesus), thirty-seven in Matthew (nine times of Jesus), eighteen in Luke (three times of Jesus), thirteen in John (twice of Jesus), and thirteen in Acts (six times of Jesus). The verb *anistēmi* occurs 108 times, again mostly of more mundane "rising" and "getting up," but nineteen times of the post-mortem raising of Jesus (five times in Mark, four times in Luke, twice in John, seven times in Acts, and once in 1 Thess 4:14). The noun *anastasis* is used forty-two times in the New Testament, mostly of the general resurrection. *The three times only that Paul uses it of Jesus are in Rom 1:4 (tradition), 6:5 (general resurrection?), and Phil 3:10.* It is in Acts (six out of eleven uses) and the later New Testament traditions (three of eleven), and particularly in the post–New Testament communities, where it is used more frequently for "the resurrection of Jesus Christ."

To do so is to begin to lose the full verbal impetus of what God has done and is doing in Christ (a *process*, begun emphatically) and to replace it with a reified noun representing an event objectified (and potentially frozen) in history. If the Corinthians are sometimes charged with an over-realized view of the resurrection, one danger for us today may well be a fixation on an over-historicized resurrection, as if our affirmation of the facticity of this past event (defined in terms of modern science and history) expresses its full significance.

In such a context, it is noteworthy that the good news proclaimed by Paul is not "the resurrection of Jesus," a static nounal statement, but "God raised Christ" (15:15, in the active form), or "Christ was raised out of the corpses" (15:12, the more common divine passive).[10] The focus of the proclamation is not on "The Resurrection" itself (its manner, its physiology, or its glory, which is why we have no need canonically for eye-witness accounts of the event itself), but on the subject (God) and object (Jesus Christ) of the raising. The meaning of "God raised Christ" is thus determined more by the nature of God and the nature of the Christ raised than by abstracting a noun from the common verb used to link them.[11] The evidence that "God raised Jesus Christ" is dependent on the subsequent diverse encounters with the one raised and the consequent engagement in mission, not on any eye-witness account of the event itself.

For these reasons, I leave open the meaning of the noun "resurrection" and follow Paul's usage more carefully by referring to Christ

---

10. Note, however, that Paul is more inclined to express the heart of his Gospel in terms of "Christ crucified" (1 Cor 1:23). Yet both affirmations ("Christ crucified" and "Jesus Christ was raised") embody the tension between identification with humanity ("crucified" and "Jesus") and the connection with the divine ("Christ" and "was raised"), and for Paul, both invite human participation: "If we have died with Christ, we believe we will also live with him" (Rom 6:8; cf. 2 Tim 2:11).

11. Here I affirm emphatically Lorenzen's major project to describe resurrection in terms of faith (as engaged belief: witness and praxis) rather than primarily in terms of abstract ontologies or doctrines. The first two-thirds of his first book, *Resurrection and Discipleship*, is a summary and critique of understandings of "The Resurrection," while the last third of that book and the majority of his second book, *Resurrection, Discipleship, Justice*, is a passionate description of what it means in practice that "God raised this Jesus whom you crucified." We considered giving this Festschrift the un-Baptist title, "The Dance of Life," in reference to Thorwald's oft-stated conviction that the only way to know the dance (or sport) is to join in, since the teachers, rules, and coaching manuals can only take us so far. And so it is with "resurrection," with "being raised"....

"being raised" when the passive of *egeirō* is used, and "resurrection" when the noun *anastasis* is used. Occasionally, as above, I will use "The Resurrection" to draw attention to the reified term in all its post-biblical theological glory. I do this not to imply criticism of "non-biblical" theology, but merely to emphasize that meanings and doctrines inevitably develop and grow—a process that can be understood and enhanced by occasional critical reflection on the earliest sources of their meaning. For the same reasons, I also use the translation "corpses" for *nekrōn*, to represent the stronger sense of that word, and "soul" and "soulish" consistently for *psychē* and *psychikon*, respectively, rather than the misleading translations, "physical" (NRSV) or "natural" (KJV, WEB).[12]

Paul's "Body Language"

The word "body" (*sōma*) is of particular significance for Paul, especially in the Corinthian correspondence, where it is used of the individual human body and the corporate body of believers (the body of Christ) in close proximity (1 Corinthians 6); of the eucharistic body of Christ (1 Corinthians 10–11); of the ecclesial body of Christ (1 Corinthians 12–14); of cosmic and other natural bodies (1 Cor 15:40); and of soulish and spiritual bodies (1 Cor 15:44).[13] All of these references imply a corporate dimension (even when we don't hear it in English), with the exception of those few (of the forty-six occurrences in 1 Corinthians!) that are explicitly singular (1 Cor 5:3; 7:4; 9:27; 13:3) or refer to a collection of individual bodies (1 Cor 6:15). For example, to make this point clear, it is the body *of all of us* that is the temple of the Holy Spirit (1 Cor 6:19; cf. 3:16), not solely our individual bodies, and we are to glorify God in *our* body (a corporate singular, 6:19). Similarly, when Paul anticipates a

---

12. In so doing, I follow the suggestions of Richard B. Hays, *First Corinthians* (Interpretation: A Bible Commentary for Teaching and Preaching; Louisville: John Knox, 1997), 253: "'resurrection of the dead' (*anastasis nekrōn*) means literally 'rising of the corpses.' For the spiritually refined Corinthians, this was not the stuff of Christian hope; it was a scenario for a horror story." The translations "physical" and "natural" reinforce the imposition of post-Cartesian categories on the text, since *physis* (usually translated as "nature") does not occur in this passage. I also use "just righteousness" and "righteous justice" interchangeably for *dikaiosunē* to convey the sense of relational righteousness implied in the term and in its Hebrew antecedents.

13. Lee, *Paul, the Stoics, and the Body of Christ*, gives an excellent analysis of the "body" and its corporate reality in Stoic literature and in 1 Corinthians, except that unfortunately she does not continue the analysis through to include chapter 15!

question from the Corinthians (15:35), he asks: "With what kind of body (singular) do they come (plural)?" again assuming a corporate identity for the risen body (singular), rather than a collection of individual bodies (plural). Here the dominant assumptions about Western individualism continue to meet a severe challenge in our (collective!) imagination, but it is one we must continually wrestle with if we are to comprehend the implications of Paul's arguments.

We should, therefore, assume that a corporate body is intended in all instances unless we are forced by the text to read it otherwise, and we should resist any arbitrary compartmentalisation of the meanings of *sōma*, as if they do not overlap in any way. Repeatedly in this letter, Paul makes the point that we are *one* body, the body of Christ (12:18, 27). On this basis then, we cannot legitimately privatize our sexual ethics ("sinning against the body," 1 Cor 6:18) as if our *porneia* is a sin only against our own individual body. Nor should we assume that Paul's exhortation to examine ourselves at the Lord's Supper is simply an invitation to individual introspection (1 Cor 11:27-34)—many African sisters and brothers would see it as a call to corporate responsibility.[14] So, too, we should be suspicious of any claim that what Paul says about our resurrection body, *not* "bodies," primarily affirms a privatized and individual postmortem existence. The body, for Paul, is to be understood as corporate, Christological, eucharistic, ecclesial, sometimes individual, sometimes fleshly, and sometimes spiritual! We should not assume that this diversity of meaning indicates that Paul is fond of using *sōma* as a metaphor, for that involves the assumption that the essential meaning of body is the physical human body (as in English).[15] Rather, we should adjust to the reality that *sōma* in Greek has an even wider repertoire of meanings than "body" in English, and that phrases such as "the body of Christ" express a "shared corporeity" and "somatic union" that go beyond analogy and metaphor to establish a relational and ethical reality.[16]

---

14. See J. Ayodeji Alewuya, "Revisiting 1 Corinthians 11.27-34: Paul's Discussion of the Lord's Supper and African Meals," *JSNT* 30 (2007) 95-112.

15. Lee, *Body of Christ*, 1-5, argues persuasively for more than simply analogy or metaphor in Paul's use of "body," though does not go so far as John A. T. Robinson, who contended that the church is "in literal fact the risen organism of Christ's person in all its concrete reality" and "literally now the resurrection *body* of Christ." See John A. T. Robinson, *The Body: A Study in Pauline Theology* (SBT 1/5; London: SCM, 1952), 51.

16. See Lee, *Paul, the Stoics, and the Body of Christ*, 4-5, who quotes these phrases from Albert Schweitzer in her helpful discussion of the views of Robinson, Schweitzer, Jewett, and Martin.

CLARIFYING THE CORINTHIAN CONTEXT

In a letter noted for its explicit and detailed interaction with the context of its hearers, it is something of a puzzle to comprehend why the longest of Paul's "discussions" with the Corinthians should have been kept until last, and why he should tackle this particular topic in this way. On the face of it, if the Corinthians really were denying "The Resurrection" (15:12), why didn't Paul tackle them about it from the outset of his letter? As Paul seems to say (but much too late, it would seem), if there is no resurrection of any kind then what is the point of it all anyway (15:17–19)? What, then, would be the purpose of Paul's prior challenges to the Corinthians about their ethics (legal, 1 Corinthians 5; sexual, 6–7; socio-political, 8–10; liturgical, 11; and ecclesial, 12–14), if the very originator of these ethics had simply been crucified as a criminal some twenty years or so previously in a distant province of the Empire? Were there not many more respectable ethicists closer at hand who could be quoted to equally good effect?

It is not really surprising, given this, that Paul's (seemingly belated) claim that "some of you say that there is no resurrection (*anastasis*) of the dead" (15:12) has led to a wide variety of interpretations since, corresponding to the many differing understandings of Paul's rhetorical strategy and of the Corinthian context. Perhaps, it has often been suggested, Paul is combating an "over-realized" eschatology that claims "resurrection" has in some sense already happened (cf. 4:8; 2 Tim 2:18), leading to an underlying theological problem that contributes to the hyper-charismatic excesses of the community?[17] But if so, why does Paul leave such a fundamental problem until last—and then describe it as a denial of resurrection, rather than as an over-emphasis on the present dimension of resurrection power? Others have reconstructed Paul's purpose as a challenge to the dominant Hellenistic understanding of the immortality of a bodiless soul—claiming that the emphasis in the charge by Paul is on the end of the sentence: "some of you say that there is no resurrection *of the dead*" (15:12, meaning "corpses," as suggested above). Thus Paul's main point, it is claimed, is to stress the embodiedness of

---

17. Anthony C. Thiselton, *The First Epistle to the Corinthians: A Commentary on the Greek Text* (NIGTC; Grand Rapids: Eerdmans, 2000), especially 1172–78, 1276–81, makes the most coherent recent defense of this position.

resurrection (from his Jewish traditions) over against an ensouled immortality (more typical of the Greco-Roman world).[18]

The prevalence of this Hellenistic belief is often asserted by citing the classic Platonic epigram: the *sōma* (body) is the *sēma* (prison) of the *psychē* (soul), expressing the widespread belief that death liberates the latter from the former. But if this is primarily what Paul is combating (rejection of bodily resurrection in favour of an immortal soul), how does appealing to what they seem to deny—the raising of Jesus—help the argument, particularly when Paul doesn't stress the *bodily* resurrection of Jesus Christ? Adding his own name (belatedly) to the list of witnesses to "The Resurrection" (15:8–9) hardly strengthens the evidence for a bodily (fleshly?) resurrection, as every "liberal" exegete in recent times likes to point out.[19] Why does Paul make no mention of an empty tomb (as in the Gospel accounts) or of "touching my body" (John 20:27) or of "flesh and bones" (Luke 24:39)? And why cap the whole argument with the assertion that "flesh and blood cannot inherit the empire of God" (15:50), when this would seem to put at risk the main point of such an argument? If Paul is attempting here to defend a physical "flesh and blood" resurrection of Jesus Christ, he seems to make rather a mess of it!

There are, of course, many refinements to these basic positions that make better sense of the objections I have raised, and it would be unfair to impose a crude polarity on the scholarly debate when I have rejected such dichotomies elsewhere. Nevertheless, within the confines of this study—and whilst affirming the relevance of some aspects of the "realized eschatology" and "immortality of the soul" arguments for understanding Paul and 1 Corinthians[20]—I argue for a modification of these

---

18. Richard A. Horsley, *1 Corinthians* (ANTC; Nashville: Abingdon, 1998), 197–220, is a recent eloquent exponent of this position.

19. This is particularly evident in the "resurrection debates" cited earlier, where the evidence of 1 Corinthians 15 is often the focus of polarized positions on what "resurrection" means.

20. The dominant Hellenistic belief in the immortality of the soul is still an important piece of the puzzle, as I argue below. I would describe my understanding of Paul as less "apocalyptic" (in the sense of expecting imminent divine intervention) than Horsley's and tending to a more "realized eschatological" position, though not in the way it has often been described in the context of the Corinthian community. I think that for Paul, despite all their shortcomings, the *ekklēsial* communities already embody the firstfruits of God's decisive and transformative intervention.

positions that takes into account the recent work, briefly outlined below, of Dale Martin, Kevin Madigan and Jon Levenson, and Dag Endsjø.[21]

Dale Martin has clarified the extraordinary difficulty we have in unravelling Corinthian (Hellenistic?), Pauline (Jewish?), and our own post-Cartesian terminology about corporeal and incorporeal, matter and non-matter, body and spirit, soul and physicality. The absolute distinctions that Descartes made in separating the proper objects of scientific enquiry from the spiritual realm of the church, coupled with the dramatic rise and dominance of the scientific paradigm since, are almost impossible for us to unravel. Nor can we easily disentangle them from the language of the Greek philosophers, whose assumptions are profoundly different although their vocabulary has often been imported into our scientific definitions of "reality" and truth. Translators of and commentators on 1 Corinthians 15 have not always helped us to appreciate the difficulties of these shifts in the meanings of our terminology over time. We do well to maintain a certain humility and sensitivity to the ambiguities of the text and its many interpretations since. Martin pushes us further still, urging that we must take responsibility for the "(often unintended) ethical ramifications and political consequences of the things we say we believe" and "examine the often unrecognized implications of our own constructions of the bodies of ourselves and others,"[22] and indeed of the body of Christ. We should start by repenting of our modernist assumption that "body" means "physical" or "material," and "spirit" means "non-material" or "ephemeral."[23] Martin demonstrates forcefully that it is not helpful for us to assume a modernist scientific description of reality as the interpretive context for a first-century text. Our polarities are not theirs—even when we think we're using the same language.

---

21. See Martin, *The Corinthian Body*; Kevin J. Madigan and Jon D. Levenson, *Resurrection: The Power of God for Christians and Jews* (New Haven: Yale University Press, 2008); and Dag Øistein Endsjø, "Immortal Bodies, before Christ: Bodily Continuity in Ancient Greece and 1 Corinthians," *JSNT* 30 (2008) 417–36.

22. Martin, *The Corinthian Body*, 251.

23. Descartes' distinctions may have served in the past to enable scientific inquiry to proceed without too much interference from the Church, but they no longer serve science well and have "misled countless readers in their reading of ancient authors, Paul especially" (Martin, *The Corinthian Body*, 5). It is clear that no one in the ancient world (and certainly neither Plato nor Paul) conceived of "body" and "spirit" in this way. We should not impose such polarities on this text!

Jon Levenson has shown that Jewish understandings of resurrection at the time of Paul were more prominent than Christian scholars have often assumed, more theologically profound (concerning the nature of God, rather than focusing on post-mortem existence as such), and thoroughly corporate in nature.[24] The latter point has often been made in Christian scholarship, but usually as a foil to emphasize the uniqueness of the resurrection of Christ, thereby missing entirely the point of Paul's use of the "firstfruits" analogy (15:20, 23). This corporate understanding of the resurrection of the corpses needs to be reasserted not only as the Jewish context for the raising of Christ but also as its fundamental nature and its consequential significance.[25] The use of the "firstfruits" analogy to describe the raising of Jesus Christ by God is not an affirmation of individual uniqueness but suggests the beginning of an ongoing collective fruitfulness. To be sure, the full harvest lies in the future ("at his *parousia*," 15:23), but the raising of Jesus ushers in a present and continuing reality: God is affirming and transforming the body of Christ through the power of the Spirit.[26] This present reality is embodied in the corporate nature of the identity of the raised Christ, indicated in so many ways by the *sōma* language throughout 1 Corinthians, and also explicitly in chapter 15 by the first- and last- or second-Adam language. The raised Christ as last Adam is the life-making Spirit (15:45) who enables and ushers in the general resurrection of the corpses at his appearance (*parousia*), a future reality that informs and shapes the present Spirit-filled life of the corporate body of Christ. Jesus Christ is raised as

---

24. See Jon Douglas Levenson, *Resurrection and the Restoration of Israel: The Ultimate Victory of the God of Life* (New Haven: Yale University Press, 2006), x: "When the programmatic question is defined as 'Will I have life after death?' the discussion has already gotten off on the wrong foot."

25. Matt 27:53 also makes this clear in a more graphic way. Indeed the connections between Paul and Matthew with regard to resurrection traditions are greater than might be expected (perhaps the Antiochene influence?), given that some locate them on opposing sides in emergent Jewish and Gentile "Christianity." Note the distinctive use of θάπτω / τάφος (bury/tomb, 1 Cor 15:4; Matt 27:61, 64, 66; 28:1) compared with the consistently non-christological usage in Luke–Acts; and also the overwhelming preference of both Paul and Matthew for *egeirō* rather than *anastasis*, again in contrast to Luke–Acts.

26. Robert C. Tannehill, *Dying and Rising with Christ: A Study in Pauline Theology* (BZNW 32; Berlin: Töppelmann, 1967), 130, contends that in Paul there is no "clear distinction between references to a present participation in new life and a rising with Christ in the future. Both ideas occur within the same passages as variations on one theme."

the representative Human One, the mythic last Adam, the forerunner, the firstfruits, the body (of humans) that is also the temple of the Holy Spirit, because God has affirmed the Way of the crucified one and of all who follow him.

Levenson and Madigan have also rightly stressed the *theology* of resurrection, namely, that resurrection is God's act and a necessary consequence of the outworking of the righteous justice of God. This is the most helpful framework within which to interpret Paul's comment that if in this life only we have hoped in Christ, then we are of all humanity the most pitiable (15:19). At the popular level, this text is often understood as an affirmation of individual life-after-death, so that the glories of heaven will make up for all that Christians have suffered or done without in this life. Coupled with a dubious belief in the "rapture of the faithful" that is somehow connected in popular thought with the *parousia* (15:23), the resultant eschatology has paralyzed many persuaded by the more apocalyptic traditions, such that present existence becomes a matter of surviving life in the dark abyss between the historical resurrection of Christ and the future hope of the general resurrection—caught in the headlights between promise and fulfillment.[27] Unfortunately, this fixation on the historicity and bodily physicality of the past and future events of resurrection can so often lead to a devaluation of the theological significance of *this* embodied life, of *this* creation, of the Way of Jesus in *this* world, in favor of hope for something better in the next.

So Paul's statement (15:19) should not be read as an affirmation that resurrection is necessary so that miserable and pitiful Christians will get their reward in the next life. Rather, consistent with Jewish tradition as described by Levenson, we can understand that in affirming the raising of those who sleep (the resurrection of the corpses) as a consequence of the raising of Jesus Christ, Paul is affirming the character of God as righteous and just beyond the limits of any one lifetime. If this is not so, and God's transforming justice (our hope in Christ) does not transcend the generations and our present experience of time and space, then we're all wasting our time, asserts Paul (15:2,13–19), since then God is not God and will never be "all in all" (15:28). So resurrection is not seen by Paul as the necessary compensation for a Christian life of denial, but as the

---

27. See Keith D. Dyer, "When Is the End Not the End? The Fate of Earth in Biblical Eschatology (Mark 13)," in *The Earth Story in the New Testament* (ed. Norman C. Habel and Vicky Balabanski; Earth Bible 5; London: Sheffield Academic, 2002), 44–56.

consequence (and *telos*) of the righteous justice of God seen in Jesus and to be lived out in his risen body, the *ekklēsia*. If there is no (corporate) resurrection, then God is not just and we are to be pitied for living in that false hope. Indeed, Paul can countenance personal *anathema* and no life after death (see Rom 9:1–5), but he cannot countenance the possibility that God is not just or that God will not be true to Israel. Resurrection, both as the raising of Christ and as the continuing and ultimate transformation of all, is confirmation of the righteous justice of God at work in the cosmos.

For these reasons, Paul frames this whole discourse on the raising of Jesus Christ and the resurrection of corpses with exhortations to continue standing firm in the good news and the salvation and work of the Lord (15:1–2; 57–58) as revealed by the life and teaching of the crucified Christ (1:23). If this embodied and relational existence is in the end irrelevant, and only the disembodied souls of those individuals considered wise remain, making their ascent into the heavens, then why should there be any urgency or even need to overcome such divisions in the *ekklēsial* body as between Jew and Gentile, weak and strong, wise and foolish, slave and free? The denial of such an embodied resurrection by some at Corinth was thus for Paul not merely a disagreement over the finer points of some future eschatological timetable. As in the church today, it had immediate implications for how life in the body of Christ was to be understood and experienced in the present, and thus also whether the righteous justice of God was in any sense an in-breaking reality or a deferred and theoretical hope for another time and place. For this reason, Paul uses the extended argument in chapter 15 as the climax to his *ekklēsial* and ethical discussions with the Corinthians: it applies across all aspects of "body life" examined within the letter and provides an overall vision—the capstone—of the embodied reality of the on-going transformative power of the Spirit—of being "in Christ" (1 Cor 1:2, 4, 30; 3:1; 4:10, 15, 17; 15:17, 22, 31; 16:24).

Even if we accept that Paul's intent is to stress the corporate, relational, and ethical implications of resurrection in the wider context of a culture hoping for (or resigned to) a future disembodied "raising up," the problem remains as to how this connects with the "raising up" of Christ. It appears that Paul appeals to the raising of Jesus Christ almost as common ground in his argument for the resurrection of the corpses—as if most accepted the former, but not the latter. It is helpful here to consider the recent work of Dag Endsjø, who shows clearly that the oft-repeated maxim that the inhabitants of the Greco-Roman world could not accept the idea of a bodily resurrection needs serious qualification. Whereas he affirms that the "idea that the body should become immortal has rightly been considered an absurdity in the context of the Greek philosophical tradition,"[28] he questions how much this intellectual elite influenced the thinking of the wider public, especially in comparison with the mythical stories of traditional Greek religion. There are numerous Greek superheroes (sometimes the mortal offspring of the gods) who are "translated" or resurrected to bodily immortality as divine beings. In this context, Endsjø points out that the proclamation that Jesus, as the mortal son of a deity, "died, was resurrected and became immortal, after which he disappeared from the ordinary world, was in complete agreement with a pattern we repeatedly find in the more general Greek tradition."[29] He gives such examples as Achilles (but not in Homer's version), Memnon, Asclepius, Melicertes, Menelaus, and Ino from the mythic past, together with Croesus and Aristeas from historical times.[30]

This translation to immortality requires, or at least assumes, the disappearance of the body, since elevation to the divine pantheon requires an embodied existence. Thus for Endsjø, there would have been no problem in theory for many in the wider Greco-Roman world to accept the "resurrection" of Jesus Christ in a similar way—as the bodily translation to immortality of some kind of superhero, chosen by the gods.[31] It would not be possible, however, to understand this kind of "resurrection" as applying in any way to long-dead corpses. That which has been destroyed or has disintegrated can no longer be restored—not even by the gods. Endsjø cites the example of Pelops, dismembered and served as a dish to the gods. The gods were able to reassemble him, but because his shoulder had already been eaten by Demeter, it had to be replaced by a prosthesis.[32] As Endsjø asks: "If this mighty assembly of Olympian gods could not recreate even the shoulder of Pelops, how, then, should anyone be able to

---

28. Endsjø, "Immortal Bodies," 418.
29. Ibid., 423.
30. Ibid., 424–25. This is a representative list only.
31. Paul's insistence on "Christ crucified" may be part of his challenge to this view of resurrection as the "glorious translation of the superhero." I am indebted to my co-editor, David Neville, for this and other insights, qualifications, and corrections.
32. Endsjø, "Immortal Bodies," 433.

recreate a whole body?"[33] In the context of this view of popular religion, we can see how it would be possible for a Corinthian to accept that an exceptional individual could be raised bodily by the gods—but not long dead, disintegrating corpses.

This reconstruction by Endsjø is helpful for clarifying how (some of) the Corinthians might more readily accept the raising of Jesus than the general resurrection of the corpses. For this reason, Paul begins his argument in 1 Corinthians 15 with the more culturally acceptable message of the raising of Jesus after three days (whose unbroken body did not require recreating), before asserting the consequential resurrection of corpses, which would be a much more difficult proposition for those with a Hellenistic background to accept. For Paul, the raising of Jesus and the resurrection of corpses are inseparable parts of the continuing transforming action of God, and they qualify and inform each other.

So the work of Endsjø clarifies another part of the jigsaw in Paul's argument, though it does not go so far as to describe what the "ordinary" Corinthian (without divine aspirations) may have understood about his or her own death and immortality. Here we return to the widely held understanding that the predominant view within all levels of Greco-Roman culture was that the soul was liberated from the body at death and freed to journey heavenwards—assuming that proper funerary rites were observed and that those remaining alive continued to aid their ancestors in the journey.[34] The archaeological evidence for the prevalence of household shrines to the ancestors, sometimes alongside shrines to other deities and emperors, is evidence of widespread belief in the immortality of the soul. Dead bodies were buried outside towns, with due respect for proper protocols, so that the continuing presence and well-being of the souls of ancestors could be ensured and celebrated daily by relatives within the home. Interestingly, in Paul's somewhat tortured discussion of the question of idol meat (1 Corinthians 8–10), he is unequivocal about shunning it in the Temple in the presence of idols (8:10–13), but far more accommodating towards eating it in the presence of household ancestors (10:27), who would inevitably have been present

---

33. Ibid.

34. Everett Ferguson, *Backgrounds of Early Christianity* (2nd ed.; Grand Rapids: Eerdmans, 1993), chapter 3, "Hellenistic-Roman Religions" (137–298), provides an overview of these elements of Greco-Roman religion.

in the home of an "unbeliever." This should alert us to some interesting consequences.

When such households were baptized and joined the body of Christ, were the ancestors (present in spirit) included in some way in the rite?[35] If Paul's corporate "body language" did not extend to include all the family connections, "fictive" and actual, past and present, what would this have said about the transforming resurrection power of God being "all in all" (15:28)? We should consider whether the practice of a household baptism that included ancestors in the body of Christ might serve to illustrate the nature of the reality of the resurrection that Paul was seeking to establish (15:29). This would not simply be some bizarre accommodation to Hellenistic folk religion, for Paul's arguments about Abraham being "included by faith" (Romans 4; Galatians 3) and the ancestors being "baptized into Moses" and drinking from "the rock which is Christ" (1 Cor 10:2–4) also assume some kind of retrospective consequences stemming from the raising of Jesus.[36] It may be difficult for Westerners who can no longer recall the names of all their grandparents to appreciate the significance of these issues or to conceive that the "great apostle of the Protestant West" could show any tolerance towards what we might call ancestor worship. Yet Paul's acquiescence in such practices would certainly be consistent with his obvious pastoral concern for those who have already died.[37] Such concerns seem to have played

---

35. I acknowledge here the helpful work in this area by my doctoral student Oh-Young Kwon, "1 Corinthians 1–4: A Rhetorical and Social Analysis and its Evaluation from a Korean-Confucian Christian Context" (Doctor of Theology thesis, Melbourne College of Divinity, 2008).

36. The role of ancestors within Hebrew culture and religion has been underestimated in Western scholarship. For a timely corrective and an indication of what difference it makes to be aware of the ancestors in and behind the text, see Mark G. Brett, *Decolonizing God: The Bible in the Tides of Empire* (The Bible in the Modern World 16; Sheffield: Sheffield Phoenix, 2008), 44–61 (chapter 3: "Ancestors and their Gifts"). Note also the comment by Levenson, *Resurrection and the Restoration of Israel*, xi: "in the Hebrew Bible, the lives of ancestors and descendants were inextricably connected in ways that modern people have enormous problems imagining."

37. Many of the theological problems we may have with such an interpretation are a product of our assumptions about the nature of post-mortem existence and our absolutizing of "personal faith." Somewhere between the insistence that only those baptized in a certain way are saved, or at a certain age or on a particular confession of personal faith, and the attempt by the Mormons to baptize everyone retrospectively, there lies a range of baptismal practices Paul seems able to accept. See the detailed discussion of thirteen of the many possible interpretations of this extraordinary comment by

a large part in prompting Paul's first (surviving) letter, 1 Thessalonians; and in 1 Corinthians 15:18, 20, 29 (using Paul's preferred vocabulary, "the ones sleeping") and 15:52 (reverting to "the corpses" to drive the point home) we can see that this issue underlies the whole discussion and is not simply a passing reference in 15:29.[38] The fate of the dead and the dying was a significant concern of everyday life in the ancient circum-Mediterranean world.

These suggestions about the Corinthian context are necessarily selective but sufficient to suggest some helpful perspectives on Paul's possible arguments and underlying assumptions in 1 Corinthians 15. We cannot, of course, lay aside all the assumptions that we bring to the text, but we do well to remain open to as many plausible new insights as we can, in order to test them—and ours—as we read the text and interpret them in dialogue with our own "*ekklēsial* body."

WHAT PAUL DOES *NOT* SAY

Paul does not primarily address the question of life after death as such—and certainly not in terms of the post-mortem fate of individuals. Life after death (in some form, and at the very least as part of the ongoing transforming life of God) is assumed both by Paul and the Corinthians; but it is whether or not our collective embodied identity is of ultimate significance, what its relationship is to Jesus Christ, and the implications of this for our present existence and ethics that are Paul's main concerns.

Paul (15:29) in Thiselton, *First Corinthians*, 1240–49; and the extensive literature cited there. Mercifully, Indigenous and Eastern scholars are beginning to challenge Western assumptions about this text and about the evils of so-called ancestor worship, and to bring us a perspective closer to a biblical world-view. We have much to learn, and I for one am only beginning.

38. I am not suggesting that the sacraments and prayers of the living "save" or even influence the dead (they are, after all, in Paul's words, the "sleeping ones"), but rather that these dead kinfolk (fictive or actual) *are* part of the household body. It is inconceivable that the household could be baptized without consideration of the continuing relationship between them all. If Paul allows that they are included in baptism, there is then the opportunity to transform the patriarchal and hierarchical nature of the entire household "body" in line with the ethical teachings that dominate the rest of the epistle. The actual fate of the (otherwise unregenerate) sleeping ones in Paul's thought is not so clear as some think. Are "the dead in-Christ-raised" or "the dead-in-Christ raised"? The former is inclusive and the latter exclusive, and, in any case, their fate is not explicitly described. See David Konstan and Ilaria Ramelli, "The Syntax of ἐν Χριστῷ in 1 Thessalonians 4:16," *JBL* 126 (2007): 579–93, who argue strongly for the inclusive reading—*all* are raised-in-Christ.

Is the future of humanity—apart from those few super-mortals who are translated to the divine ranks—to be visualized as rotting corpses buried in the earth while the souls ascend through the heavens, or does God continue to act decisively to bring justice and transformation to the whole cosmos even beyond the end of our mortal lives? It is therefore not so much a question of, Do we live beyond death? as, Does the righteous justice and transforming power of God continue beyond death? that dominates Paul's thinking.

We can also see from the language Paul uses here that it is not the physicality of the resurrection body that seems to be Paul's concern. That question may well have been ours in more recent times due to the post-Cartesian polarization of our sense of reality into matter or non-matter, physical or spiritual, scientific or theological. But for Paul the affirmation that we are raised immortal as an embodied spirit (1 Cor 15:44) does not imply a non-material, earth-denying existence. Indeed, all creation undergoes the same transformation and groans in longing for it (Rom 8:18–25). God gives all sorts of bodies to all kinds of cosmic and created entities (1 Cor 15:35–41), so why should humans conceive of ultimate reality as disembodied unless they wish to escape responsibility for their embodied existence, their relationships and ethics?

It has also become clear that Paul is not interested in presenting Jesus as the "firstfruit" but as the "firstfruits," that is, not as the first of many individuals to be raised out of death but as the beginning of a continuing harvest, all interrelated in one cosmic body.[39] To assert the truth of individual bodily resurrection in the context of 1 Corinthians 15 is rather like insisting that you (singular) were present at the Lincoln Memorial in Washington when Martin Luther King Jr. shared his dream or, indeed, at Chicago's Grant Park when Barack Obama was elected president. Though such a truth may be existentially relevant, even life-changing for those who really were there (and make for a great testimony!), it hardly encapsulates the wider significance of the event itself. Bigger and more important things were happening! Indeed, Paul does affirm specifically,

---

39. Brett, *Decolonizing God*, 171, argues strongly for Paul's embrace of cultural hybridity in his body language, and quotes with approval Miroslav Volf's claim that the "Pauline move is not from the particularity of the body to the universality of the spirit, but from separated bodies to the community of interrelated bodies." See Miroslav Volf, *Exclusion and Embrace: A Theological Exploration of Identity, Otherness, and Reconciliation* (Nashville: Abingdon, 1996), 47–48. I agree but suggest that Paul might have rephrased this last clause as: "to the body of interrelated communities."

in places, the participation of the individual in God's wider work; but his overwhelming emphasis is on the collective, corporate body of Christ and our role in the building up of that transformed and transformative community. So for us to assert, on the basis of 1 Corinthians 15, the reality and importance of our own individual post-mortem existence would be to ignore the vast crowd surrounding us and to shut our ears to the one articulating the vision. There are bigger moves afoot....

WHAT PAUL *DOES* SAY

The basic argument Paul makes is simple and clear, as stated in the headline sentences of each section, beginning with verses 1, 3, 12, 20, 35, and 58:

> 1–2 *Hold fast to the good news I proclaimed, you received, in which you stand and by which you are being saved.*

Note also the other end of this ethical *inclusio* in v. 58. The framework for this whole discussion is the lived reality of the good news of Jesus.

> 3–11: *I passed onto you what I received: that God raised Jesus Christ, and he was seen by many witnesses, last and least of all by me.*

It is clear that Paul argues for both continuity and discontinuity between God raising Jesus and the resurrection of the corpses. On the one hand, he differentiates between historical encounters with Jesus after he was raised by God (15:3–11) and subsequent access to that reality ("I passed on to you . . ." [15:3]), since Paul claims to be the last and least of those witnesses (15:8–9).[40] On the other hand, he argues explicitly and emphatically for continuity between Jesus' being raised out of the corpses, and the resurrection of corpses (15:12–13; 15–17; 20!; 29–35; 42; see text columns below). For Paul, again I stress, the raising of Jesus by God constitutes the firstfruits of the general resurrection of

---

40. At this point Paul asserts a certain discontinuity between the earliest encounters of the risen Jesus and later secondary experiences. It may well be that some still experience mystical encounters with the risen Christ today, but they are neither normative for the church nor part of the earliest testimony that describes and tests such experiences. Religious experience alone cannot define the meaning or verify the reality of "resurrection"; it must also be tested by Scripture, in the *ekklēsia*, and by action in the world. I am grateful to my colleague Ross Klinger for the benefit of his wisdom and experience in this area.

the corpses (15:23)—the present evidence of a future and already in-breaking reality.

> 12–19: *Given this message that Jesus has been raised out of the corpses, how can some of you say there is no resurrection of corpses? The former truth guarantees the latter. If not, we're all wasting our time.*

Thus Paul wants to make it absolutely clear to the Corinthians that the raising up of Jesus by God necessitates, and cannot be separated from, the raising up of all, including even long-dead corpses. Nothing is beyond God's transforming power. It becomes very clear if we map the interchanging terms (Table 1) used by Paul throughout chapter 15 that Paul's preferred language (on the left, the "raising up of Christ") is brought into relationship with popular disparaging usage (on the right, the "resurrection of corpses") to reinterpret and ultimately redefine it (culminating in 15:52).[41]

Evidently Paul is concerned to establish here that the proclamation that "Christ was raised out of the corpses" (explicitly in 15:12 and 20, and in abbreviated form six times in between) is a truth that overlaps with the reality of the "resurrection of corpses" (ἀνάστασις νεκρῶν in 15:12, 13, and 42; and in abbreviated and sometimes overlapping form using *egeirō* some eight times in between). For Paul, what God has done in raising Jesus is used to redefine whatever was understood by the "resurrection of the corpses." The fulcrum in this semantic clarification is the statement in verses 20–21, where the last Adam (see also 15:45–47) is named as the one who foreshadows and initiates the "resurrection of the corpses" (*anastasis nekrōn*), and this formulation is as close as Paul gets to speaking of "the resurrection (*anastasis*) of Christ" as distinct from "Christ being raised (*egeirō*)." One has the sense that Paul carefully makes a connection between his own preferred semantics (Christ "being raised") and the wider pejorative discourse about the "resurrection of corpses," an obvious taunt directed at the crudity of Jewish and Christian belief by more sophisticated Hellenists. Paul himself would much rather speak about the raising of those "who have fallen asleep" (7:39; 11:30;

---

41. As noted earlier (footnote 9), Paul only ever uses *anastasis* three times in connection with Jesus Christ: once in citing the tradition (Rom 1:4), once inclusive of the general resurrection (Rom 6:5), and once in Phil 3:10. The phrase ἀνάστασις νεκρῶν occurs nowhere in the Septuagint, whereas ἐγείρω and νεκρός occur together two times (Isa 26:19 [cf. Book of Odes 5:19]; Sir 48:5).

Table 1

Language Used of Christ	Language Used of the General Resurrection
v. 4: ἐγήγερται (*egēgertai*) (on the third day)	
v. 12: ἐκ νεκρῶν ἐγήγερται	v. 12: ἀνάστασις νεκρῶν (*anastasis nekrōn*)
	v. 13: ἀνάστασις νεκρῶν οὐκ ἔστιν
v. 13: οὐδὲ Χριστὸς ἐγήγερται	
v. 14: Χριστὸς οὐκ ἐγήγερται	
v. 15: κατὰ τοῦ θεοῦ ὅτι ἤγειρεν τὸν Χριστόν	v. 15: νεκροὶ οὐκ ἐγείρονται
	v. 16: νεκροὶ οὐκ ἐγείρονται
v. 16: οὐδὲ Χριστὸς ἐγήγερται	
v. 17: Χριστὸς οὐκ ἐγήγερται	
v. 20: Χριστὸς ἐγήγερται ἐκ νεκρῶν	
v. 21: Second Adam—ἀνάστασις νεκρῶν	
v. 23: in/at his appearance/coming—ἐν τῇ παρουσίᾳ αὐτοῦ	
	v. 29: νεκροὶ οὐκ ἐγείρονται
	v. 32: νεκροὶ οὐκ ἐγείρονται
	v. 35: ἐγείρονται οἱ νεκροί
	v. 42: ἀνάστασις τῶν νεκρῶν, followed by ἐγείρεται used of mortals, seeds, and so on.
	v. 52: οἱ νεκροὶ ἐγερθήσονται

15:6, 18, 20), but he tackles the ridicule of resurrection head-on by adopting the language of the critics and building connections between it and the raising of Jesus (note the careful interweaving of *egeirō* language and *anastasis* language with reference to the corpses). Paul is not prepared to acquiesce by adopting a more culturally acceptable understanding of "resurrection." This is because the rejection of any bodily dimension to immortality has been used by some at Corinth to frustrate and deny the reality of God's transforming power within the corporate body of Christ, especially with regard to the many ethical issues tackled by Paul in the rest of the letter.[42]

> 20–34: *Christ has been raised out of the corpses, the firstfruits of the resurrection of all corpses and the guarantee that all enemies, including death, will be defeated in Christ so that God might be all in all.*

The locus of this connection and the means of its fulfilment are explained in terms of the παρουσία (*parousia*) of the "life-giving spirit," whereby the confession that Χριστὸς ἐγήγερται ἐκ νεκρῶν means that the last Adam has inaugurated the ἀνάστασις νεκρῶν. Otherwise, what is the point of baptizing your ancestors together with your household if the "whole of the corpses" (ὅλως νεκροί, 15:29) are not raised? What is the point of baptizing a body (both the individual and corporate body) if the body is not raised? And what is the point in risking danger and death every day in order to live in this transformed light? Why not party and give up on ethics altogether (15:32)!

> 35–57: *The implications of all this for understanding the nature of God's cosmic transformation are spelled out:* ἀνάστασις *is mentioned once more in v. 42 and is redefined in terms of* ἐγείρω *and applied to all creation, concluding with the triumphant* οἱ νεκροὶ ἐγερθήσονται *(the corpses shall be raised, v. 52).*

The point of Paul's analogy about the embodied stars is that the creator God can give to us any kind of transformed body, and is not limited by the constraints of "flesh and blood." It is also an allusion to the stars of Dan 12:3, where again there is an inseparable link between

---

42. I recall in this context the frustration of one student in Professor Lorenzen's resurrection class: "Why is he going on about Aborigines, refugees, and the ordination of women? What have they got to do with resurrection? I thought this was a theology class!" Fortunately, most students come around to seeing the connections.

transformed bodies and the in-breaking justice of God ("leading many to righteousness/justice").[43]

> 58: *Be steadfast, immovable, always excelling in the work of the Lord, because you know that your labor in the Lord is not in vain.*

This is the other end of the ethical *inclusio* (see vv. 1–2 above), demonstrating that this section is not to be taken as an abstract theological defense of resurrection—nor as an attempt to verify it historically—but as an exhortation to *live* the reality of the resurrection. Because this is our future, let us work at it also being our present, especially in the midst of suffering.

WHAT MAY WE SAY?

In these days when the search for Higgs boson commences (intermittently) in the bowels of the Swiss-French Alps—pushing towards the point (moment?) where time and matter intersect (time zero?)—Paul's words still issue a challenge: "in an atom (ἐν ἀτόμῳ, *en atomō*), in the blink of an eye, we shall all be transformed" (15:52). Even the smallest indivisible unit (whether "atom" or "boson," whether of time or "matter") will not escape the transforming power of God. This is not to be understood as a new process, since the work of transformation has already begun in the Spirit and in the body of Christ, but it represents the fulfillment and goal (*telos*) of that process. Paul's insistence that there is continuity between this transformed reality and the previous reality, between the sowing of the soulish body and the raising of the spiritual body (15:44), means that this embodied life counts—"matter" matters—especially *because* the transformative power of God in Christ is able to renew all things. For Paul, it is important to conclude this letter containing his most extended and varied treatment of "body" ethics with an affirmation of the ultimate significance of those ethics for the resurrection body—or rather, for the "body-being-raised." This glimpse of the *telos* in turn shines backwards like an eschatological fire (3:13–15) to test the fruit of our lives—our actions and ethics as the body of Christ (15:1–2, 58).

There are, of course, many current ethical questions for which our understanding of resurrection has direct implications. Some major

---

43. See Levenson, *Resurrection and the Restoration of Israel*, 190: "The spiritual body (to use Paul's term) with which they will be raised will have the permanence and radiance of astral bodies, but it is not one of them."

unfinished business remains from the time of Paul: the equality and mutuality of male and female (1 Cor 7:4!), the ending of the abuse of slaves (1 Corinthians 6–7), the pre-eminence of love (1 Corinthians 13) and its application to body ethics (1 Corinthians 12–14). Other issues become more pressing as the legacy of colonialism and the deterioration of the environment continue to dominate the news. Whether it is kinder to the wider creation to leave our dead "a-moldering in the grave" or to reduce them to ashes first to speed the process is a question I am not scientifically equipped to answer. But given that we honor our dead, their material bodies and the manner of their departing—and especially their transformed and transforming presence among us—we continue in the hope that every atom of their being (indeed, every boson, should they be found!) will continue to participate in God's transformation of the cosmos until the *telos*, when God will be all in all (15:28). And until then, they share with the body of Christ as the firstfruits of that resurrection of the corpses. Why should we retreat from the truth that Christ has indeed been raised into "the *ekklēsia*" and "the *ekklēsia*" is being raised into Christ? It is *not* the whole truth, of course, but it is a very significant part of what Paul has to say to the Corinthians. Rather than the idea that the *sōma* is the *sēma* of the *psychē* (that our earthly existence prevents the flight of our real identity to a greater heavenly reality), for Paul, the collective *sōma* is the shrine (*naos*, 1 Cor 3:16; 6:19) of the spirit, the *sōma* of the risen Christ, and death itself cannot prevail against it.

There are implications here also for a deeper appreciation of the role of our ancestors ("the cloud of witnesses," Heb 12:1) and for a greater awareness of the "Spirit of Place,"[44] that is, our connectedness to our environment and to those who inhabited it before us. We see the existential importance of this in the roadside shrines remembering those killed in automobile accidents and in the garish concrete and marble mausoleums in our cemeteries—sometimes decked out in plastic flowers and color photographs of the departed. Such shrines are ecologically unsustainable and may even desecrate the very location and memory they seek to honor. But they represent a profound truth—that here in

---

44. See the comments of Jürgen Moltmann, "Ancestor Respect and the Hope of Resurrection," *Sino-Christian Studies: An International Journal of Bible, Theology & Philosophy* 1 (2006) 13–26: "in modern Western countries (people) need a new culture of memory in order no longer to live (their) days as individuals, but rather to look beyond those days" (21).

this place, this soulish body was crushed under the wheels, planted as a seed, scattered as ashes, drowned in the deep; yet even so, not one atom will be lost in God's transforming work. Even as the flesh decays and the atoms are reabsorbed into God's creation, the firstfruits of God's affirmation of Jesus continue to be reborn in all who walk his way, and their identities, their embodied spirits, are caught up in God's renewed creation. These are they who go first to welcome the appearance and coming (*parousia*) of the Christ and all that the Christ stands for, who embody those hopes, and who live forever in the very being of God who is becoming "all in all" (1 Cor 15:28).

So what does affirming the "resurrection of the corpses" mean in our context? It is not merely a matter of asserting the physicality or materiality of individual post-mortem life (of Jesus or of ourselves), since the only claims Paul makes in this respect (1 Cor 15:45, 50) actually challenge our post-Cartesian categories and assumptions about resurrection bodies. Rather, affirming the "raising up of the corpses" is to affirm that "God will be all in all" (15:28), and that the just righteousness of God embodied in Jesus Christ will ultimately prevail—even beyond death. If this conflict over righteous justice is conceived as a cosmic battle (15:20–28), then affirmation of resurrection means that God "wins" over evil through Jesus Christ (15:28). If described in terms of mythic typologies, then resurrection means that primeval humanity (the first Adam) has been reconfigured by the transforming humanity of the last Adam, the life-making Spirit (15:21–23, 45–49). If expressed in terms of the transformation of God's people, then resurrection means that the *ekklēsia*—the risen body of Christ—continues to grow and to sustain those who suffer (15:30–34, 58) and eventually die, and we are irreversibly raised (raised immortal and imperishable, 15:53–54) as the dead precede the living to welcome the coming of the crucified and raised Christ (15:23, 52).

PART THREE
Ethical Engagements

9

Human Rights in Early Christian Perspective

The Distribution of Wealth

E. Glenn Hinson

Most studies of early Christian perspectives on human rights have focused on concern for religious liberty, perspectives that changed dramatically as Christianity shifted from persecuted minority to favored religion as a result of Constantine's conversion. In this essay, however, I examine an issue of human rights not accorded so much attention, but which is of immense importance in today's world—the distribution of wealth. Is distribution of wealth a human rights issue? Article 25 of the Universal Declaration of Human Rights adopted by the United Nations in 1948 declares:

1. Everyone has the right to a standard of living adequate for the health and well-being of himself and of his family, including food, clothing, housing and medical care and necessary social services, and the right of security in the event of unemployment, sickness, disability, widowhood, old age or other lack of livelihood in circumstances beyond his control.

2. Motherhood and childhood are entitled to special care and assistance. All children, whether born in or out of wedlock, shall enjoy the same social protection.

In the United States of America today it is more typical perhaps to think of *poverty* as the problem, and I could easily write about early Christian attitudes toward poverty. Something Clarence Jordan, the founder of Koinonia Farm in Americus, Georgia, once said to me when I referred to "the problem of poverty," however, prompts me to proceed in a different direction. "Glenn, the problem is not *poverty* but *wealth*. Too few people have got too much money; too many of us don't have enough." As usual, in his homely way, Clarence hit dead center the most critical issue in the laissez-faire, free-enterprise culture that has run rampant in the United States since the United Nations adopted its human rights declaration. What I seek to discover in this study is how the current situation in America looks in light of early Christian thinking.

First, a few facts about distribution of wealth or goods and services in America today: One percent of American citizens lays claim to just under twenty percent of the nation's income, far more than the 100 million people (33 percent) on the bottom receive. Ten percent pulls in just a little less than 40 percent of all household income, and 20 percent claims half. Tax rates on the super-wealthy fell from 91 percent in the 1950s to 35 percent today, corporate rates from 35 percent in 1945 to 10 percent today. Whereas in 1980 the average CEO received forty-two times the pay of the average worker, in 2004 the CEO "merited" 358 times as much. Translated into human statistics, 13 percent of Americans, mostly single-parent families, fall below the poverty line. Twenty percent of America's children live in poverty. There are 750,000 homeless Americans. Forty-seven million have no health insurance. In a recent study the United States ranked thirty-seventh among nations with respect to health care provided to its citizens.

The United States is often lauded for its philanthropic millionaires, and the Roman Empire did not lack largesse or philanthropy, either from private citizens or from the public purse. Romans displayed admirable generosity in erecting grand public buildings, constructing aqueducts and sanitary systems, building baths and gymnasia, paving streets and roads, sponsoring religious and public festivals, paying for and distributing grain and other commodities, giving handouts of cash and clothing, purchasing freedom of slaves, adopting orphans, supplying scholarly stipends for needy students, and rendering a multitude of other services. Where their altruism broke down and where Christianity built a highway into Roman society, however, as pagan commentators such as Celsus were quick to point out, was among the neglected lower classes and the truly impoverished. These, even the most partisan classicist concedes,[1] received scant mention in Hellenistic writings, and Rome

---

1. See, for example, Henricus Bolkestein, *Wohlgetätigkeit und Armenpflege im vorchristlichen Altertum. Ein Beitrag zum Problem "Moral und Gesellschaft"* (Utrecht: Oosthoek, 1939).

never contrived any systematic plan to care for them. In fact, in Roman society they were commonly characterized with opprobrious epithets such as *leves* (crooked), *iniquinati* (evil), *improbi* (immoral), and *scelerati* (wicked)—characterizations far removed from the Hebrew Bible and early Christian identification of them as "the pious." Greeks and Romans sought to deal with the problem of poverty by forced emigration, hiring out the poor as mercenary soldiers, or by "regulating births." Infant exposure was common among the lower classes. Orphans of lower-class citizens did not know the protections and solicitude enjoyed by those in the moneyed estate. There were no orphanages or hospitals in the true sense. The motto of classical humanism was not to "give to the penniless" but to give to those who are deserving.[2] Although the Cynics, among others, may have anticipated the Christian ethic of total renunciation, they did not proceed beyond that point to actually meet the needs of the poor. Their weakness, as W. W. Tarn has remarked, was that "they saved their souls by living on common people who had no time to save their own."[3] Thus the poor were left to fend for themselves. They formed *collegia* or guilds for mutual aid, especially for burial of the dead. In the main, they represented the disinherited of society whose lot scarcely equalled that of slaves.

Christians of the first several centuries, of course, did not talk about the problem as one of equitable or inequitable distribution of wealth. Within an Empire plagued with much the same disparities evident in the United States today, however, they manifested an awareness of the problem in their strongly voiced reservations about wealth and the wealthy, in the partiality they displayed toward the poor and the many services they rendered them, and in the powerful countercultural movement of monasticism, which gained momentum as persecution abated in the late third century and became a flood thereafter.

WEALTH AND THE WEALTHY

One prong of the Christian response to great disparities was focused on wealth and the wealthy. The primitive catechism contained teach-

---

2. Cf. Cicero, *De officiis* 2.15.54; Seneca, *De vita beata* 23–24; A. R. Hands, *Charities and Social Aid in Greece and Rome* (Aspects of Greek and Roman Life; Ithaca: Cornell University Press, 1968), 64–76.

3. W. W. Tarn, *Hellenistic Civilization* (3rd ed., revised by G. T. Griffith; London: Arnold, 1952), 326.

ings from the Hebrew Bible and the sayings of Jesus concerning the evils or dangers of wealth and the obligation to share. Until Clement of Alexandria sought to rescue the rich by allegorizing Mark 10:17–31, Christians had few good words and little hope for those who, as in the Hebrew Bible, were seen as the virtual symbol of evil.[4] The wealthy were granted scarcely a whisper of a chance of entering the Kingdom of God.[5] To the contrary, in God's intervention in human history in Jesus, God repudiated the rich and chose the poor as instruments of salvation (cf. Luke 1:53; 1 Cor 1:5; 2 Cor 8:9; Jas 2:5). If the rich dared to boast at all, it should be in their humility, for they would be frustrated in their desires.[6] They could place no confidence in how much wealth they could display (1 Tim 6:17). Converts were repeatedly admonished about the treachery of material possessions. A disciple of Jesus cannot serve both God and mammon. Lust for money chokes the word of God (Matt 13:22 // Mark 4:19 // Luke 8:14); the rich are like thistles among the wheat stalks.[7] Love of money is "the root of all evil."[8] Aspirants to wealth easily fall prey to the devil (1 Tim 6:9). Luke and Hermas denounced the selfish rich with particular zest. Those who cling so fast to their earthly treasures would suffer a woeful fate like Dives (Luke 16:19–31), Ananias and Sapphira (Acts 5:1–6), or Simon Magus (Acts 8:9–13).[9]

The salvation of the rich, therefore, lay in distributing their wealth. In its most radical form, this involved complete community of goods. Such appears to have been Luke's leaning. Thus he shared with Mark and Matthew Jesus' counsel to the rich youth to divest himself of all his property and possessions, give them to the poor, and follow him (Luke 18:18–23 = Mark 10:17–22; Matt 19:16–22). He depicted the Jerusalem community achieving the ideal when all of the faithful "held everything in common, sold their possessions and properties, and distributed them to all according to each person's need" (Acts 2:44–45). He saw in Barnabas, who sold a field and placed the proceeds at the apostles' feet, the ideal Christian (Acts 2:44–45). The *Didache* and the Epistle of Barnabas both urged complete community of "corruptible things"

---

4. Cf. *2 Clem.* 20:1; Jas 5:2.
5. Matt 19:23–24 // Mark 10:25 // Luke 18:25; Herm. *Sim.* 9.20.2.
6. Jas 1:10–11; *1 Clem.* 13:1.
7. Herm. *Sim.* 9.20.1.
8. 1 Tim 6:10; Pol. *Phil* 4.1.
9. Luke 6:24; Herm. *Sim.* 9.20; Herm. *Vis.* 1.1.8–9; 3.6.

on analogy to the complete community of "incorruptible."[10] Lucian also knew Christians who "despise all things equally and count them common property..."[11] Tertullian boasted that African Christians held "all things in common, except their wives,"[12] although his words have a rhetorical ring about them. Nevertheless, the ideal of Jesus' challenge to the rich youth and the primitive Jerusalem community motivated many Christians to strive for communal living throughout the patristic era. Origen commended highly the primitive practice in commenting on Matt 19:16–30. Furthermore, from Anthony on, Christian monasticism erected itself upon the same ideal. Dozens of wealthy and cultured men and women, encouraged by bishops and monks, headed the challenge in the fourth and fifth centuries. According to Ambrose, "Natural law created everything to be shared, usurpation made it private."[13]

If the complete rejection of private ownership was an ideal of many, it was not necessarily the goal of all. Indeed, Ernst Troeltsch saw in it "no idea of doing away" with private property per se, but "only a challenge to energetic charitable giving."[14] The fact is that from the outset Christianity attracted a few wealthy converts and received them as welcome and valuable additions to the church. Instead of denouncing them and their possessions out of hand, more pragmatic leaders inculcated generous stewardship. The wealthy opened their homes to Christian assemblies and supplied the food for *agapae* (Christian "love meals"). Paul taught liberality: "from each according to his ability, to each according to his need." According to Acts 20:35, he undergirded his last plea in Ephesus with a word of Jesus, "It is more blessed to give than to receive." For the relief offering to the poor in Jerusalem, he pulled out all stops in his appeal to the Corinthians (especially in 2 Cor 9:6–11). Other early writings abound in directives to all persons of means to share unstintingly. Christians were to be rich in benefactions (Heb 13:16; 1 Tim 6:17–19). In an elaborate appeal for stewardship, Hermas counseled the rich to "circumcise" their riches if they wanted to be useful to the church and

---

10. *Did.* 1; *Barn.* 19.8.

11. Lucian, *Peregrinus* 13.

12. Tertullian, *Apology* 39.11–13.

13. Ambrose, *De officiis* 1.28; cf. Basil of Caesarea, *Homilies* 12.18; Jerome, *Epistle to Helvidius*.

14. Ernst Troeltsch, *The Social Teaching of the Christian Churches*, Vol. 1 (trans. Olive Wyon; Halley Stewart Publications 1; New York: Macmillan, 1931), 115.

obtain salvation: "For just as the round stone cannot be square unless some of it is cut and pared away, so also those now rich cannot be useful to the Lord unless their wealth be cut."[15] Elsewhere he explained the grounds for the rich person's poverty—the distraction of possessions from piety. In assisting the poor, however, the rich may become rich by way of the poor's intercession for them (a Stoic twist!). The two thus become partners in righteousness. "Blessed are those who have and understand that they are made rich by the Lord."[16] Clement of Alexandria, confronted with a previously unparalleled entrance of converts of means, took pains to justify the rich person's place in the church against critics who operated on the earlier, more negative attitude. Wealth is a burden, he admitted. It endangers salvation, but it does not hopelessly prevent it. By a wave of his allegorical wand he converted Jesus' harsh command to the rich youth into a negation of excessive craving for and attachment to riches. Wealthy Christians can use their substance for righteous ends and need only repudiate unrighteous ones. The true rich are those who are rich in virtues.[17]

OF ALMS AND THE POOR

As one might expect, the second prong of early Christian response to mal-distribution of wealth was aimed directly at redistribution. Latin Americans came pretty close to the early Christian perspective when they spoke about "God's preferential option for the poor." Most early Christians would have assumed that because of their wealth, the rich, though fewer in number, didn't need advocates as badly as the poor did. Consequently, again as in the Hebrew Bible, they virtually equated authentic piety with almsgiving—that is, showing mercy—to the poor. So characteristic was this that Matthew could speak of doing "righteousness," the ideal of religious service in Jewish thought, and almsgiving almost synonymously (Matt 6:1–2; cf. Acts 10:35; 1 John 2:29; 3:7, 10;

---

15. Herm. *Vis.* 3.6.6.
16. Herm. *Sim.* 2.10.
17. Clement, *Which Rich Person Can Be Saved?* 11–19. C. J. Cadoux, *The Early Church and the World* (Edinburgh: T. & T. Clark, 1925), 450–51, defended Clement as making "a legitimate attempt to apply the central principles of the Gospel-teaching on the matter to Christian life under its altered conditions, and as such it is of considerable importance."

Rev 22:11). As Judaism did,[18] so early Christianity also ascribed immense religious potency to almsgiving and other acts of charity. God returns mercy in kind.[19] It was a short step from this conviction to the belief that almsgiving and charity are means of repentance for sins.[20] For many, philanthropy or charity supplied the ultimate test of true worship and faith. If, as T. F. Torrance has contended, this represented a lapse from the New Testament (or, more accurately, Pauline) doctrine of grace,[21] it represented a lapse in the direction of love in deed rather than in mere word.[22] Even Paul's writings, strong as is their emphasis upon God's free gift in human salvation, contain vigorous exhortations to "good deeds" for which God will assess us in the final judgment (Rom 2:6; 1 Cor 3:13ff.; Col 1:10; 2 Thess 2:17). A virtual slogan of some early writings is "equipped for every good deed" and analogous phrases.[23] The Jewish-Christian *Clementine Homilies* and *Recognitions* cite the Golden Rule as the test of true worship and several times expound its demands: "to feed the hungry, to give drink to the thirsty, to clothe the naked, to visit the sick."[24] To distribute to the needy, to do any good deed or to show mercy, according to Origen, is the Christian's sacrifice.[25] Cyprian pulled out all the stops in his treatise *On (Good) Works and Almsgiving*.[26] God the Father and Christ the Son have given liberally in their provision for our redemption. God provided almsgiving as a means of erasing post-baptismal pollution. The Scriptures of both Testaments encourage almsgiving. Jesus enjoined it. We must not worry about using up all of our possessions; God has promised to take care of the merciful and doers of good. Fears that produce miserliness show preoccupation with riches and a lack of faith, neither of which belongs in the church. Christians

18. See Tob 4:10; Sir 3:30; Acts 10:4, 31.

19. Matt 5:7; *Did.* 2.7; *1 Clem.* 13:2; Pol. *Phil* 2:3.

20. *2 Clem.* 16:4; Origen, *On Leviticus Homily* 3.4; Cyprian, *On the Lapsed* 35; *On (Good) Works and Almsgiving* 1, 4.

21. T. F. Torrance, *The Doctrine of Grace in the Apostolic Fathers* (Grand Rapids: Eerdmans, 1959), 70, 116–17; Eugene, OR: Wipf & Stock, 1996. Citations are to the Eerdmans edition.

22. 1 John 3:18; *1 Clem.* 30:3; 38:2; *2 Clem.* 4:3; 12:4.

23. See 1 Tim 2:10; 5:10; 2 Tim 2:21; 3:17; Titus 2:14; 3:1; Heb 10:24; 13:21; *1 Clem.* 2:7; 33:1, 7.

24. *Clementine Homilies* 12.32.

25. Origen, *On Numbers Homily* 11.9.

26. Cf. also *Testimonia* 3.1–3; 9.26.

must share their worldly wealth with Christ so as to share in Christ's heavenly wealth. How shameful for the rich not to bring something for the *agape* ("love meal") but to feed on that brought by the poor! That they have children to care for is no excuse. The one who has many children is obligated even more on the children's account. Their best provision is to turn one's patrimony and inheritance over to God for safekeeping. To give a gift with Christ present is far more glorious than giving in the presence of proconsuls and emperors. What a fearful judgment awaits those who fail to give (citing Matt 25:31–46), but what great rewards for those who follow the apostolic example.

Irenaeus and the *Apostolic Constitutions* conceded no relaxation of the Old Testament requirement of oblations for the clergy and the poor under the gospel, the latter refusing only offerings of the corrupt.[27] Wealthy individuals made handsome private gifts. Marcion, an affluent shipbuilder, gave the Roman church two hundred thousand *sesterces*, though the church returned it when it excluded him for heresy.[28] Cyprian donated one hundred thousand *sesterces* to the church of Carthage.[29] All gifts except "firstfruits,"[30] however, were solicited on a purely voluntary basis. Tithing did not become a rule of the churches until later.[31] Cyprian and Origen strongly commended tithing but laid down no law about it.[32] The *Apostolic Constitutions* required a tithe of produce ("firstfruits") for the needy.[33] Chrysostom and Augustine shamed their hearers for doing less than the Jews in regard to tithing.[34] Jerome demanded tithes as if the Old Testament commandment had never been questioned.[35]

Most of the alms and other gifts doubtless went to the Christian poor, for the resources were too limited to expect more. Nevertheless, the Didachist's advice to "let your alms sweat in your hands" is exceptional,

---

27. Irenaeus, *Against Heresies* 4.18; *Apostolic Constitutions* 2.35; 7.2.29; 4.5.19.

28. Tertullian, *Prescriptions against Heretics* 30.

29. Cyprian, *Epistle* 39; Pontius, *Life of Cyprian* 2.

30. *Did.* 13:7; Clement of Alexandria, *Stromateis* 2.18.86.3.

31. Edwin Hatch, *The Growth of Church Institutions*, 4th ed. (London: Hodder & Stoughton, 1895), 102, attributed this institution to the Carolingian reformation of the eighth century.

32. Cyprian, *On the Unity of the Church* 26; Origen, *On Numbers Homily* 11.1.

33. *Apostolic Constitutions* 7.29.

34. Chrysostom, *On Ephesians Homily* 2; Augustine, *Sermons* 9.16; 95.5.

35. Jerome, *Commentary on Matthew* 2.22. See further Lukas Vischer, *Tithing in the Early Church* (trans. R. C. Schultz; Facet Books; Historical Series 3; Philadelphia: Fortress, 1966).

obviously sensitive to abuses.³⁶ Actually, he contradicted his own reserve in quoting the words of Jesus, "Give to everyone who asks."³⁷ It was more characteristic to give without attaching strings. Hermas, for example, insisted, "Give to all who are in want unreservedly (*haplos*), not distinguishing between those to whom you give or those to whom you do not give. Give to all, for God wishes that all be given some of their own free gifts."³⁸ Clement of Alexandria forbade too close a scrutiny.³⁹ Lucian's story of Peregrinus or Proteus tends to prove that Christians erred on the side of naiveté. In Palestine this second-century master of deception picked up a smattering of Christian theology and proceeded to foist himself off as a prophet, priest, and head of a "synagogue" (church). When at last he was apprehended and thrown into prison, Christians turned every stone to have him freed. Unsuccessful in that, they then showed him every kindness. Widows and orphans waited near the prison from daybreak on to see him. Officials visited him in his cell, had elaborate meals brought and studied the Scriptures with him, their "new Socrates." Christians from as far away as Asia were sent at common expense to aid, defend, and encourage him. They supplied him with money. "So if any charlatan or trickster," Lucian concluded, "able to profit by affairs, comes among them, he quickly acquires sudden wealth by imposing on simple folk."⁴⁰

There is not room here to discuss the remarkable range of Christian charity. It included care of widows and orphans; the sick, poor, and disabled; prisoners and captives; burial of the poor and other dead; emancipation of slaves; furnishing work; and care for victims of calamities. Even before the Constantinian era, certainly when judged in terms of the meagerness of resources, the extent of these was astonishing. A superlative example appears in Cornelius' report to Fabius of Antioch in 251 CE, that the Roman church, in addition to clergy, had over fifteen hundred widows and indigents on its relief rolls.⁴¹ This astounding figure attests the success of the Roman church in persuading wealthier converts to open their purses and to care for the most neglected elements of Roman society. In order to place the issue of distribution in proper perspective,

36. *Did.* 1:5; cf. chapters 11–13.
37. Luke 6:30 // Matt 5:42; *Did.* 1.5.
38. Herm. *Mand.* 2.4.6; cf. Jas 1:5; *Barn.* 19:11; *2 Clem.* 16:4.
39. Clement of Alexandria, *The Instructor* 3.6.36.
40. Lucian, *Peregrinus* 13.
41. Cornelius in Eusebius, *History of the Church* 6.43.

permit me to focus on popular attitudes toward and provision for the neglected and despised masses of the poor.

A. R. Hands has given strong evidence for questioning whether the benefactions of the early Empire, though quite substantial, filtered down to the genuinely impoverished at all—either basic commodities, educational advantages, health aid, or medical care.[42] Small wonder Christian attitudes and aid proved so attractive! Christian writings of the first two centuries leave the distinct impression that God sent the Son and commissioned God's people for the care of the poor, God's own "righteous ones." According to Luke, Jesus himself inaugurated his ministry by reading Isa 61:1, "For [the Lord] anointed me to proclaim good news to the poor" (Septuagint).[43] In agreement with the Psalms, Jesus called the poor "fortunate" and promised them a share in God's Kingdom.[44] He taught his disciples to invite the poor and unfortunate to share meals (Luke 14:13, 21) and commanded the rich to sell their possessions and distribute the proceeds to the poor (Matt 19:21 // Mark 10:21 // Luke 18:22). Luke even edited the story of Jesus' anointment for burial lest Jesus' words "The poor you have with you always" undercut the churches' concern for the poor (Matt 26:11 // Mark 14:7 // John 12:8; Luke 7:44–50).

Nothing evoked stronger censure among early Christian writers than neglecting or demeaning the poor. The primitive catechetical document called the "Two Ways" listed lack of pity for the poor under "the way of death."[45] James 2:2–6 savaged his addressees for showing deference to the wealthy who, on rare occasions, visited Christian assemblies. Ignatius condemned the Asian heretics for having no concern for any of the distressed—widows, orphans, the afflicted, prisoners, the hungry and thirsty.[46] On the other hand, early writings repeatedly invoked the gospel and the Scriptures in support of liberality toward the needy. *Didache* 13:2 enjoins giving "first fruits" of wine, grain, oxen, and sheep, and also of clothing and money, to the prophets, and, if a community had no prophet, to the poor. The rich persons' duty, according to early Roman

---

42. Hands, *Charities and Social Aid in Greece and Rome*, 64–65.

43. Luke 4:18; cf. 7:22; Justin, *Dialogue with Trypho* 12.2; 34.3; 64.6.

44. Luke 6:20 // Matt 5:3, 8; Jas 2:5; Pol. *Phil* 2:3. Which reading is original is debated, but Luke's special interest in the poor favors a deletion of "in spirit."

45. *Did.* 5:2; *Barn.* 20.

46. Ign. *Smyrn.* 6:2.

writings, was to supply what the poor needed; the duty of the poor was to praise God and to intercede for the rich.[47] True fasting, in line with Isa 58:1–2, involved sharing one's bread with the hungry, sheltering the homeless, and clothing the naked.[48] Clement of Rome claimed to know Christians who became indentured servants in order to use the money to feed the poor.[49]

The conversion of Constantine opened the doors upon a vast new treasure house for the favored religion. "As its wealth grew," S. L. Greenslade correctly remarked, "it was taken for granted that the church would care for the poor."[50] Already in the peaceful era from Gallienus on, devout Christians like Anthony of Egypt had begun to take literally the Lord's command to the rich youth. As the monastic ideals of poverty and community of goods caught on, the church found its stores for charity overflowing. When the Empire became Christian, the resources multiplied again. The removal of restrictions alone assured that,[51] but the state also came directly to the church's aid.

Bishops played a broad social role, not only interceding on behalf of the poor and supplying aid but also adjudicating both civil and religious cases. A Valentinian decree in 364 CE charged bishops specifically with the duty of watching out for the poor and saving them from unfair exactions.[52] As a superlative example of episcopal involvement, one may cite Basil of Caesarea. His extant letters to public officials contain an entreaty to an official on behalf of Dorotheus, a presbyter, whose grain had been seized;[53] a plea to a tax collector for an extension of time for payment;[54] an appeal on behalf of a widow, requesting fair treatment by a Count Helladius;[55] an intercession with the prefect Modestus to

---

47. *1 Clem.* 38:2; Herm. *Sim.* 2.

48. Justin, *Dialogue with Trypho* 15.

49. *1 Clem.* 55:2.

50. S. L. Greenslade, *The Church and the Social Order: A Historical Sketch* (London: SCM, 1948), 22.

51. *Codex Theodosianum* 5.31. Theodosius and Valentinian decreed that property of clergy and monks or nuns dying intestate would go to the church.

52. *Corpus juris* 1.3.32.

53. Basil of Caesarea, *Epistles* 86, 87.

54. Basil of Caesarea, *Epistles* 88.

55. Basil of Caesarea, *Epistles* 107–9.

alleviate the tax burden of iron workers in the Taurus mountains;[56] and a variety of personal pleas.[57] Basil himself manifested a keen interest in the plight of the poor.[58] Accordingly, he assigned a prominent place to charity in his monastic rules[59] and appointed suffragans to assist him in meeting the need. In 373 he arranged with the prefect of Cappadocia's *numerarii* (accountants) certain special considerations for Christian alms-houses that he had placed in the charge of his suffragans. In a letter to one *numerarius* he expressed confidence that the latter would do all he could for the poor as the suffragan directed, visit the alms-house (*ptochotrophia*) in his district, and exempt it from all taxes.[60] In a letter to the second *numerarius* he expressed regrets that he could not make a person-to-person entreaty but felt assured that the official would heed the suffragan's counsel and grant him whatever he requested when the former visited the alms-house in his district. He added punch to his request by citing the concession gained from the other accountant and by inserting parenthetically a rumor that the second *numerarius* had already founded an alms-house at his own expense in Amaseia.[61]

Basil's Western contemporary, Ambrose, evinced a similar mindset. His rejoinder to the pagan senator Symmachus' charges of imperial favoritism toward the church, resulting in confiscation of pagan property, was as follows:

> The Church possesses nothing but her faith. These are her rents, her revenues. The wealth of the Church is the support of the poor. Let them [the pagans] count up how many prisoners the temples have ransomed, what support they have afforded to the poor, to how many exiles they have ministered the means of life.[62]

He stoutly defended the action of Paulinus of Nola and his wife, Therasia, in selling their possessions and giving the proceeds to the poor "in order to serve God more diligently."[63] Ambrose idealized the

56. Basil of Caesarea, *Epistles* 110.
57. Basil of Caesarea, *Epistles* 35; 111–12; 147–49.
58. Cf. Basil of Caesarea, *Epistles* 144.
59. Basil of Caesarea, *Moralia* 38, 48. The *Moralia* is a collection of eighty rules on the ascetic life.
60. Basil of Caesarea, *Epistles* 142.
61. Basil of Caesarea, *Epistles* 143.
62. Ambrose of Milan, *Epistles* 18.17.
63. Ambrose of Milan, *Epistles* 58.1–2.

primitive "classless" society, where each bore the burden of the state.⁶⁴ He eulogized his brother Satyrus and others for their dispensations to the poor.⁶⁵ He counted charity the key virtue of the clergy and love of money a great sin.⁶⁶ He once melted the communion vessels to ransom captives, sustaining his action by citing the story of the martyr Lawrence, who, told to collect the treasures of the church, brought the poor. The vessels, he insisted, could not be broken up for base uses but could be for the sustenance of the poor.⁶⁷

RADICAL RENUNCIATION

The third prong of early Christian response to the mal-distribution of wealth took the form of radical renunciation. The ascetic surge of the late fourth century, to be sure, cannot be ascribed only to concern about economic inequities in Roman society. Spurring it on was the apocalyptic situation created by the Germanic invasions of the Roman Empire, when it made little sense to devout Christians to hold tenaciously to things of the earth. The tenuousness of life in this context produced an almost wanton abandonment of private ownership, as some have contended, even to the detriment of stable society in the West.⁶⁸ Notable examples included the two Melanias;⁶⁹ Marcella and Paula in Rome;⁷⁰ Paulinus of Nola and his wife, Theresia;⁷¹ the Roman senator Pammachius;⁷² and Ambrose's sister, Marcellina. Melania the Elder gave lavishly of her massive fortune for thirty-seven years and then proceeded to Jerusalem, where she spent forty days distributing what remained just before her

---

64. Ambrose, *Hexameron* 5.15.
65. Ambrose, *On the Death of Satyrus* 1.59–60.
66. Ambrose, *On Duties* 1.32.169; 2.15; 2.27.134.
67. Ambrose, *On Duties* 2.28.
68. In *The History of the Decline and Fall of the Roman Empire*, Vol. 3 (Philadelphia: John D. Morris & Co., circa 1845), 665–87, Edward Gibbon lampooned the monastic movement. At the conclusion of his depiction he charged: "The progress of Christianity has been marked by two glorious and decisive victories—over the learned and luxurious citizens of the Roman empire; and over the war-like barbarians of Scythia and Germany, who subverted the empire and embraced the religion of the Romans" (687).
69. Cf. Palladius, *Historia Lausiaca* 54, 61.
70. Cf. Jerome, *Epistles* 46, 108.
71. Cf. Ambrose, *Epistle* 58.
72. Cf. Jerome, *Epistle* 66.

death.⁷³ In the mid-fourth century, as Germanic tribes advanced on Rome, Marcella, a young widow, gathered other women of wealth and culture in her palace on the Aventine Hill in Rome to form a circle for study of the Scriptures and cultivation of the devout life. One of the Aventine Circle, Paula, funded Jerome's flight from Rome to Bethlehem in 385 and established there two monasteries, one for women, which she headed, and the other for men, led by Jerome. Paulinus, born of a wealthy and noble family of Bordeaux, gave up a public career and, after a few years of leisure, took up the ascetic and contemplative life with his wife and began to distribute his fortune to the church and the poor. In 394 he and Theresia founded a home for monks and the poor at Nola and lived lives of great austerity. In 409 he became bishop of Nola. Pammachius, a Roman senator of the Furian family and husband of Paula's daughter Paulina, embraced the monastic life when the latter died, and devoted the fortune he had inherited to the care of the indigent. Among other things, he and Fabiola erected a hospital for pilgrims at Portus. Thanks to his sister, Marcellina, Ambrose was one of the stoutest defenders of the ascetic life in his treatise on *The Virgins*.

Although a fear motive played strongly into this powerful movement, we must not overlook the intensity of concern to be faithful to Jesus' call to discipleship, interpreted more-or-less literally. The death of his parents when he was eighteen or twenty plunged Anthony, previously not a very serious youth, into a period of soul searching. He thought about the way the apostles had forsaken everything to follow Jesus, and how early Christians in Jerusalem had laid all of their possessions at the feet of the apostles. On entering a church, he heard Jesus' words to the rich youth read. They spoke directly to him. Leaving the church, he proceeded to arrange with nuns for the care of a younger sister and gave away the rest of his property to the poor.⁷⁴ He took up the life of a hermit. The story of Anthony's conversion impacted upon the lives of numerous others. None is better known than the effect it had on Augustine at a critical moment in his personal struggle with his sexual impulses. As he described the episode in his *Confessions*, a Roman friend named Ponticianus joined the little band at Cassiciacum and started telling how two young Roman nobles had forsaken their fiancées upon hearing the story of Anthony's conversion. As Augustine recounted,

73. Palladius, *Historia Lausiaca* 54.2–6.
74. Athanasius, *Life of Anthony* §§1–3.

> Ponticianus told us this story, and as he spoke, you, O Lord, turned me back upon myself. You took me from behind my own back, where I had placed myself because I did not wish to look upon myself. You stood me face to face with myself, so that I might see how foul I was, how deformed and defiled, how covered with stains and sores. I looked, and I was filled with horror, but there was no place for me to flee to away from myself. If I tried to turn my gaze from myself, he still went on with the story that he was telling, and once again you placed me in front of myself, and thrust me before my own eyes, so that I might find out my iniquity and hate it. I knew what it was, but I pretended not to; I refused to look at it, and put it out of my memory.[75]

Born and reared in modest circumstances, Augustine, of course, did not have wealth to distribute following his conversion, but on returning to Thagaste in Numidia he formed a monastic circle. He became, like his mentor, Ambrose, one of the strong proponents of monasticism and a major monastic figure in the West, setting the ideal of Christian devotion. Jerome, likewise, articulated with special fervor a case for the preferential treatment of the poor, first in Rome and then in Palestine. He lauded Fabiola for selling and distributing her possessions and claimed for her the honor of founding the first hospital, "into which she might gather sufferers out of the streets, and where she might nurse the unfortunate victims of sickness and want."[76] He eulogized Nebridius, not only because his own gifts had hardly any rival, but because he had a special knack of obtaining aid from the emperor for the poor, for captives, or for the afflicted.[77] In other letters he singled out the remarkable generosity of Pammachius, Paulinus, and Paula.[78]

Of special interest to my case for redistribution of wealth is the fact that monks set the standard for others with respect to care of the poor and needy. Though records of their feats have a legendary quality, trustworthy instances still leave an amazing testimony. According to a *Life of Pachomius*, originator of communal (coenobitic) monasticism, the coenobites once gave so liberally that they themselves ran out of bread. Palladius' monastic sketches abound with deeds of self-denial for the

---

75. Augustine, *Confessions of St. Augustine* 8.7.16 (trans. John K. Ryan; Garden City, NY: Image, 1960), 193.

76. Jerome, *Epistles* 77.6.

77. Jerome, *Epistles* 79.6.

78. Jerome, *Epistles* 66; 118; 108.30.

sake of the "poor," often meaning the monks themselves but also including others. Apollonius, a businessman, renounced all, bought medicines and foodstuffs to care for five thousand monks, and retired to Mount Nitria.[79] Two Spanish brothers, Paesius and Isaiah, used their fortunes to build monasteries that "took in every stranger, every invalid, every old man, and every poor one as well, setting up three or four tables every Saturday and Sunday."[80]

ANY HOPE OF MORE EQUITABLE DISTRIBUTION OF WEALTH TODAY?

Now comes the question of applicability. A century ago, Walter Rauschenbusch challenged Christians to respond to the same social crisis. He spoke with great fervor and hopefulness. "The social body needs moral innervation," he declared, "and the spread of men who combine religious faith, moral enthusiasm, and economic information, and apply the combined result to public morality, promises to create a moral sensitiveness never yet known."[81] Real hope rested, he thought, on informed preaching of social responsibility; on recovering the Christian conception of life and property; on creating customs and institutions for social concern, generous stewardship, and sharing by people of wealth; on the increase of "communism" of the type depicted in Acts; and on the upward movement of the working class. Sadly, although the movement he envisioned got off to a promising start, it soon ran out of steam. So I return to the question, is there any hope of a more equitable distribution of wealth today, especially in a country where a majority of the population claims Christian credentials?

Lest it make any reader anxious, let me say that we have no reason to expect in Europe or the United States a resurgence of the ascetic and contemplative movement that claimed the allegiance of so many of the best and brightest youth in the fourth century and after. Recent studies indicate that monasticism continues to thrive and to grow in the southern hemisphere, especially in Asia, Africa, and Latin America, where poverty is rife. In the northern hemisphere, however, it attracts far fewer

---

79. Palladius, *Historia Lausiaca* 13.1–2.

80. Palladius, *Historia Lausiaca* 14.3.

81. Walter Rauschenbusch, *Christianity and the Social Crisis* (ed. Robert D. Cross; New York: Harper & Row, 1907, 1964), 397.

persons, though a growing number is turning to religious orders of the world's religions for spiritual guidance.

Looking at the figures cited in the introduction to this study, I think we will have to recognize that recovery of early Christian attitudes toward distribution of wealth would necessitate a colossal change of heart not only on the part of the populace in general but also on the part of Christians themselves. Prospects for such change do not look encouraging. For one thing, since the mid-nineteenth century business has imposed itself as the prevailing social model in American life. Early on, business moguls such as Andrew Carnegie and John D. Rockefeller established themselves as icons of the American way of life with their vast accumulation of wealth and their philanthropies. A new generation of fantastically wealthy entrepreneurs such as Bill Gates and the Walton family, whose fortunes are reported to be in billions rather than millions, have succeeded them.

For another thing, the business model has imposed itself on church life at all levels. In the case of Baptists, whose congregational polity has made them more susceptible to the prevailing culture, church has become a business. In 1923 at the Southern Baptist Theological Seminary in Louisville, Kentucky, Gaines S. Dobbins, previously Professor of Sunday School Pedagogy, became Professor of Church Efficiency and published a book, based on his inaugural address, titled *The Efficient Church*, in which he depicted Jesus as a model entrepreneur! Church is a business, he contended, and it should be conducted with the same expectations as any other business, namely, for success. By the time our new millennium rolled around, the prevailing object of religion was successful marketing and the purpose of the gospel was prosperity.

The "prosperity gospel" is evident in many mega-churches today, but it seems to have seeped most deeply into the pores of Pentecostalism, the fastest-growing Christian religious movement in the world today, especially in the southern hemisphere.[82] According to Paul Gifford, an expert on African religion, "In this form of Christianity, a believer is successful; if not, something is wrong."[83] The fastest-growing group, revealingly named Winners, promise success in all areas of life, but "material

---

82. See Philip Jenkins, *The Next Christendom: The Coming of Global Christianity* (Oxford: Oxford University Press, 2002), 7-8, 61-66, 68-69, 73-77.

83. Paul Gifford, "Expecting Miracles: The Prosperity Gospel in Africa," *Christian Century*, July 10, 2007, 20.

success is paramount." The leader of the Redeemed Christian Church of God in Lagos, Nigeria, Enoch Adejare Adeboye, claims that whereas God commanded Moses to "Go and set my people free," God commanded him to "Make my people rich." His model is not Jesus but Bill Gates.[84] The notable exponent of the "prosperity gospel" in the United States is T. D. Jakes, pastor of a nondenominational mega-church in Dallas called The Potter's House. Jakes focuses on economic empowerment and has certainly empowered himself, earning $100 million "by marketing and selling every aspect of his ministry." As Jonathan L. Walton has remarked, "Like Donald Trump, Anthony Robbins, and televangelist Joel Osteen, Jakes has entrepreneurial impulses, business savvy and unbridled ambition. He knows what Americans want and is unapologetic about selling his recipe."[85] Not many persons attracted to either of these evangelists succeed in the way they promise, but it seems not to disrupt the business, for the leader has absolute control.

As regards a recovery of early Christian concern for more equitable distribution of wealth, therefore, I do not see anything either in society or in the church applying the brakes to a runaway train. Bill and Melinda Gates, of course, are deserving of kudos for sharing much of their vast fortune to address the AIDS crisis in Africa, just as Andrew Carnegie was for erecting libraries and John D. Rockefeller for re-founding the University of Chicago. They do show some generosity of stewardship. Not all persons of wealth, however, are so generous, or generous at all. For many, love of money is an end in itself, as was seen in President George W. Bush's efforts to prevent redistribution of wealth through taxes on inheritances. Moving in the direction of a Christian concept of sharing of goods and services will require far more drastic change in the whole economic system.

The magnitude of the problem is overwhelming. It could cause us to throw up our hands in despair and do nothing. We might take a lesson here, however, from the American Quaker saint, John Woolman (1720–1772), who spent the greater part of his life persuading Quakers to free their slaves. As he traveled the American colonies as a "minister" of the Quaker society in 1746, he saw the awful plight of people living in servitude. From that time until his death of smallpox in England in

---

84. Gifford, "Expecting Miracles," 21.

85. Jonathan L. Walton, "Empowered: The Entrepreneurial Ministry of T. D. Jakes," *Christian Century*, July 10, 2007, 28.

1772, he spent about one month every year touring the American colonies and placing his heart's concern before Quaker Meetings. He gave up a prospering merchandising business and learned the tailor's trade lest he be "too encumbered" by the affairs of this life to follow God's leading. In 1763 he stopped riding on horseback or in carriages because slaves were not permitted to ride. He gave up sugar, rum, and molasses made in the West Indies because that was produced by slave labor. Yet he worried whether too many would follow his lead and bring hurt to the ones he wanted to help. He no longer wore dyed suits because the dye was made from indigo, and indigo came from slave labor. Little by little, he began to see that injustice came not from an intention to hurt others but from unthinking. Slave owners, at least Quaker owners, did not intend to inflict hurt on blacks, but for the sake of their own comforts and convenience they did so unthinkingly. Woolman discerned the same thing in the case of whites violating treaties with Indians, ship owners' treatment of sailors, and the hurts inflicted on young post-boys in the stagecoach traffic in England.

What I think John Woolman teaches us, above all, is that we must not let ourselves be so overwhelmed by the magnitude of problems that we do nothing. Woolman lived by Rom 8:28—not in the King James Version but in a version that fits the context better: "We know that in everything, God is working together for good with those who love God, with those who are called according to God's purpose." To Woolman this said, "Little efforts matter." He did not live to see the end of slavery, even among Quakers, but by 1787, largely because of his quiet revolution, no American Quaker owned a slave.

The Woolman approach comports with that of the early Christians. Until well after Constantine's conversion, they numbered too few to expect to transform Roman society or to stamp a Christian imprint on it. Certainly they did not count enough people of wealth and influence to make a difference. Aware of such limitations, they threw up little straws into the wind. They recognized that wealth can create a false sense of security and lead us away from God. When persons of wealth entered into a covenant with God, they did their best to liberate themselves from that false dependence on wealth. They identified the poor as the church's true wealth and did everything they could to extend to them the compassion of God. When Constantine's conversion radically altered the church's situation and some forgot, many did their level best to go on following

Jesus no matter how much it cost. Is Woolman's and the early Christians' way a place to start? How else can resurrection hope begin to become an embodied reality?

10

The Challenge of the State-Church System to Religious Liberty and Human Rights

Per Midteide

THE RELATIONSHIP BETWEEN CHURCH and state has been a vexed issue throughout the history of the Christian church. Even in the New Testament, the issue was raised when Jesus was confronted by his opponents with the question: "Is it lawful to pay taxes to Caesar, or not?" He replied: "Render therefore to Caesar the things that are Caesar's, and to God the things that are God's" (Matt 22:15–22; Mark 12:13–17; Luke 20:20–26). We should not read too much of the arguments of our time into this saying, but at least Jesus' reply recognizes the state as legitimate, and that relationship to God belongs to a separate sphere.

The question of the relationship between religion and the state is a burning question. Daily we read about tensions this issue raises, especially in the Muslim world. During the spring of 2007 we witnessed massive demonstrations in Turkey in favor of retaining the separation of state and religion. The fear of increased influence from religious leaders in political life is real. We see similar developments in Eastern Europe, in the former Soviet Union states, as well as in most countries in the Far East and the Middle East, where the tension between the State and religious communities constantly produces unrest and challenges human rights and freedom of religion or belief. But even in Western democracies, where these values might be expected to be respected and held in high esteem, minorities face problems, and the relationship between church and state is frequently debated.

Here we look more closely into the situation in Europe, both historically and at the present time, and we argue that the closer the relationship between church and state is, the more this relationship represents a challenge to human rights. There are few real "state churches" left in Europe, but in this respect we take a closer look at Scandinavian models, and the Norwegian one in particular. Then we offer some reflections, including a theological perspective to which Thorwald Lorenzen has made a valuable contribution. The essay will include a brief historical sketch of the relationship between the state and the church, and also will present the most important declarations from the international community concerning human rights.

During the first centuries after the initial spread of the Christian faith, Rome as well as local governors had a hostile attitude to this new religion. The same was true on the part of other religions and faiths in the Roman Empire. When Christians refused to honor the Roman gods and the emperor, it resulted in waves of heavy persecution up to the time of Constantine.[1]

During the reign of the emperor Constantine (288–337 CE), this situation changed dramatically. In 309 Christianity was declared a lawful religion. Although Constantine tolerated other cults, he favored Christianity, and during his reign the Roman Empire developed into a so-called Christian empire. Through this development the emperor was in the position to influence the leadership of the Christian church. He convened and presided over the Council of Nicea in 325 and thus evolved the idea of ecumenical councils.[2]

This was the first time in the history of the Christian church that a head of state had presided over a church council, and without doubt this had a decisive influence on the conclusions drawn at this meeting. The church had obtained official status and remained fairly autonomous. However, during the fourth century the emperor increasingly demanded influence over church matters. In the Byzantine Empire during the sixth century, Justinian was the ruler of the church and state equally, and for a long period of time the state had dominion over the church. In reality, the state church was now formally established.[3]

---

1. Hjalmar Holmquist and Jens Nørregaard, *Kirkehistorie*, Bind 1, *Oldtid og Middelalder* (Copenhagen: Schultz, 1946; Akademisk, 1992), 102.

2. Hans Lietzmann, *A History of the Early Church* (Meridian Books; Cleveland: World, 1961), 116.

3. Lorenz Bergman, *Kirkehistorie* (Copenhagen: Haase & Soens, 1958), 86.

As the empire started to disintegrate, this influence diminished; and during the Ottoman period, in Constantinople, the situation was turned upside down, and the patriarch of the Orthodox Church was given political power over the laity of the church.

In the West, partly due to the absence of a strong central power, the church, through the position of the pope, gained strong influence not only in matters concerning the church but also in the political arena. As strong political powers developed in Europe, the competition between church and state—that is, who was the head of the other—became intense. The issue was, is the emperor, the king (as ruler by divine right) the supreme head of the church as well as the state, or is the pope (as vicar of God on earth), the supervisor of the state as well as the church? The clashes between popes and kings were frequent, violent, and bitter.

The Reformation period changed much in the church picture, but it did not introduce a fundamental change in the discussion of the relationship between church and state—apart from the fact that some Protestant groups (among them the Baptists as the strongest voice) advocated a complete separation of church and state.

In the United States, Baptists, Methodists, and Congregationalists who had fled from religious persecution in Europe found a safe haven and advocated a complete separation of Church and State. This was expressed in Thomas Jefferson's Virginia Statute of Religious Freedom and in the First Amendment of the Constitution of the United States.

The separation of church and state is still an important part of American society, although what this principle means is still disputed. In fact, we today can observe attempts from ultraconservative Christian groups in the U.S.A. to challenge the intentions of the First Amendment. These groups play a significant political role by rallying behind conservative candidates for the presidency and for state governorships. They want to introduce very conservative Christian education in public schools, and seek religious control over political institutions. President Jimmy Carter has convincingly documented this development in his recent book, *Our Endangered Values: America's Moral Crisis*.[4]

In Northern Europe in particular, the Lutheran reformation created state churches in which the faith of the king or the ruler became the religion of the state. Other faiths were not tolerated, and religious freedom,

---

4. Jimmy Carter, *Our Endangered Values: America's Moral Crisis* (New York: Simon & Schuster, 2005).

as we understand it today, was nonexistent. However, in recent decades, most European countries have adjusted their constitutions to meet the new understanding of Human Rights and Freedom of Religion.

INTERNATIONAL DECLARATIONS

The international community does not specify in any document or charter how the relationship between church and state should be organized, but there exist, as most observers know, a number of statements concerning the relationship between human rights and liberty of religion. The *United Nations (UN) Declaration of Human Rights* (adopted in 1948) contains a number of articles concerning this issue. Article 2 states:

> Everyone is entitled to all the rights and freedoms set forth in this Declaration, without distinction of any kind, such as race, colour, sex, language, religion, political or other opinion, national or social origin, property, birth or other status. Furthermore, no distinction shall be made on the basis of the political, jurisdictional or international status of the country or territory to which a person belongs, whether it be independent, trust, non-self-governing or under any other limitation of sovereignty.

This is expanded in Article 18:

> Everyone has the right to freedom of thought, conscience and religion; this right includes freedom to change his religion or belief, and freedom, either alone or in community with others and in public or private, to manifest his religion or belief in teaching, practice, worship and observance.

More specifically, the issue of discrimination on the basis of religion or belief is manifested in the UN Declaration on the Elimination of All Forms of Intolerance and of Discrimination Based on Religion or Belief, approved by the General Assembly in 1981. "Considering that religion or belief, for anyone who professes either, is one of the fundamental elements in his conception of life and that freedom of religion or belief should be fully respected and guaranteed," the Declaration proclaims.

> *Article 1*
>
> 1. Everyone shall have the right to freedom of thought, conscience and religion. This right shall include freedom to have a religion or whatever belief of his choice, and freedom, either individually or in community with others and in public or private, to manifest

his religion or belief in worship, observance, practice and teaching....

Article 2

No one shall be subject to discrimination by any State, institution, group of persons, or person on the grounds of religion or other belief....

Article 3

Discrimination between human beings on the grounds of religion or belief constitutes an affront to human dignity and a disavowal of the principles of the Charter of the United Nations, and shall be condemned as a violation of the human rights and fundamental freedoms proclaimed in the Universal Declaration of Human Rights and enunciated in detail in the International Covenants on Human Rights, and as an obstacle to friendly and peaceful relations between nations.

Article 4

1. All States shall take effective measures to prevent and eliminate discrimination on the grounds of religion or belief in the recognition, exercise and enjoyment of human rights and fundamental freedoms in all fields of civil, economic, political, social and cultural life.

2. All States shall make all efforts to enact or rescind legislation where necessary to prohibit any such discrimination, and to take all appropriate measures to combat intolerance on the grounds of religion or other beliefs in this matter.

The text is detailed in its definition of the right of the individual to practice his or her faith. Moreover, article 2 explicitly states that "any distinction, exclusion, restriction or preference based on religion or belief is to be defined as discrimination." These articles, as well as others not quoted here, also give specific direction concerning protection from intolerance.

In the spirit of the UN Declaration of Human Rights, the European Council adopted its own European Convention on Human Rights (Rome, 1950). This convention was later supplemented by five protocols—the latest during 1966 in Strasbourg. This Convention states the following:

Article 9

> Everyone has the right to freedom of thought, conscience and religion; this right includes freedom to change his religion or belief, and freedom, either alone or in community with others and in public or private, to manifest his religion or belief, in worship, teaching, practice and observance ...

In many parts of the world, the freedom of citizens to practice their religion and to express their faith publicly is limited to the extent that persecution is the order of the day. Facing the threat on this aspect of human rights, an international conference was arranged in Oslo, Norway, in 1998 in connection with the fiftieth anniversary of the UN Declaration of Human Rights. After the conference, the Oslo Declaration on Freedom of Religion or Belief was published. In part it read:

> Whereas the Oslo Conference on Freedom of Religion or Belief, meeting in celebration of the fiftieth anniversary of the Universal Declaration of Human Rights, reaffirms that every person has the right to freedom of religion or belief;
>
> The participants in the Oslo Conference:
>
> Recognize that religions and beliefs may be misused to cause intolerance, discrimination and prejudice, and have all too often been used to deny the rights and freedoms of others;
>
> Affirm that every human being has a responsibility to condemn discrimination and intolerance based on religion or belief, and to apply religion or belief in support of human dignity and peace;
>
> Confirm that Article 18 of both the Universal Declaration of Human Rights and of the International Covenant on Civil and Political Rights together with other instruments create both a mandate for freedom of religion or belief and a universal standard around which we wish to rally.

This declaration does not explicitly mention church-state relations, however, but reaffirms the Declaration of 1981 concerning the elimination of all forms of intolerance and of discrimination based on religion or belief.

CHURCH AND STATE IN WESTERN EUROPE

After the sixteenth-century Reformation, the church scene was dramatically changed in Europe. Broadly speaking, southern Europe remained Roman Catholic (except for Greece, where nearly all citizens were Orthodox) while Britain and northern Europe were divided among different Protestant denominations—mainly Lutheran, Reformed, and Anglican. But the concept of religious freedom was not respected in any part of Europe, and northern Europe ended up with state churches of different characters.

The debate about the new Constitution of the European Union also caused disagreement with respect to the Christian faith. Should the preamble of the Constitution include a reference to Europe's Christian tradition constituting or expressing the basic values of the Union? Should such a reference be made, or would that be read as discrimination against the growing Muslim community in Europe and other non-Christian groups? The strongest opposition to such a reference came from France and the Nordic members of the Union, who argued that a Constitution for the European Union should be secular and respect all religions and traditions alike!

In recent years, European states have adjusted their legislation in order to meet international agreements on religious liberty and human rights. The relationships between church and state vary considerably, but in principle they generally follow a two-pronged approach. There should be no formal links between church and state and no constitutional legislation concerning churches or religious groups, but on the other hand constitutional articles about state neutrality in matters of religion or beliefs have been promulgated. We find a variety of regulations and agreements between majority churches and the state, and in most cases majority churches have specific rights over against religious minorities.

One could argue that it is a human-rights issue in countries where one church is favored by the state through special legislation and agreements, as the general understanding of the rights of citizens demands that every citizen be treated with equal status by the state.

Italy is dominated by the Catholic Church in many ways. But there is no constitutional link between the state and the Catholic Church. The Constitution of Italy reads:

> 3. All citizens have equal social dignity and are equal before the law, without distinction of sex, race, language, religion, political opinions, personal and social conditions. It is the duty of the Republic to remove those obstacles of an economic and social nature which limit the freedom and equality of citizens, impede the full development of the human person....
>
> 7. The State and the Catholic Church are, each within its own order, independent and sovereign. Their relations are regulated by the Lateran Treaties. Changes to the Treaties accepted by both parties do not require the procedure for constitutional amendment.
>
> 8. All religious confessions are equally free before the law. Religious confessions other than Catholic have the right to organize in accordance with their own statutes, in so far as they are not in conflict with Italian laws ...

In spite of this, religious minorities have faced a number of obstacles through the years. As in Italy, Spain also has a system in which religious communities are differently categorized and have different legal status in society.

In Greece, the Orthodox Church is described in the Constitution as the predominant form of religion, and both Christian minorities and Muslims face societal problems. The Parliament is responsible for approving the framework for the church as such, but the church decides on internal legal matters.

In England, one religious denomination is formally recognized and given a privileged status by the state. It is the "established" church of the nation, and the Church of England, or the Anglican Church, still holds onto the name "Church of England," despite the fact that only about 30 percent of the population has membership in this church. The English sovereign remains the head of the Anglican Church, and the Church could therefore be seen as a state church. The bishops of the Church of England must still take the oath of loyalty to the English monarch: "I accept Your Majesty as the sole source of ecclesiastical, spiritual and temporal power." The call for disestablishing the privileged position of the Church of England has come from both liberal and conservative politicians but thus far has not gained the momentum necessary to make a radical change. Since 1919, however, the Anglican Church has developed and decided upon its own laws and regulations, although some of these must still be approved by Parliament.

In Scotland, the Presbyterian Church enjoys the same position as the Anglican Church in England, the Queen (or reigning sovereign) being the head also of this church.

The French Constitution has the following opening article: "France shall be an indivisible, secular, democratic and social Republic. It shall ensure the equality of all citizens before the law, without distinction of origin, race or religion. It shall respect all beliefs. . . ." France did away with the state-church system more than a century ago, in spite of the fact that the country is predominantly Catholic. Churches can be registered as "cultural organizations," and as such they are entitled to tax deductions. Religious groups that are not registered may face problems, even in performing their normal religious activities.

The German Constitution contains the following articles:

Article 3 (Equality before the law).

All persons are equal before the law. Men and women have equal rights. No one may be prejudiced or favored because of his sex, his parentage, his race, his language, his homeland and origin, his faith or his religious or political opinions.

Article 4 (Freedom of faith, of conscience and of creed).

Freedom of faith and of conscience, and freedom of creed religious or ideological, are inviolable. The undisturbed practice of religion is guaranteed. No one may be compelled against his conscience to render war service as an armed combatant. Details will be regulated by a Federal law.

The relations between the churches and the State are regulated by separate agreements. The two major churches, Lutheran and Reformed, have attained the status of "Public legislative corporations" and handle their own matters without any interference from the state.

Belgium has no state church, but the Catholic Church is the dominant church in the country. The United Protestant Church of Belgium is officially recognized by the state, but a number of smaller churches and religious communities have faced severe problems as a result of not being recognized. They have been labelled officially as cults and have not enjoyed the same rights as churches recognized by the state.

CHURCH AND STATE IN PARTS OF EASTERN EUROPE

With the expansion of the European Union in recent years, following the collapse of the Soviet Union, to speak of Eastern Europe may seem out of place. But since a number of eastern European countries continue to face demanding challenges with respect to human rights and the relation between church and state, it may be appropriate to present a few examples.

During the Communist era in Poland, the church was separated from the state. But the Catholic Church played a vital political role in the opposition that led to change in 1989. The vast majority of Poland's thirty-four million inhabitants belong to the Roman Catholic Church. Religious freedom is granted in the Constitution, and Catholics, Orthodox, Jewish, and Protestant communities are treated as equals in the legal system. The Constitution also affirms the separation of church and state, but crucifixes are found in Parliament, and Christian education is provided in public schools.

In Bulgaria, about 86 percent of the population has membership in the Bulgarian Orthodox Church. The 1991 Constitution proclaims religious freedom and separation of church and state. In spite of this, the Orthodox Church is labelled "the traditional religion in the Republic of Bulgaria," and other churches have experienced serious difficulties in their relations with the state. The ties between the Orthodox Church and the state are still strong, and there is still some way to go before "non-traditional" religious groups enjoy the same recognition as the Orthodox Church.

In Romania, the situation is much the same as in Bulgaria. About 86 percent of the population belongs to the Romanian Orthodox Church. During the period of Communist rule, there was separation between church and state, although the 1948 "Law of Cults" gave the State strict control over the church. Since 1989, the Constitution (article 4,2) prohibits any discrimination on account of religion, and article 6 expresses freedom for "national minorities" to develop their religious identity.

In the Balkans, we see a particularly interesting relationship between the Church—or Islam—and the state. In Serbia, the church is in theory separated from the state. But the ties between the two are so strong that it is seen as virtually a national obligation to belong to the Serbian Orthodox Church—if one wants to be a true Serb. In Kosovo, with its 95 percent Albanian population, it is a matter of course to be

Muslim, although one finds a very secular society in this province. In the serious tension between Serbia and Kosovo, religion combined with nationalism plays a significant role.

NORDIC COUNTRIES

Although human rights and religious freedom are highly regarded in Nordic countries, until recently nowhere else have the constitutional ties between church and state been as close as in these countries. All the majority churches in Denmark, Finland, Iceland, Norway, and Sweden have been state churches, and all of them still enjoy a privileged position in relation to the state.

In Denmark, 84 percent of the population belongs to the Evangelical Lutheran Church. The rest belong to smaller free churches or non-Christian organizations. The Constitution states that the Evangelical Lutheran Church remains the Danish national church and as such is entitled to judicial, financial, and political support from the state, and the king or queen is obliged to belong to this confession. Bishops in this national church are formally appointed by the queen (i.e., the government), according to the vote of the Church's different departments. This national church is financed by a general church tax, which every citizen is obliged to pay, regardless of church affiliation. Although members of other churches are entitled to tax reduction for financial support of their own churches, this praxis obviously represents a challenge to human rights, because nobody should be compelled to support a state church of which they are not a member.

Finland has no state church as such, but strong bonds remain between the Evangelical Lutheran Church and the state. This church includes 85 percent of the total population. The Evangelical Lutheran Church along with the Orthodox Church have special constitutional agreements and are assured a public legal status in the society and thereby enjoy certain privileges. The government appoints one member from its own constituency as a member of the highest authoritative councils and committees of these two main churches.

In Iceland, 84 percent of the approximately three hundred thousand inhabitants belongs to the Evangelical Lutheran Church. Freedom of religion is upheld in the Constitution of 1874, but it also recognizes the Evangelical Lutheran Church as the "National Church." As such, this church is "protected and supported" by the state. This "National Church" is largely self-governing, but vicars are still appointed by the minister of church matters in the government (following recommendations from priests), and bishops are (at least formally) appointed by the president of Iceland.

Sweden used to have a state church, but in 2000 the Constitution was changed, and the formal ties between the state and the Church of Sweden were severed. Seventy-eight percent of the Swedish population still belongs to this church. Freedom of religion is explicitly affirmed in the Constitution, and the relationship between other churches and the state is formalized through separate legislation. The relations between the Church of Sweden and the state are addressed in a separate law, which states that this church be an "Evangelical Lutheran, open, democratic and nation-wide church." The king of Sweden must still belong to the Church of Sweden.

The Reformation in Europe had a decisive influence on the Scandinavian development with respect to church-state relations. Norway was at that time in a forced union with Denmark, so the king of Denmark was also the king of Norway. When the king converted from Catholicism to the Lutheran faith, the church in both countries had to follow. There was no room for religious freedom for any member of either society. The 1687 Law of Norway clearly stated that the religion of the state—the Lutheran Church—was the only form of religion tolerated in the country. Those who departed from this faith were severely punished or expelled from their homeland.

When in 1814, Norway ended its four-hundred-year union with Denmark, and the union with Sweden was established, Norway created its own constitution: the Constitution of 1814. Little changed, however, with respect to the provision of religious freedom under this Constitution. In fact, a passage in which freedom for "Christian sects" to practice their faith was accepted, but for some reason this passage never found its way into the Constitution.

This new Constitution represented an important step on Norway's road to complete independence. (The union with Sweden was dissolved in 1905.) However, it included less-flattering articles: for example, articles denying entry into the country to Jews and Jesuits. The article denying Jews admission was removed from the text in 1851, but the passage concerning Jesuits remained until 1956 (although by then it had been a dormant article for many years).

Before 1845, no Norwegian citizen was allowed to leave the state church. That year the Parliament approved a new law concerning "Dissenters," which provided constitutional recognition to other Christian churches. Gradually, as the idea of religious freedom gained increasing public support, various articles blocking Human Rights were removed from the text. Among these were articles prohibiting people who did not belong to the State Church from serving in public positions.

The public school system was based on laws dating back to 1737, when general education for all children was introduced. The schools were then regarded as Church schools leading up to confirmation in the Lutheran state church. As a result, it was not possible for teachers who did not belong to the state church to teach religion in public schools. This blocked non-members from employment in a number of cases where all teachers were expected to teach religion. These laws also prevented non-members of the state church from serving as headmasters of any public school. Only in recent years, when religious education ceased to function as Christian education for the state church and no longer served as a confessional introduction to the Lutheran faith, has the situation for teachers changed.

The Dissenter Law remained with minor changes in 1891, and this law regulated the relationship between the state church, other churches, and non-church members until 1969, when a new law was introduced removing some of the former, discriminating practices. For example, before 1919 all members of the Norwegian government had to be members of the official church. The new arrangement after 1969 was that more than half the members of the cabinet had to belong to the state church—an arrangement still in place. Article 12 stipulates:

> The King himself chooses a Council from among Norwegian citizens who are entitled to vote. This Council shall consist of a Prime Minister and at least seven other Members. More than half the number of the Members of the Council of State shall profess the official religion of the State.

The King himself has no choice, for as article 4 states: "The King shall at all times profess the Evangelical-Lutheran religion, and uphold and protect the same."

Norway still has a constitutional state church. No other country has a constitution which in a number of articles defines the position of the country's official church. The key article concerning the church-state relationship in the Norwegian Constitution, Article 2, reads as follows:

> All inhabitants of the Realm shall have the right to free exercise of their religion.
>
> The Evangelical-Lutheran religion shall remain the official religion of the State. The inhabitants professing it are bound to bring up their children in the same.

Since believers and members of many non-religious groups are severely persecuted in many non-European countries, lacking the most elementary protection against harassment from the state, it may seem insensitive to their situation to discuss human-rights problems in Western democracies. Nevertheless, we find it useful and necessary to ask, does the state-church system represent a challenge to religious liberty and human rights?

THE STATE-CHURCH SYSTEM: A CHALLENGE TO RELIGIOUS LIBERTY AND HUMAN RIGHTS?

For decades the discussion about the relationship between church and state in Norway has been heated. Opinion polls show that the attitude is divided, both inside and outside the state church (or the Church of Norway, as it is generally labelled). Extensive reports commissioned by the state have been published (the last one presented in 2006).[5] Most conclude with recommendations for more-or-less radical changes in the relationship between the state and the Church of Norway.

The argumentation follows different paths. Those who would prefer to retain the status quo, or who favor only minor changes in the state-church relationship, put forward the following considerations:

1. Why change a system that seems to function well? We know what we have, but we don't know what we might get if we change.

2. A separation of church and state would have serious implications for the church's financial situation, since presently the state and local municipalities cover all expenses for running the church, including the cost of church buildings.

---

5. NOU (Norwegian Public Reports) 2006, 2. Official report presented by a State Commission on "The State and the Church of Norway." (I am indebted to this report for quotations from the Norwegian Constitution.)

3. A "free" church or "folk-church" will be a far more closed church and will open the way for conservative elements within it to "take over" the leadership, resulting in the vast majority of members being estranged from the Church. This argument comes from the more open-minded and "liberal" part of the Church.
4. A separation of church and state will cause an exodus from the Church by those members who have a more distant relationship with the Church.

On the other hand, those who want to see a separation of church and state argue:

1. The state-church system belongs to a time long past and represents an anachronism in a modern society.
2. The church should not be ruled by the state but should have the right to decide any church matter without interference from the state. (Bishops are still appointed by the king.)
3. The state-church system conflicts with the principles of human rights and freedom of religion.

From a political perspective, any government would have an interest in influencing a Church that includes eighty-four percent of the population, especially as the State pays the Church's bills. From that perspective, it would be in the interest of the State to retain and to make use of the rest of the power the State-Church system makes possible. Having the mandate to appoint all bishops of the Church of Norway means that the State still has a key role in who represents the spiritual leadership of the Church.

An illustrative example of politicians' determination to maintain this influence over the Church was presented in March 2007 by the Prime Minister on behalf of his Labour Party, which is the largest in the Parliament: He wanted to change or delete the articles in the Constitution that mention the Evangelical Lutheran Church as the official religion of the State but still wanted to uphold the State Church and continue the arrangement under which the bishops of this Church would be appointed by the Government. No State religion but a State Church with State control! This represents a pragmatic approach to the issue of the relation between Church and State that completely lacks any consideration of consequences with respect to Human Rights.

There are voices insisting that the Constitution allow for and respect full freedom of religion because the Constitution explicitly guarantees all citizens the right to practice their religion. However, the same article, in the next paragraph, declares that "The Evangelical Lutheran Religion remains the official Religion of the State." Obviously there is a tension between the two paragraphs that some find impossible to reconcile. The problem increases dramatically in that Article 4 of the same Constitution states that "the King has to confess the Evangelical Lutheran Religion." Clearly the King of Norway does not have the freedom to choose his religious belief.

Further on, in Article 12, the text stipulates that more than half of the members of Cabinet must belong to the State Church. This represents another limitation on Freedom of Religion or Belief for people in the political leadership of the country. Article 16 gives the King authority over religious meetings and affairs, and also to ensure that religious teachers follow the prescribed norms. (Presently the King of Norway has only a formal and symbolic position, with no genuine political power, although he still presides over the Cabinet meetings, which are held in the King's Palace every Friday. This means that the political power of the King expressed in the Constitution is taken over by the Prime Minister and Cabinet.) Article 27 also states that members of the Cabinet who are not members of the State Church do not take part in deliberations and decisions concerning this Church.

It could be argued that the Constitution, through these articles, creates an impression of a modern democratic country having only limited freedom of religion and therefore being in conflict with international understandings of Human Rights. The Norwegian philosopher, Tore Lindholm, who is working with the Norwegian Center for Human Rights, argues that: "From the idea of freedom of religion and beliefs, the State should respect *all* religions and beliefs, and it should not identify itself with any particular form of belief."[6] In line with his thinking, the former labor leader, Reiulf Steen, is convinced that: "As long as the Evangelical Lutheran faith retains the status of official State-religion, we label other Christian groups as secondary. This is discrimination."[7]

---

6. Tore Lindholm, "Statens verdigrunnlag og menneskerettighetene," in *Stat, Kirke og Menneskerettigheter: Essays* (ed. Njaal Hoestmaelingen, Tore Lindholm, and Ingvill T. Plesner; Oslo: Abstrakt, 2006), 198.

7. Reiulf Steen, "State, Church and Human Rights," *Vaart Land*, January 24, 2007, 24.

Some defenders of the State-Church system within the Lutheran Church argue that it must be up to the Church itself to decide upon its relationship to the State. But they fail to realize that the issue of a State-Church system is not an internal Church matter. When a church demands an exclusive relationship with the State, through which it enjoys services and favors denied to other churches or religious groups, this represents a challenge to international understanding and Human Rights.

Most of the Church-State debate in Norway has evolved from the question of how the Church should organize its relation to the State. Much less of the debate has originated from another equally important starting point: What kind of State do we want to have? In a society that is becoming more and more pluralistic and in which the number of non-Christian beliefs and groups are growing and as many Norwegians go to church in churches outside the State Church, do we really want a State that favors one particular group, even if this group still nominally represents the majority of the population? Is there such a thing as a "Christian State"?

Most people in a modern democracy expect the State to treat its citizens in a way that gives them equal rights and opportunities in all matters of society. The question is whether this is at all possible within a State-Church system.

Norway has signed all the international Human Rights Conventions and Declarations and is obliged to honor all of them. Commenting on a case raised in Sweden in 1998, the European Human Rights Commission stated that: "A State Church system cannot in itself be considered to violate Article 9 of the Convention . . . However, a State Church system must, in order to satisfy the requirements of Article 9, include specific safeguards for the individual's freedom of religion . . ."

In 1993, the United Nations Human Rights Commission commented on the issue of the State Church, saying: "The fact that a religion is recognized as a State religion or that it is established as official or traditional, or that its followers comprise the majority of the population, shall not result in any impairment of the enjoyment of any rights under the Covenant, including articles 18 and 27, nor in any discrimination against adherents to other religions or non-believers" (referring to articles 18 and 27 in the UN Convention on Civil and Political Rights 1966). If discrimination is understood as the failure to grant all citizens equal rights and opportunities in all areas of public life, the State-Church system is hardly compatible with the intention of the international conventions on religious freedom and Human Rights.

In Norway this issue has been debated for half a century, and the disagreement seems to be as heated as ever. The main problem seems to be that until now few discuss the principles of Human Rights, equity and justice grounded in international Human Rights declarations as well as in the biblical material. Rather, the questions asked include: What serves the Church best? Who should have the decisive power in church matters? How can we avoid a split in what now is a State Church if and when the ties between Church and State are severed? How can the State Church within the present system gain more independence from the State and retain its privileges?

The King himself is not allowed to have a public opinion on this matter, but the President of the Parliament, who ranks second to the King, has publicly stated that the State-Church system is incompatible with the international standards of Human Rights and religious freedom.[8] It is a promising sign that influential people who are able to detach themselves from issues of personal interest are now focusing on the challenges the State-Church system represent to the most important issue: How can we have a Church-State relation which provides for citizens of all faiths the highest possible degree of Human Rights and Freedom of Religion or Belief?

Some would ask whether this problem is a theological issue. According to Lutheran theology, the relation between Church and State is a pragmatic matter. "The question is which relationship gives the Church the optimal working condition," says the Lutheran theologian, Dag Thorkildsen.[9] This position may be derived from the Lutheran teaching of "the two regiments," but whether this can be maintained in a modern society is doubtful, both from a theological and Human Rights persepective.

This thinking seems to be widespread within the State Church. In 2006, the Center for Church Research published a collection of essays entitled *Change and Belonging: The Issue of State Church in Perspective*.[10]

---

8. Thorbjoern Jagland in a public statement in Oslo, January 2007.

9. Dag Thorkildsen, "Demokrati foerst, ordninger saa," in *Stat, Kirke og Menneskerettigheter: Essays* (ed. Hoestmaelingen, Lindholm and Plesner), 109.

10. Ulla Schmidt, ed., *Endring og Tilhoerighet, Statskirkespoersmaalet i persepktiv*

The essays discuss a number of issues related to the Lutheran Church's position in society, in politics, and in relation to other beliefs and confessions. The Human Rights perspective, however, is not included in the discussion.

In his work on the resurrection, Thorwald Lorenzen has offered an extremely valuable contribution to "rediscovering" the centrality of the resurrection in New Testament theology. The resurrection is, for Lorenzen, "the ontological foundation for Christian faith and its social dimension, the Christian Church."[11] He further argues that this understanding of the centrality of the resurrection offers a theological basis for the Christian understanding of Human Rights.

As we have seen, the UN Declaration of Human Rights states that "all human beings are born free and equal in dignity and rights." Lorenzen searches for "a universally valid moral foundation for human rights," without which "human rights will be increasingly emptied of their validity and authority . . ." And this foundation he finds in the Christian message of God raising Jesus from the dead: "Christians are clear and transparent at this point. Their ethical vision is grounded in God's raising the crucified One from death . . . [T]his foundational event implies a vision of reality in which the equality of all people is ontologically grounded."[12]

Lorenzen underlines the importance of the biblical concept of equality. Galatians 3:28 declares that "there is no longer Jew or Greek, there is no longer slave or free, there is no longer male and female, for all of you are one in Jesus Christ." This is made reality through the resurrection of Jesus. Through this event, "the reality of God's *shalom* has broken into history in a new and intensive way."[13] Lorenzen argues that since all men and women, through the resurrection of Jesus, are equal and with equal rights, there is no room for discrimination of any kind. It could be argued that he is drawing too far-reaching conclusions from the importance of the resurrection of Jesus. But as the life and preaching of Jesus bear witness to his deep-rooted sense of justice and respect for

---

(KIFO Perpsektiv [Church Research Perspectives] 16; Trondheim: Tapir Akademisk, 2006).

11. Thorwald Lorenzen, *Resurrection, Discipleship, Justice: Affirming the Resurrection of Jesus Christ Today* (Macon, GA: Smyth & Helwys, 2003), 37.

12. Ibid., 103.

13. Ibid., 104.

all human beings, his message is authorized by God's raising him from death. This, we think, makes Lorenzen's conclusions valid. His book, *Resurrection—Discipleship—Justice*, represents a very important contribution in establishing a theological foundation for Christian reflection and involvement in Human Rights issues.

The Baptist tradition, to which Lorenzen belongs, has always advocated freedom of religion and has paid a price for this conviction.[14] Likewise, the separation of Church and State is deeply rooted in Baptist theological reflection.[15] Denton Lotz, former General Secretary of the Baptist World Alliance, is the President of the International Religious Liberty Association (IRLA). Addressing the IRLA World Congress in February 2007, he stated:

> Religious freedom is the basis of all freedoms. Where religious freedom is denied, all other freedoms are weakened and threatened. Separation of religion from the State strengthens religious freedom. Such separation guarantees religion its freedom and at the same time frees the State to be tolerant of all traditions and neutral in the face of conflicting religions and ideologies. The history of religions shows that when religion uses the State to enforce its doctrine, and when the State uses religion to control people, both the State and religion suffer.

In the West, we look with great concern at Muslim states in which Islam is made the State religion. But in our considerations concerning the State-Church system, we should include a closer look at the relation between State and Religion in Muslim countries. In a lecture entitled "Religious Freedom and the State Church," the Methodist theologian, Peder Borgen, argues that "the State-Religion in Norway should be compared with state-religions in, for example, Islamic countries." He presents two reasons for this: first, the growing number of Muslims in our country makes it important to have insight into their understanding of Islam as state-religion; and second, the issue of religious freedom in relation to the State Church needs to receive input from the study of similarities

---

14. James E. Wood, Jr., "Baptists and Human Rights," in *Faith, Life, and Witness: The Papers of the Study and Research Division of the Baptist World Alliance 1986–1990* (ed. William H. Brackney with Ruby J. Burke; Birmingham: Samford University Press, 1990), 257–67.

15. Heather M. Vose, "Our Baptist Heritage: Christian Citizenship and Church/State Relations," in *Faith, Life, and Witness*, ed. Brackney with Burke, 193–203.

with and differences from Islam as state-religion.[16] We would argue that unless the State gives every citizen and every religious group equal status and equal rights in a democratic society, the system does not comply with internationally accepted understandings of Human Rights.

---

16. Peder Borgen, "Religious Freedom and the State Church," lecture given in Trondheim 1995, p. 10.

11

Ethos, Compassion, and Human Rights

A Foundation for Homiletical Ethics

David Albert Farmer

UPON INITIAL CONSIDERATION, ONE would assume that reminding clergypersons to present ethically in the pulpit would be unnecessary—a waste of words, a stating of the obvious. Yet, a glance through preaching practices today and through the ages reveals a frequent lack of ethics on the part of those who claim to speak into their contexts the word of the living God. This chapter seeks to establish the need for homiletical ethics and moves to name the components of a foundation for such ethics.

ETHICS AS A VITAL COMPONENT IN THE STUDY OF HOMILETICS

Though often not recognized as such, homiletics in the theological curriculum is one of the few disciplines that, properly taught and guided, allows for full integration of the disparate components of a theological education. A preaching professor will have the most opportunities for success with students who, before enrolling in her or his basic preaching course, have already done some study of both Hebrew and Christian Scriptures, at least one of the biblical languages, the general flow of the history of the church, systematic theology, and, if possible, pastoral care. Learning to preach well is in part pulling these areas together in such a way that a relevant, inspiring, and well-reasoned message may be presented to modern hearers. While, indeed, as someone said long ago, the preacher doesn't bring the pots and pans to the dining table at meal time, she or he nonetheless serves a homiletical meal that has been prepared with the finest pots and pans of theological education.

In addition, the professor of preaching will be reminding her or his students about a number of basic skills that, hopefully, students have brought with them to their formal study of the theory and practice of preaching. For example, students who have not taken a basic speech course will require some coaching in the importance of eye contact with an audience, elocution, formatting and structuring content for oral presentation, introducing, concluding, illustrating, and so on.

I fear it is the norm, however, for students of preaching never to have any professorial reminders about the importance of ethics in preaching. Many of them thus launch out on their preaching careers thinking that anything goes in sermon preparation and delivery as long as a sermon, almost any kind of sermon, is delivered come Sunday.

This is an error on the part of divinity schools and preaching professors. In a foundational preaching course, the basics are part and parcel of core content, and, therefore, mention of any aspect of the preaching process is never out of line. After all, in any skills-development process, consistent returning to the basics is how advanced performance is ultimately achieved—and maintained. Even the greatest of instrumentalists still return to their musical scales in most practice sessions. Athletes prepare for any game or competition by warming up with the most basic skills that a beginner to that sport would be trying to master. A student of preaching needs to be taught that ethical standards in preaching are a vital part of every sermon-preparation process and every finished sermon. And by "taught," I don't mean a brief, cursory mention in a single lecture.

We cannot assume, given the frequent appearance of charlatan preachers in the world and the prevalence of out-and-out lies coming from persons across all our cultures whom we are supposed to trust (politicians, media professionals, and others), that preachers-to-be have, on their own, connected effective preaching to inviolable ethical norms. Eisegesis, plagiarism, and preaching without an honest love and respect for one's hearers (along with numerous other ethical infractions) are simply unacceptable, and in the long run damaging and damning to the ongoing Jesus movement. The church always pays a heavy price, sometimes in literal currencies, when it allows or overlooks violations of ethical norms. If the preacher is telling lies from the pulpit, what will listeners think of that preacher and the preaching process when they discover the truth?

AN EXCURSUS ON TRUTH IN THE CHRISTIAN COMMUNITY

We live in an era when truth is negotiable; maybe it always has been. Maybe because information exchange has exploded, there are just that many more opportunities to lie. A few years ago, when the then pastor/staff-relations committee in the congregation I serve as pastor released a booklet of my sermons under a title my older son suggested, some friends and foes had problems with the title and its various implications. That infamous title, which—strangely enough—didn't make it to the *New York Times* bestseller list, was *Lies My Sunday School Teacher Told Me*. One of my dearest friends in the entire world was one of those who called foul. He is one of the people whose opinion I value and respect in full; never would I intentionally do or say anything to hurt him. What he said was that the dedicated Sunday-school teachers who taught him during his church upbringing may have told him things that he later found out to be incorrect, but they were sharing what they took to be the truth. His teachers didn't intentionally mislead him or tell untruths; they just didn't know better. They loved him and cared about him, and as far as the content of their lessons was concerned, they did the best they could.

The hang-up, obviously, is the word *lies*. My friend, who is much nicer than I am all around, would have preferred that I not use the term *lies* to refer to inaccurate information transmitted unintentionally. And I certainly recognize that tension. Perhaps there should be a distinction drawn between malicious, intentional lies, on the one hand, and unintentional lies, on the other, which, of course, my kind friend wouldn't even term *lies*. At the end of the day, however, whether intentionally or unintentionally, misinformation—and often damaging misinformation—has been shared.

One of the problems with naming unintentionally shared bits of misinformation *lies* is that uninformed Sunday-school teachers aren't the only culprits. Schoolteachers, parents, and preachers also have to come under review. Isn't there a possibility—yea, a probability—that we speak of so-called truths we haven't confirmed or possibly can't confirm? Isn't the typical pattern for most people in most cultures around the world simply to pass on as truth what their forebears and mentors have passed on to them as true without taking the initiative or the responsibility of finding out for themselves? (Let me be quick to say that many people in the world have no choice in these matters. They do not have access to information beyond what their governments make available to them. Their minds are controlled from birth to death. These are not the kinds of people or situations I am addressing. I'm talking about people who have much more information available to them than they bother to access.)

Another problem is the wide variety of information we allow others to share with our children and with us. If we were to stay with the simple reality, "God is love," let's say, there would be much less chance of passing along inaccurate information about God than when we go into such detail about our dogma that we are inevitably taken out on thin ice. Whatever happened to the good old, "There are several perspectives on this issue, and here are a few of them. The one I personally favor is . . ."?

Still another problem is that *truth* itself needs to be defined. Philosophers have always debated the nature of truth, and the debate still ensues. There isn't a firm resolution about the matter, and there isn't likely to be one any time soon.

Philosopher Alfred North Whitehead stated, "There are no whole truths; all truths are half-truths. It is trying to treat them as whole truths that plays the devil."[1] Although I certainly believe there are "whole truths," Whitehead's point is well taken. On many points, what we call truth is nothing more than our attempt to universalize what worked well for us once or twice; the legitimate difference of opinion on the nature of truth leads people who don't wish to debate or justify an opinion or an action to say, "Well, it's *my* truth."

Mahatma Gandhi's autobiography was subtitled *The Story of My Experiments with Truth*. That conjures up bold and enticing mental images, doesn't it? The following comments should stick in consciousness and dwell with us for at least a while:

> I would say with those who say, "God is Love," God is Love. But deep down in me I used to say that though God may be Love, God is Truth above all. If it is possible for the human tongue to give the fullest description of God, I have come to the conclusion that God is Truth. . . . I went a step further and said that Truth is

---

1. Whitehead, *Dialogues of Alfred North Whitehead* (Boston: Little, Brown, 1954) prologue.

God. You will see the fine distinction between the two statements, "God is Truth" and "Truth is God." I came to that conclusion after a continuous and relentless search after truth, which [spanned] fifty years... I then found that the nearest approach to truth was through love.[2]

Here's an example of "truth" versus "non-truth" that constantly comes up in the world of religion. The beautiful creation stories that open the book of Genesis, both versions of how the created order came to be, are not "true" by laws of the very nature they purport to describe. The two broad responses to this fact we know all too well. One has been a "digging in of heels" that tries to use this pre-scientific literature to match up with or even to inform modern science. Those who hold to this view define *truth* as historically, scientifically verifiable facts, using the ancient literature itself to determine what is accurate or inaccurate. In other words, the ancient Hebrew creation myths are used to establish what is factual, and then they and they alone are used to determine if any material or ideas extraneous to the stories themselves can be true. This closed system, of necessity, rejects any information about the creation of the world not already contained in the stories, so it's easy to spot what creationists call falsehoods.

In stark contrast are those who take the ancient stories to be true in their overall affirmations that the world came to be with the creative God calling the cosmos into being and that the processes were orderly and even "logical." In this way of thinking, our cosmos didn't "just happen." Therefore, the truth of the Genesis creation stories is affirmed even though the intricate details of "what happened when" and God's infamous "day off" are questionable and may be all wrong.

The book that many folks in my congregation's midweek study group read for our summer 2007 sessions was both informative and disturbing—truthful most of the way through and in places untruthful only by reason of overgeneralization. In any case, Christopher Hitchens, who seems to have been moved to embrace atheism because of the considerable and horrific failures of institutional religion, is especially critical of modern religious movements who know good and well that the ancient stories cannot be true according to modern factual definitions of *truth*, but who pretend that the old configurations are true by

---

2. I stumbled upon this life-changing insight from the great M. K. Gandhi at this Internet site: http://die_meistersinger.tripod.com/gandhi8.html/.

today's standards anyway. Hitchens wrote *God is not Great: How Religion Poisons Everything*. He is much better quoted than explained: "In our new semi-secular and mediocre condition, even the religious will speak with embarrassment of the time when theologians would dispute over futile propositions with fanatical intensity: measuring the length of angels' wings, for example, or debating how many such mythical creatures would dance on the head of a pin."[3]

The one-chapter biblical book, 2 John, fascinates me. This is true for several reasons. For one, it's addressed to a lady. For another, it's warm and personal. For a third, truth and love are tied together and in a very interesting way.

> The presbyter to the elect lady and her children, whom I love in the truth, and not only I but also all who know the truth, because of the truth that abides in us and that will be with us forever. Grace, mercy, and peace will be with us from God and from Jesus, the Anointed One, God's Child, in truth and love. I was overjoyed to find some of your children walking in the truth, just as we have been commanded by God. But now, dear lady, I ask you, not as though I were writing you a new commandment, but one we have had from the beginning: let us love one another. And this is love, that we walk according to God's commandments; this is the commandment just as you have heard it from the beginning—you must walk in it (2 John 1–6; preacher's paraphrase).

By the way, all uses of the word "love" here are *agape* forms, so we know more precisely what kind of love the author is speaking about.

What we typically see translated as "the lady" may have been a reference to an individual whose name was *Kyria*, who was known to be an elect (*eklektē*) one. *Kyria* can mean "lady," but it can also be a proper noun. And, by the way, it is the feminine form of the word of respect that people often used for Jesus: *kyrios* ("mister," "sir," or "lord"). "Elect lady" may also have referred to a particular, but unnamed, congregation. (Why not? *Ekklesia* is a feminine noun.)

In any case, the church members are called upon to make truth a living, active truth—something that shapes how they "walk," how they actually live their lives. They are also called to love each other, and the writer says that we show our love by living according to the standards

---

3. Christopher Hitchens, *God Is Not Great: How Religion Poisons Everything* (New York: Twelve, 2007), 68.

for love established by God Godself. This is what the writer means by referring to "commandments" in this context.

The word translated as "truth" in English seems simple enough, but it actually isn't. Translators can't convey the depth of this word, *alētheia*, with a single English word. What many of us think of as truth in our world and in our vernacular is simply getting the facts straight, and, indeed, honesty and forthrightness are vitally important. The meaning of the word in Greek, however, is more complex; it conjures up a picture of something that drives us to grasp truth as much more profound than many of us have ever imagined.

The *alpha* here is a negating prefix. The *lēthē* part of this word means "forgetting" in its root. So, what we translate as "truth" in English for the ancient Greeks meant something like *non-forgetting* or *unforgetting*.[4] Truth, then, is refusing to forget what we once knew deep down in our being to be correct and right. It is more than just knowing and affirming facts.

In Greek mythology, *Lethe* was a river and a river goddess. The River Lethe was one of five rivers encircling *Hades*, the abode of the dead. Lethe was the river of forgetfulness.[5] In the land of the dead to which all people went (since there was not any conception of a heaven in the ancient Greek mindset), part of coping meant forgetting. Those who dwelled in the abode of the dead had sort of "half lives" in a shadowy existence. Part of coping meant not remembering what life on earth had been like. So while one was robbed of her or his memories of the happy times of life, she or he was also relieved of memories of pain and suffering—to say nothing of the worries that would inevitably arise in regard to loved ones left behind.

A-lētheia, then, was un-forgetting, refusing to let go of acquired knowledge and experience of what in my depths I have known to be right and correct. *That* I will not forget. *That* I will not surrender. This understanding of truth can only partially be about gathered proofs that appeal to rationality alone.

It was the Fourth Gospel's Jesus who is said to have uttered one of the most stirring and insightful and inspiring ideas associated with

---

4. See philosopher Peter Suber's 1992 baccalaureate address from Earlham College: "When We Leave Our Desks." Online: http://www.earlham.edu/~peters/writing/bacc2.htm/.

5. Suber credits Martin Heidegger as the originator of this etymological insight.

the first-century Jewish carpenter who merely wished to reform his beloved Judaism: "You will know the truth, and the truth will make you free" (John 8:32). Now that we know the meaning of *truth* in the New Testament, we can restate Jesus' words: You will unite yourself with unforgetting, and that will make you free!

THE CONSISTENT CALL FOR ETHICS IN SECULAR SPEECHMAKING AND THE STRANGE SILENCE OF DEMANDS FOR ETHICAL FOUNDATIONS FOR PREACHING

Pick up practically any ancient or modern "classic" handbook for public speaking, and you will be confronted by consistent calls for ethical standards in the preparation and delivery of any and every speech. At Wilmington College, where I teach humanities and basic speech courses to undergraduate students, our required textbook over several years and editions has been Albert J. Vasile's *Speak with Confidence: A Practical Guide*. Within the first few pages of the first chapter of the present edition, and of all previous editions I can remember, Professor Vasile brings to the attention of beginning public speakers the importance of ethics in public speaking: "As a competent public speaker you should always strive for excellence, which includes high ethical standards."[6] He stresses in a general way, before getting to the details, that "being ethical is being honest, truthful, fair, decent, and considerate, and having high morals."[7] If those are the rapid-fire tests for an ethical speech, most political speeches and many sermons in the English-speaking world absolutely fail.

Professor Vasile lists seven standards by which any ethical speaker is bound.[8] I describe these in my own words, but he devised the list:

1. A speaker makes it her or his business, in so far as possible, to know the makeup of the audience that will hear the speech (political groups, ethnic groups, and so on).

2. The speaker possesses sufficient compassion and common sense to understand how the speech might impact on the hearers.

---

6. Albert J. Vasile, *Speak with Confidence: A Practical Guide* (9th ed.; Boston: Pearson, Allyn & Bacon, 2004), 15.

7. Ibid.

8. Ibid., 16.

3. An effective public speaker, an ethical public speaker, is always fully prepared. She or he wouldn't think of wasting the time of people who are giving their time to listen to what the speaker has to say.

4. The responsible speaker tells the whole truth, not just one side of a story; she or he does not exclude pertinent information. I always tell my speech students, as well as my preaching students at Palmer Seminary, not to make an opponent's case, not to cause the opposing view to sound more appealing or sensible than the position the speaker or preacher claims as her or his own. Even so, in fairness, the fact that there are views held other than the one stressed in a particular public address needs to be mentioned (never given center stage!).

5. The believable public speaker clearly understands the difference between what is fact and what is opinion and makes certain that the audience grasps the difference as well.

6. Any borrowed words or ideas are credited in a speech prepared and delivered according to ethical standards.

7. If there is to be a question-and-answer session following the speech itself, the speaker with integrity answers straightforwardly, revealing pertinent information or saying, "I don't know."

Let us not leave these seven standards too quickly. They must inform homiletical ethics, as a sermon is one of several types of public address; indeed, a sermon is one of several speech types.

THE GOAL OF ETHICAL NORMS IN THE PRACTICE OF PREACHING

Faithfully preaching the truths of Jesus' message often, in our day, takes a backseat to means-justifies-the-end messages that primarily intend to indoctrinate or manipulate. The evident goal of most first-world preaching today is to add numbers to membership rolls or to build an army of adherents who fear to differ theologically with the preacher to whom they yield their right to think and reason. Too often, preaching is about job keeping—not upsetting the apple carts of either local congregations or denominational hierarchies. Also, all too many preachers pretend with their congregants that effective preaching can be done without adequate preparation, and thus that all the fevered activities required to keep parishioners entertained by church-as-social-club are infinitely more important than the prayerful meditation, reflection, and diligent study required to preach consistently thoughtful, focused messages that are appropriately pastoral and, simultaneously, appropriately challenging to individuals and corrupt governments and other institutions. Participating in this sham is unethical.

Who will speak out against this rampant absence of ethics in preaching today? Faithful preaching is so rare and preachers who preach consistently by ethical standards so much in the minority that there are few preachers to call for change.

As this article is written, there is an active, ongoing debate in the United States about whether or not plagiarism is an acceptable practice in preaching. That matter is debatable? How can plagiarism ever be considered either ethical or acceptable? Some of the clergy advocating plagiarism happen to be those who have their sermons for sale!

For eighteen years, I edited the preaching journal *Pulpit Digest*. Thorwald Lorenzen was one of our fine contributing editors. The journal ceased publication in early 2001 after a sixty-four-year run—before there were many homiletics sources available online. Even so, we had a few subscribers who consistently bought two subscriptions mailed to the same name and address. Only finally did we realize what was happening! One copy was to be stored and kept for future reference; the other, ostensibly, was marked up and cut out and perhaps carried directly into the pulpit.

Evidently, as the years have passed and *Pulpit Digest* is no more, sermon copying has escalated. In *The Wall Street Journal Online* November 15, 2006 edition, the financial world caught moneymaking preachers with their robes down in the act of profiting, many of them shamelessly so.

> The Rev. Brian Moon [in August of 2006] . . . preached about "God's Math."
>
> "People are drowning, drowning in their marriages, drowning in their careers, drowning in hurtful habits," Mr. Moon told his congregation at Church of the Suncoast, in Land o' Lakes, Fla. "They need someone to rescue them and bring them on the raft. They need people driven by God's addition."
>
> Those words, it turns out, were first uttered three years ago by the Rev. Ed Young, pastor of Fellowship Church in Grapevine,

Texas. His Web site, creativepastors.com, sells transcripts of this and other sermons for $10 each.

Mr. Moon says he delivered about 75% of Mr. Young's sermon, "just because it was really good." That included a white-water rafting anecdote similar to Mr. Young's in the original. Mr. Moon, who has now been a pastor for seven months, didn't give credit to Mr. Young, and he makes no apologies for using a recycled sermon.

"Truth is truth, there's no sense reinventing the wheel," Mr. Moon says. "If you got something that's a good product, why go out and beat your head against the wall and try to come up with it yourself?"

The widespread buying of packaged wisdom has touched off a debate about ethics, especially after incidents in which pastors have resigned over plagiarism allegations. Some members of the clergy say sermon sales diminish religious oratory and undermine both scholarship and the trust between ministers and their flocks.

"Every minister owes his congregation a fresh act of interpretation," says Thomas G. Long, a preaching professor at the Candler School of Theology at Emory University in Atlanta. "To play easy with the truth, to be deceptive about where the ideas come from, is a lie."[9]

Obviously, Professor Long appropriately holds us all to ministerial integrity. There are also other issues to consider when it comes to preaching and ethics.

More than twenty years ago, while teaching as a guest professor of homiletics at the International Baptist Theological Seminary in Rüschlikon, Switzerland, where I first met Thorwald Lorenzen, I attempted a lecture, near the end of the semester, on ethics in preaching. I was thirty or so minutes into a two-hour lecture when one of my Italian students interrupted me by saying, "Excuse me, Professor, but if I may say so, you don't know what you're talking about."

I was shocked and embarrassed. I was also perplexed because I knew this student well and considered him a friend. I didn't expect that kind of challenge. The other students in the room were also taken aback. I tried to reduce the awkward moment by saying, "Oh, you've been talking to my wife again." But his concern was significant enough that hu-

---

9. Suzanne Sataline, "The Sermon You Heard on Sunday May Be from the Web," *The Wall Street Journal Online*, November 15, 2006, p. 1.

mor could not minimize what he needed to say. "Tell us what is on your mind," I urged, and what came out of Rafaelle Volpe's mouth that day marked a turning point for me—both in terms of how I thought about preaching and ethics, and in terms of how I understood the whole world as influential in determining what preaching is, can be, and should be.

He said, "When I leave your classroom and this seminary, I will go back to my country and become a pastor. I will probably serve three churches in order to make a modest living, and in those three small churches there will be many prostitutes. They do not want to be prostitutes, but that is the only way they as mothers can support their children. I don't think your American churches welcome prostitutes as members, but maybe, anyway, you can tell me what my ethical responsibilities are as a preacher to these women." I had tears in my eyes by the time he finished—both because I had been painfully naïve, and because of the plight of the prostitutes to whom he referred, as well as the plight of who knew how many other people, excluded rather than included in God's circle of love by the preaching of practically every preacher since Jesus. I asked the class to take a ten-minute break, during which time I slipped away to dry my eyes, trash my lecture notes, and find the strongest cup of coffee I could locate. Back in class, I opened the floor for discussion for the remainder of our class time together that day, and I learned tremendously from my international community of fellow learners.

Incidentally, I attended a luncheon not long after the incident I have just described at which the Reverend Howard Moody was the speaker. Moody had been pastor of New York's Judson Memorial Church from 1956 to 1992. Moody had never been afraid of conflict or of standing up for justice, regardless of the unpopularity of the cause. I learned from his speech that day that he had angered plenty of New Yorkers and others by pushing for the decriminalization of prostitution. In support of that initiative, Moody and some of his parishioners once set up at a meeting of the Republican National Convention in New York, coffee-service areas for prostitutes servicing the Republican delegates in town to help democracy move forward.

ETHOS

Aristotle's thorough studies of the art or science of public speaking will likely never be superseded in a world that values and practices various types of planned and organized public oral discourses. Said the late

Professor Lane Cooper of Cornell University, one of Aristotle's most ardent students, translators, and interpreters in relatively recent times:

> The *Rhetoric* of Aristotle is a practical psychology, and the most helpful book extant for writers of prose and for speakers of every sort. Every one whose business it is to persuade others—lawyers, legislators, statesmen, clergymen, editors, teachers—will find the book useful when it is read with attention. And the modern psychologist commonly will find that he has observed the behavior of human beings less carefully than did Aristotle, even though the author keeps reminding us that in the *Rhetoric* his analysis of thought and conduct is practical, not scientifically precise and complete.[10]

In Aristotle's pre-Christian era (the three books of *Rhetoric* having initially been compiled in about 350 BCE), his primary concern was with persuasion and how effectively and ethically to persuade hearers in judicial settings as well as in gatherings of the general public who needed to hear about various matters of import. He defined *rhetoric* as the faculty or power, in any given case, of discovering every available means of persuasion.[11] The speech itself provides for three possible means or types of persuasion; these, over time, have collectively come to be referred to as the Aristotelian triad:

1. *Ethos* was the word Aristotle selected to refer to the public speaker's character. Character, thought Aristotle, was the primary characteristic for making a speaker credible.

2. Hearers are also persuaded by the state or level of emotion (*pathos*) to which the speech brings them.

3. Finally, those who hear a speech may be persuaded by the logic (*logos*) of the speaker's arguments.

---

10. *The Rhetoric of Aristotle* (ed. and trans. Lane Cooper; Englewood Cliffs: Prentice-Hall, Inc., 1932), xvii. The exclusively masculine references to the professions in this passage reflected both the accepted style of "inclusive" writing in the English-speaking world of the early 1930s as well as Professor Cooper's cultural context in which a very limited number of female clergy, politicians, and helping professionals were known to him. While I have left the masculine exclusivity as originally published, neither the person honored by this Festschrift nor I practice the use of non-inclusive language. Nor do we, for that matter, miss out on the privilege of affirming women in all facets of the ministry and, of course, every other profession.

11. Cooper, *The Rhetoric of Aristotle*, 7.

Character, emotion, and logic are the means through which a speaker may persuade an audience, and first on Aristotle's list is the speaker's character, *ethos*.

> [A]s a rule we trust men of probity [uprightness, integrity] more, and more quickly, about things in general, while on points outside the realm of exact knowledge, where opinion is divided, we trust them absolutely. This trust, however, should be created by the speech itself, and not left to depend upon an antecedent impression that the speaker is this or that kind of man. It is not true, as some writers on the art maintain, that the probity of the speaker contributes nothing to his persuasiveness; on the contrary, we might almost affirm that his character is the most potent means to persuasion.[12]

Most of us, including those who hear us preach, want to hear persons of high moral character speak about the truly significant aspects of living. We react negatively to those who preach one thing and live in a way that contradicts it. An obvious example would be a well-known media evangelist's preaching the importance of sacrificial financial giving to her or his ministry, only to have brought to light this preacher's lavish lifestyle funded by monies promised for the truly needy people of the world, who were never given a single coin to help alleviate a part of their suffering.

There have been and are too many preachers who are closeted, and probably self-hating, homosexuals; most of them are married and may also be parents, and they may well seek out secretive sexual encounters online or in the next town. They serve homophobic congregations, so to keep the salaries flowing these gay and lesbian preachers gay-bash from the pulpit. What a sick and painful way to live! Their enduring anger at themselves spews forth in the form of some of the most vitriolic vendettas imaginable. To hear these preachers tell it, murderous terrorists have a better shot at claiming a place in God's realm than do homosexuals. Of course, in these cases, the preacher alone is not at fault; whole congregations as well as whole religious or denominational groups share the blame for promoting and allowing such hatred of members of God's family to become institutionalized.

---

12. Cooper, *The Rhetoric of Aristotle*, 8–9. There is no historical evidence that any women were public speakers during the lifetime of Aristotle either in Athens, where he first studied and then taught with Plato, or while Aristotle was tutor to Alexander the Great.

Augustine of Hippo (another great rhetorician who single-handedly baptized or Christianized the pre-Christian perspective on rhetoric as developed by Aristotle) found himself embroiled in one of the church's earliest major controversies over ministerial ethics. Church historians have called this inner-Church conflict the Donatist controversy. The problems that brought this controversy to a head date back to the persecution of Christians by the Roman emperor Diocletian, whose reign extended from 284 to 305 CE.

About two years before he voluntarily retired as emperor, Diocletian published his Edict against the Christians. Places of Christian worship began to be destroyed, and copies of Christian Scriptures were confiscated by Rome. Christians were ordered not to assemble for worship. Things would get much worse before they got better. Even so, in this first round of Christian persecution, there was within the Christian community great attention given to how priests and bishops responded to the demand by Rome that copies of Scripture be surrendered. Some of these clergypersons without resistance turned Scriptures over to Roman representatives. Some absolutely refused and thus were taken into custody; in addition to those who died for refusing to turn over their copies of Scripture, some of the priests and bishops neither complied nor resisted; they ran!

Many years after the Edict of Milan brought these horrible persecutions to an end, the behavior of bishops and priests regarding the release of Scriptures was still being discussed. To oversimplify, Bishop Donatus took the position that the clergy who had given in to the demands of Rome had sacrificed their rights to practice ministry; every religious act that they performed after their cowardice was invalid. A service of holy matrimony performed by a priest who had failed to resist Roman demands was not a true marriage. A lapsed bishop who participated in the consecration of a fellow bishop had nothing to offer, according to Donatus, because he had lost the validity of his office as a result of his previous actions; the bishop or bishops whom he had consecrated were as a result not bishops at all.

Bishop Augustine took the opposing view and condemned the stance of Donatus. According to Augustine, a clergyperson's credibility in the performance of ministerial tasks does not rest on the priest's personal holiness but rather upon the credentials given by the church. One duly ordained may indeed fail to live up to proper personal standards, but the absence of personal holiness and responsible decision-making cannot take away the power of what the church has authorized. Augustine believed that the priests who kowtowed to Roman rules regarding the Scriptures should do penance, but their acts after their poor judgment calls were just as valid as those performed before Diocletian had begun his rampage against Christians.

While all preachers fall short of human perfection (whatever that is), if they see themselves and present themselves to their congregants as fellow seekers and strugglers and not as examples of how others should live their lives, many of the possible problems about the preacher's character are immediately resolved. This is not to say that we preachers should stop trying to be our best selves. This is not to say that there are ethical standards for laypersons and another set for clergypersons. This is not to say that the preacher is ever relieved of the responsibility of trying to live by the same standards to which she or he points a congregation.

COMPASSION

The Dalai Lama has said that compassion is the radicalism of our time. If that is true (and who can dispute it?), how sad! Is compassion really so rare that someone who lives compassionately is a contemporary radical? Well, how many people do you, the reader of this book, know who are truly compassionate? I think I know a few, but I don't know many truly, consistently compassionate people.

We all realize that even some of the students whom we teach in divinity schools, and the churches that many of them go out to serve, lack fundamental human compassion. Oh, there may be a smattering here and there, but too many acts of so-called compassion, if they exist at all in those contexts, turn out to be self-serving to some degree. Compassion is a natural, an unstoppable, outgrowth of God's kind of unconditional love for all people. There is no such thing as Christian preaching that lacks compassion in its heart and soul.

Love has become as subject to personal whim and contextual application as has truth in the modern world. Love is what I want it to be when I want to express it as I see fit. Of course, just because someone claims to feel love or to be acting in love, this doesn't mean love is involved in any way.

The old standby volume Vine's *Word Studies in the Greek New Testament* still does a good job of helping us to grasp the meaning of *agape*. The author says that God's kind of love is a more reasoned love based on the unswerving conviction that the object of love is worthy of love; it would be possible, then, to love someone in this manner without feeling all warm and fuzzy inside. When someone angers you and makes you crazy, if you love that person with *agape* love, then you love her or him with your actions despite your anger or frustration or disappointment. The emotional component may or may not be present, and when it's not, we still act in love; we act in the person's best interest, anyway.

Any of us preaching regularly to the same congregations undoubtedly have people in our churches who have irritated us to the point that our ability to feel compassion for those persons is sorely tested. (And if any one of my congregants is reading this book, I'm definitely *not* talking about you; it's someone else!) I won't allow myself to feel guilty for having honest human emotions, but I will try to be courageous enough to keep remembering Abraham Joshua Heschel's description of a religious person. A religious person, he believed, held both God and humanity together in all of her or his thoughts and suffered when fellow humans suffered; a religious person's greatest passion, as he said it, was compassion.

HUMAN RIGHTS

It was the self-proclaimed atheist Bertrand Russell who looked back over his life and said that three passions had gripped him: his longings to love and be loved, his search for knowledge, and his pity for fellow humans who suffered. Oh yeah, there's that pesky passage where the Matthean Jesus asks his hearers, "For if you love those who love you, what reward do you have? Do not even the tax collectors do the same" (Matt 5:46, NRSV)?

Professors Catherine and Justo Gonzalez, a church historian and historical theologian respectively, have contributed a great deal to modern preaching as a result of their insights about the true preaching context. What follows from Gonzalez and Gonzalez grips me and requires all of us, I think, who dare to preach to refuse to get caught up in the selfish limitations of preaching as if all that matters is addressing the interests of the gathered crowd:

> [P]reaching should always take into account, not only the immediate context of the congregation, but also that wider context of

the community of faith throughout the world. Preaching should certainly address the situation of the hearers. If it takes place, for instance, in a middle-class suburban congregation in the United States, it must deal with the issues and concerns of that congregation, but it must not do so at the expense of its catholic context ... Preaching must be addressed to the needs of a parish; but it must not be parochial, for one of the needs of every parish is to be connected to the church universal. People in the above-mentioned suburban parish need to recognize that they are part of the same church that struggles for justice in South Africa and gathers for worship under a thatched roof in a village in India.[13]

I would say that another reason for the need to be connected with a world context when preaching (other than the reality of the church universal) is that all humanity is interconnected. As many others have said more eloquently than I, when one fellow human suffers, we all suffer. People who are starving in distant parts of the world I may never see are, even so, members of my family. How can I ignore them? How can I make myself not care? People who are not free to seek or to serve God as they feel called and led are, despite my own great freedoms, members of my family, and I cannot direct my thoughts away from them.

If we were to take the lead established by Catherine and Justo Gonzalez and connect it to an active awareness of agencies such as Amnesty International, our preaching would be properly focused and directed. Immediately, we would see, for example, how petty and pointless is preaching that seeks only to further a nationalistic agenda or that intends only to press hearers to embrace the right doctrines ("right" almost always meaning agreeing with the preacher). We cannot preach ethically if we are self-centered or self-serving.

Do preachers need to be taught or reminded that there are ethical and unethical ways to preach? If you agree with me that they/we do, then let the new learning or the relearning begin at once. At the core of ethical preaching will be preachers of high moral character (still with flaws, much to the dismay of plenty of congregants), and these will be preachers who reveal much more compassion in their preaching than we have been hearing from most pulpits for decades. These preachers who preach ethically will not allow their congregations to believe that the gospel has been

---

13. Justo L. Gonzalez and Catherine G. Gonzalez, "The Larger Context." In *Preaching as a Social Act: Theology & Practice*, edited by Arthur Van Seters (Nashville: Abingdon, 1988). Online: http://www.religion-online.org/showchapter.asp?title=1084&C=1106/.

preached unless the pains and struggles of all those who suffer across this fragile globe have been acknowledged and responded to.

"Teacher, which commandment in the law is the greatest?"

He said to him, "'You shall love the Lord your God with all your heart, and with all your soul, and with all your mind.' This is the greatest and first commandment. And a second is like it: 'You shall love your neighbor as yourself.' On these two commandments hang all the law and the prophets." (Matt 22:36–40, NRSV)

12

From Terri Schiavo toward a Theology of Dying

D. Dixon Sutherland

ON MARCH 31, 2005, at 9:05 A.M., Theresa ("Terri") Schiavo died at the Hospice of the Florida Suncoast in Pinellas Park, Florida. Her condition was diagnosed medically as *Persistent Vegetative State* (PVS), which developed after she collapsed in her home on February 25, 1990, from respiratory and cardiac arrest. As a result of the collapse, she suffered brain damage and became institutionally dependent on a gastric feeding tube (PEG tube) for the next fifteen years. After fourteen appeals in Florida courts, five District court battles, a Florida law passed and rejected as unconstitutional by the Florida Supreme Court, special United States Congress legislation that moved President Bush to fly back to Washington, DC, from his home in Crawford, Texas, to sign, as well as four denials to hear her case before the Supreme Court of the United States, Terri Schiavo's feeding tube was finally removed (it had already been removed and reinserted by order of Florida Governor Jeb Bush), and she died.

During the last months of her life, Terri's case was reported around the world. Rare was the person who did not see video clips showing her watching balloons, with her mother talking to her—a video that her parents, Robert and Mary Schindler, said proved that their daughter was conscious and communicative. Outside Terri's room became ground zero for a constant protest vigil, a *cause célèbre* for Christian pro-life forces, arguing that the removal of her feeding tube would constitute killing her by slow starvation. A literal media circus ensued. There was even a Christian juggler who came because "God told me to come."[1]

---

1. Jamie Thompson, "Juggler Says, 'God Told Me to Come,'" *St. Petersburg Times*, March 31, 2005.

During the heat of the battle, Pope John Paul II made remarks that were more than coincidental about the use of feeding tubes, announcing that their use was not a medical treatment but natural, not extraordinary but ordinary care—and thus morally obligatory. Failure to continue their use, even on a vegetative person, was, the Pope announced, "euthanasia by omission."[2]

Theological convictions were the driving force behind the legal battles. The Schiavo case was in the end not about medicine or law but about religion. "The Christian right" unabashedly maintained that they represented "*the* Christian position." Their claims of absolute dogmatic correctness about when and how human life should end were bolstered by their corresponding absolutist declarations about the Bible.

POLITICS AT THE DEATHBED

Added to this theological debate were the political implications, which dug the lines in the sand even deeper. Lead counsel for the Schindlers was David Gibbs III, who is part of a self-proclaimed "pro-life" law firm in central Florida.[3]

Once it became clear that the Schindlers would not succeed in their efforts to stop removal of the PEG tube, they challenged Terri's diagnosis. The public rhetoric regarding Terri spoke of her as if she was not in PVS. Gibbs's statement is representative:

> Terri is as alive as you are. You may be sitting here thinking, "Well, I've heard she is on a ventilator; she is being kept alive by tubes, and so on." But as we sit here today, Terri Schiavo is every bit as alive as you and I . . . Terri goes to bed at night. She wakes up in the morning. She functions throughout the day.[4]

---

2. Pope John Paul II, "Address of Pope John Paul II to the Participants of the International Congress on Life-Sustaining Treatments and Vegetative State: Scientific Advances and Ethical Dilemmas," 02/03/2004, Section 3–4, United States Conference of Catholic Bishops: http://www.usccb.org/prolife/issues/euthanas/index.shtml (accessed August 2, 2007).

3. Gibbs's father leads the "Christian Law Association." A video of Gibbs giving a description of Terri's condition can be found at http://www.christianlaw.org/. There he details a picture of Terri as a severely disabled woman who attempted to communicate and respond to others, and whose only problem was that she could not feed herself. He vilifies Michael Schiavo with details that frankly contradict court evidence and the Guardian *ad litem's* report both in substance and intent.

4. David C. Gibbs III, "Gibbs on Schiavo," *Stetson Law Review* 35/1 (Fall 2005): 17.

Yet no credible medical evidence was ever presented to refute her diagnosis. Gibbs denied the autopsy report that she was blind and contended that she followed items and focused on people's faces.[5]

Casting this picture of Terri Schiavo as if she was "just like us" heightened public awareness and allowed the heavy political hand of the "Christian right" to thrust the case into the U.S. Congress. Word was put out that political survival of anyone in Washington, including the President, was dependent on taking action to reverse the courts' decisions to remove Terri's PEG tube. Astoundingly, on Palm Sunday Congress met in an unprecedented emergency session to pass a law aimed at one individual—Terri Schiavo. President Bush flew back from Texas to Washington in order to sign the legislation. Debate in Congress was filled with theological presuppositions and medical fallacies. For example, according to Congressman Tom DeLay (primary sponsor of the bill):

> She is not a vegetable. She is handicapped like many millions of people walking around today . . . A young woman in Florida is being dehydrated and starved to death. For 58 long hours, her mouth has been parched and her hunger pangs have been throbbing. If we do not act, she will die of thirst. However helpless, Mr. Speaker, she is alive. She is still one of us. And this cannot stand. Terri Schiavo survived her Passion this weekend, and she has not been forsaken.[6]

And according to Congressman Phil Gingrey, MD:

> I am not playing doctor, for indeed I am one . . . since Terri Schiavo's brain injury 15 years ago, she has been profoundly disabled. She is not, however, in a coma. She responds to people around her; she smiles and she can feel. Terri is very much alive . . . Terri's condition can improve. Terri responds to verbal, auditory, and visual stimuli, normally breathes on her own and can move her limbs on command . . .[7]

---

5. For the autopsy report, see http://fl1.findlaw.com/news.findlaw.com/hdocs/docs/schiavo/61305autopsyrpt.pdf.

6. 151 Cong. Rec. at H1725, cited in George Annas, "'I Want to Live': Medicine Betrayed by Ideology in the Political Debate over Terri Schiavo," *Stetson Law Review* 35/1 (Fall 2005): 61.

7. See Annas, "I Want to Live," 62.

These emotional pleas defied years of court evidence. As a recent study shows, the *Schiavo* case produced the highest quality evidence and judicial review of any end-of-life guardianship case in U.S. history. Furthermore, far from being unusual, the manner and decision in which the case was made "reflected a broad medical, legal, and ethical consensus."[8]

While space limitations prohibit further analysis here, it should be evident that theological assumptions about the meaning of human sanctity drove the *Schiavo* case to be politicized almost beyond coherence. This played more into the *political* agenda of the "Christian right" than serving any clarifying purpose about end-of-life decision-making. Generally, the impression was consciously spread that Terri was being killed at the hands of a heartless judiciary system and rogue doctors supporting a rogue husband. As the saying goes, perception is two-thirds of reality. Yet the reality is that Terri Schiavo's brain was not impaired. It was, as the autopsy showed, absent. To call her "disabled" is like calling the hurricane-force winds and rain of Katrina "precipitation." Technically it is, but the difference is so drastic in degree that it is different *in kind*.[9]

Many Christians have merely assumed that the public portrayal of "the Christian Right" was normative, and that Christianity would unilaterally oppose allowing Schiavo to die. Yet, as this essay shows, the decision to allow her to die is theologically well grounded in Christian tradition and ethics. First, what is it about PVS that makes such an action feasible?

---

8. Joshua E. Perry, Larry R. Churchill, and Howard S. Kirshner, "The Terri Schiavo Case: Legal, Ethical, and Medical Perspectives," *Annals of Internal Medicine* 143/10 (November 15, 2005) 744–48.

9. Dissenters often claim that since recoveries have been reported, we should not give up. But the evidence for such recoveries is slim, indeed. Most have been false claims, misdiagnosis, or not verifiable. Medically verifiable "recoveries" of PVS patients are rare. Only eleven have been reported through the study of the Multi-Society Task Force on PVS, the world's authoritative study that includes all English-speaking medical literature. The term "recovery" should be considered carefully. All of these patients remained severely disabled. In many cases the situation became worse, since patients began to feel pain and intense suffering physically and emotionally. See Bryan Jennett, *The Vegetative State: Medical Facts, Ethical and Legal Dilemmas* (Cambridge: Cambridge University Press, 2002), 57–71.

WHAT IS PERSISTENT VEGETATIVE STATE?

Persistent Vegetative State is a diagnosis that doctors use to represent the most severe of three medical diagnoses:

1. "The vegetative state" refers to the condition soon after insult to the brain.
2. "The continuing vegetative state" refers to the condition that has lasted more than four weeks.
3. "The persistent vegetative state" represents a diagnosis that is considered irreversible.

These three types of vegetative state *must not be confused with coma or minimally conscious state patients.*[10]

The terms "vegetative" and "persistent" have been questioned. The Pro-Life Committee of Catholic Bishops in the U.S. expressed concern that the word "vegetative" could suggest that the patient is subhuman and is therefore demeaning. Pope John Paul II firmly restated that concern in his statements to the World Federation of Catholic Medical Associations and Pontifical Academy for Life Congress in 2004.[11] As the authors of the term have argued, however, the term "vegetative" is not obscure and is descriptive of the patient's medical condition, not their status as a human being. It reflects a physical life, devoid of intellectual activity or social intercourse, "an organic body capable of growth and development but devoid of sensation and thought."[12] Since the early-1970s, its authors have suggested that a more accurate description would be *permanent*, as opposed to "persistent," reflecting the irreversible nature of PVS. The term "persistent," however, retains common usage as reference to PVS.[13]

The medical diagnosis of PVS is therefore very specific to a set of criteria. It reflects a diagnosis in which a patient's upper brain functions

---

10. See Jennett, *The Vegetative State*, 2–3. As Jennett's study states (p. 28), after three to six months, medical research shows a dramatic consistency in diagnosis and prognosis.

11. Committee for Pro-Life Activities of the National Conference of Catholic Bishops, "Nutrition and Hydration: Moral and Pastoral Reflections," 1991, 6 (1), United States Conference of Catholic Bishops: http://www.usccb.org/prolife/issues/euthanas/nutqa.shtml (accessed January 8, 2007); Pope John Paul II, "Life-Sustaining Treatments, section 4."

12. Jennett, *The Vegetative State*, 4.

13. Ibid., 5.

are no longer present but the functions of the lower brain, the brain stem, are intact. Thus, patients in PVS perceive neither themselves nor their surroundings. They are unconscious. Complex functions such as sensory perception, motor commands, spatial reasoning, conscious thought, and language are absent. From a neurological standpoint, they do not experience pain, suffering, or cognition. While the "higher" brain functions of a PVS patient have been irreversibly damaged, the "lower," involuntary biological functions controlled by the hypothalamus and brain stem continue, preserving respiration and circulation. Connected to the spinal cord, primitive responses to external stimuli survive and there is some preservation of autonomic regulation of the body.[14] The patient will have sleep-wake cycles, with their eyes opening and closing. They may smile, grimace, or display roving eye movements. They may track moving objects. They may turn reflexively if a loud noise is made. For loved ones and the lay observer, these traits can easily mislead them into thinking that the person is conscious or aware of their presence.[15]

The definition of death within medical science currently rests on what is known as "whole brain death." This means that both the cerebral cortex and brain stem must cease functioning permanently in order for brain death to be declared.[16] If the brain stem continues to function, by medical standards a PVS patient such as Terri Schiavo is technically (and technologically) still alive. Yet a re-reading of the U.S. politicians with medical backgrounds shows how misinformed their statements were about both her condition and the removal of her PEG tube.

---

14. Ronald Cranford, "Patients with Permanent Loss of Consciousness," in *By No Extraordinary Means: The Choice to Forgo Life-Sustaining Food and Water* (ed. Joanne Lynn; Bloomington: Indiana University Press, 1989), 187. See also Jennett, *The Vegetative State*, 4.

15. Jennett, *The Vegetative State*, 7–32. These criteria for diagnosis have been established in multiple studies by the American Neurological Association and The Multi-Society Task Force on PVS, representing five American professional bodies. The Royal College of Physicians in London and the Japanese Neurosurgical Society have also produced similar sets of criteria. References to these studies can be found in Jennett, *The Vegetative State*.

16. President's Commission, "Defining Death: Medical, Legal, and Ethical Issues in the Determination of Death," *President's Commission for the Study of Ethical Problems in Medicine and Biomedical and Behavioral Research* (ed. Morris Abram; Washington, DC: U.S. Government Printing Office, 1981): http://www.bioethics.gov/reports/past_commissions/defining_death.pdf.

RELIGION IN END OF LIFE CASES

How do theological beliefs about life and death figure into the picture? Ironically, in the first landmark cases, the theological beliefs of the families affected and Christian leaders advising them led them *not to seek the continuation of treatment but for the removal of life support*. This theological orientation preceded social norms at the time, since removal of any measure keeping a person alive was considered a crime punishable with the charge of homicide.

Religious belief played a crucial role in the 1976 case of Karen Ann Quinlan, the first person for whom a respirator was removed. Ten years later, Paul Brophy became the first person from whom a PEG tube was also withdrawn. These cases set the stage for how other cases of PVS patients were dealt with, especially that of Anthony Bland in Great Britain, in which the British court dealt directly with the substance of the theological concept of "sanctity of life." This case will be dealt with in the context of that discussion below.[17]

Karen Ann Quinlan

Karen Ann Quinlan was a twenty-one-year-old who in 1975 was found unconscious in bed at a friend's home. After five months, the Supreme Court of New Jersey granted Joseph Quinlan's request that the respirator be removed. The *Quinlan* decision became the landmark case to which others inside and outside of the U.S. would turn for direction.[18]

Theological convictions and conscience functioned at the very core of making this decision—not for the court, but for Karen's parents, Joe and Julia Quinlan. The court record testifies to the high degree of familial love that pervaded the Quinlans' home. They were deeply religious Roman Catholics. The court notes testimony that Joe spent months of "tortured indecision" because of his sense of Christian moral conviction. He first sought solace in private prayer, asking God to grant Karen recovery, but if that were not possible, guidance with respect to the deci-

---

17 The *Bland* case was the first of its kind in Great Britain. Bland's medical condition was PVS for over three years, with all the symptoms described for such a diagnosis. In contrast to Schiavo, his feeding was by nasogastric instead of a PEG tube, and he was also on a respirator. His cerebral cortex is described as having "resolved into a watery mass," as was Schiavo's. *Airdale N.H.S. v Bland*, 2 WLR 316 (1993), cited in http://www.swarb.co.uk/c/hl/1993airedale_bland.html.

18 *In re Quinlan*, 70 N.J. 10, 355 A.2d 647 (1976).

sion of what the right thing to do would be in the context of his faith in God.[19] Joe consulted with his parish priest and later with the Catholic chaplain of the hospital to seek moral advice about what to do. The court accepted *Amicus curiae* (a supporting document representing someone who is not party to the case but may have a vested interest in the decision) from the New Jersey Catholic Conference, speaking for the bishops of New Jersey. The Conference findings were:

1. Verification of the fact of death or of Karen Ann's medical diagnosis cannot be deduced from any religious or moral principle, and is outside the competence of the church. On these points, the church must be dependent upon medical standards. By these medical standards, the church considers Karen Ann Quinlan to be alive.

2. The medical procedure is characterized as "an extraordinary means of treatment" and the request of the Quinlans to terminate this treatment would therefore not constitute euthanasia. In other words, it would not be an act of killing Karen Ann. The bishops cited Pope Pius XII in support of the idea that use of an artificial respiration apparatus constitutes extraordinary means of preserving life, and families are bound only to the use of ordinary means of support.[20]

The New Jersey Supreme Court concluded that from the perspective of the Catholic Church, "The continuance of mechanical supportive measures to sustain continuation of [Karen Ann's] body functions and her life constitute extraordinary means of treatment. *Therefore, the decision of Joseph Quinlan to request the discontinuance of this treatment is, according to the teachings of the Catholic Church, a morally correct decision.*"[21] As Joseph Quinlan stated, "my experience and my faith are one. I cannot separate the two."[22]

---

19. Ibid., at 658.
20. Ibid., at 658.
21. Ibid., at 659 (emphasis in original).
22. University of Minnesota, *Joseph Quinlan Speaks about Karen Ann*, Managing Mortality: Ethics, Euthanasia, and the Termination of Treatment (Hotel Sofitel: Center of Bioethics, University of Minnesota, December 3–5, 1992).

Paul Brophy

A forty-seven-year-old former fire-fighter and emergency medical technician in Massachusetts, Paul Brophy, suffered hemorrhage from a basilar artery aneurysm in March 1983, leaving him in PVS. In February 1985, the Probate court heard Patricia Brophy's request to withdraw the PEG tube. Unlike Quinlan, Paul Brophy had made several explicit statements regarding his wishes after seeing people he rescued linger on life support. The judge accepted Brophy's statements as clear evidence showing that he would have refused artificial feeding. The family, consisting of seven brothers and sisters and five adult children, unanimously agreed. Despite this, however, the Probate judge concluded that the PEG tube was in no way burdensome, and that state interest in preserving life outweighed Brophy's right to choose his own treatment: "The proper focus should be on the quality of treatment . . . furnished to Brophy, and not on the quality of Brophy's life."[23] Further, the judge found that the feeding tube was not invasive, since according to testimony it did not make Brophy physically uncomfortable. The judge also noted that its withdrawal would not relieve burden, but cause Brophy's death, which was not otherwise imminent. Such an action would be tantamount to euthanasia, he concluded. Despite accepting the evidence that Brophy could not feel pain, the judge said that removal of the PEG tube would result in a "cruel and violent death of slow dehydration."[24]

The Supreme Court of Massachusetts reversed the Probate judge's decision in September 1986. The Supreme Court Justices spoke directly to each of the claims made by the Probate judge. Several important points are instructive for our purposes:

1. *Medical evidence shows that people in PVS do not feel pain.* Thus, graphic descriptions that Paul Brophy would die a cruel and painful death by starvation and dehydration are incorrect.

2. *A feeding tube is invasive and not an ordinary means of nutrition.* It is a medical treatment like other invasive and artificial aspects of medical care. The court opinion found:

   > . . . to state that the maintenance of nutrition and hydration by the use of the existing G-tube is only ordinary is to ignore

---

23. *Brophy vs. New England Sinai Hospital, Inc.*, 398 Mass. 417, 497 N.E.2d 626, 444–48 (1986).

24. Ibid., at 444.

the total circumstances of Brophy's situation. He cannot swallow. The judge found that Brophy may be maintained by the use of the G-tube for "several years," the longest recorded survival by such means extending for thirty-seven years. Clearly, to be maintained by such artificial means over an extended period is not only intrusive but extraordinary.[25]

3. *Removal of the PEG tube from a PVS patient is not the cause of death.* Death occurs from the underlying condition that put him in this situation. Accusations of euthanasia or suicide are inappropriate.[26]

These points should be instructive to Christians attempting to understand the complexities of making a responsible decision in such a case. The Massachusetts Supreme Court reflects the sobering but accurate medical data regarding PVS patients and their prospects. It also reflects pertinent legal orientations toward such cases.

Also significant is the role of Patricia Brophy's Christian faith in making her decision about what to do. Again, as a devout Roman Catholic, Patricia immediately sought help from prayer, asking for help and guidance. She made her decision to remove Paul's PEG tube with the counsel of her priest. She turned to scripture daily, finding Rom 8:28 and Mic 6:8 especially helpful. For these reasons, Patricia was taken by surprise when "pro-life" forces showed up and harshly condemned her. Accusations were made that she was trying to kill Paul.[27] Patricia's reasoning also came out of her Christian faith. She asked, "What moral obligation does Paul have to live like this? The so called 'pro-life' groups are not for Paul. They fight their cause and Paul is left out."[28]

HOW SHALL WE DIE?

The purpose of reviewing these cases is to remind us that the hard choices that faced the Schiavo and Schindler families are not new. The *Schiavo* case had a history in medicine and law, not only in the U.S. but in most

25. Ibid., at 437.

26. Ibid., at 439.

27. University of Minnesota, *Patricia Brophy Speaks about Paul*, Managing Mortality: Ethics, Euthanasia, and the Termination of Treatment (Hotel Sofitel: Center of Bioethics, University of Minnesota, December 3–5, 1992).

28. *Patricia Brophy Speaks about Paul.*

of the developed world. The Quinlans and Brophys broke new ground, and in doing so they relied not only on medical data but on their faith. Christian leaders and theologians sought to reflect the best of Christian tradition and logic, concluding that the best moral choice would be the removal of life support. But with Schiavo all this unraveled.

What can these landmark cases teach us about theological basics regarding end-of-life decision-making? If we give proper respect to scripture, experience, tradition and reason, what "landmark" theological issues need addressing? I would suggest it is time for Christians to give sober consideration to these issues *not in abstraction but in correlation with the realities of our world*. Given our current state of affairs in relation to the medicalization of death, we need a theological primer of sorts. Once again, Christians need to address the issues of what medieval Christianity called *ars moriendi*, "the art of dying," but for different reasons than they had. Their context was the reality of a lack of life-saving treatments and technologies. Life expectancy was barely thirty years, and Christianity responded to the constant fear of succumbing to illnesses leading to death. Yet, even where medical technologies are available, our situation is more similar to medieval Christianity than we would like. We, too, live with the possibility of staring death in the face daily, not because of the lack of medical advancements but because of them. What we fear now is not so much death but a living death—a death that cannot be attained, held just beyond reach by modern medicine.

"SACREDNESS OF LIFE"

The concept that life is sacred (also called the sanctity of life principle) is not a medical or legal concept. It is distinctly *theological* in nature and content. It stood center-stage for the Schindlers in their efforts to stop removal of the PEG tube. Not surprisingly, "sacredness of life" is at the heart of the "pro-life" movement, which understands the *Schiavo* case as the *Roe v. Wade* of euthanasia.

Because "all life is sacred," argued the Schindlers, medical treatment should be administered until the patient dies with medical treatment in place. They would therefore keep Terri alive "at any and all costs." In court, hypothetical examples were given to which the Schindler family agreed. If Terri should contract diabetes and subsequent gangrene in each of her limbs, the parents agreed that they would amputate each limb if necessary. If diagnosed with heart disease, they would order open-heart surgery. This theological ideology extended to the Schindlers' refusal to stop treatment if Terri were to wake up and tell them of her intention to withdraw artificial nutrition.[29]

The Schindlers are certainly entitled to their theological views. The problem comes, however, when this understanding of the sanctity of life is touted as *the* Christian belief. Public statements about what sanctity of life means have been loudest from people such as Randall Terry, Paul Schenck, and, most influential politically, James Dobson. Terry was the official spokesperson for the Schindler family, and Schenck was interviewed on television, arguing that this view is normative for Christianity. Terry's statement is typical: "any life remaining at all, it must be protected, no matter how conscious, compromised, or debilitated that person is."[30]

Yet making the statement, "life is sacred," the basis for preservation of any form of life to any extent or cost has many problems theologically. To begin with, the statement refers to *human* life alone. Its proponents do not regard animals, the earth, or nature as sacred. Yet when it comes to human life, they must qualify the limits of sanctity. Not *all* human life is sacred. Those holding this position are not usually pacifists. They tend to condone capital punishment, the war in Iraq, and violence against clinics and doctors performing abortions. Terry has called for the deaths of abortion doctors.

Another problem is that proponents claim that sacredness of life is supported as a major concept in the Bible. This claim lacks evidence. Even the casual reader of the Bible encounters just the opposite. Life is cheap in many of the biblical stories. Concepts of human sacredness (holiness) in the Bible correctly focus on one's devotion and loyalty to God. The emphasis is not on elevation of the quantitative worth of one's biological existence or the holiness of the flesh. The biblical impulse does not encourage us to ask, "What are we willing to live for?" but rather, "What are we willing to *die* for?"

Many who assume that the concept is straightforwardly in the Bible claim to read it literally and therefore point to particular verses that

29. Jay Wolfson, "A Report to Governor Jeb Bush and the 6th Judicial Circuit in the Matter of Theresa Marie Schiavo," December 1, 2003, 1–38: http://abstractappeal.com/schiavo/WolfsonReport.pdf (accessed December 1, 2007). During the Guardian *ad litem*'s investigation, the Schindlers retracted these intentions.

30. Cited in John A. Robertson, "Schiavo and Its (In)Significance," *Stetson Law Review* 35/1 (Fall 2005): 113. This emphasis can be found in many places in "pro-life" materials and is articulated as if it represents unilaterally the *only* Christian position.

they think state that life is sacred for its own sake. Passages such as Gen 1:27–28; Exod 20:13; Ps 139:13–16; Prov 24:10–12, 31:8; and Eccl 3:1–3 are central, along with a myriad of others. Yet in any text the concept of sacredness must be developed *theologically*. Human sacredness is not the basis for the sanction against killing (Exod 20:13) nor the result of being created in the image of God (Gen 1:27–28). We may certainly make a theological case for human sanctity from scripture (and while pro-life proponents reject it, also for nature), but we must do some very hard work theologically to extrapolate *what that means*. One of the affirmations of this essay is that the church needs to begin this task in earnest, with transparency, instead of defending abstractions. The "pro-life" view of the sacredness of life is not so much biblical as indicative of an anthropocentrism reflecting a biological idolatry.

One of the main arguments for an absolutist view of human sanctity is that we are created in "the image of God" (*imago dei*). Because we are created in God's image, we have a moral obligation to preserve life at all costs. Commonly connected to this idea is the human "soul," assumedly present as long as there is life. Paul Schenck of the National Pro-Life Action Center is representative of this view when speaking about Terri's condition: "A person is alive when their soul is united to their body. And the evidence of this is the physical and natural breath. As long as the breath is in the body and the person is breathing, their soul is united to their body and they are a full person."[31]

In fact, the history of Christian theology is replete with intellectual giants struggling over what exactly the image of God or soul is. One thing is clear: the theological concept that the *imago dei* corresponds to mere human existence does not occur amongst them. Christian thinkers up to Aquinas associated it with human reason. Augustine interpreted the image of God as the "powers of the soul," specifically found in memory, mind, and will. His work deeply influenced the thought of Aquinas, Luther and Calvin, all of whom located the *imago dei* substantively in one way or another, but ultimately tied to the human intellect.

Karl Barth made a major theological shift when he interpreted the *imago dei* relationally. The image of God is not something that we possess or that can be located in the body. Rather, it consists of the

---

31. "CNN Sunday Morning," Interview with Paul Schenck and John Shelby Spong: http://transcripts.cnn.com/TRANSCRIPTS/0503/27/sm.01.html (accessed June 15, 2007).

human ability of relationship with God and subsequently with each other, profoundly resonating in the inseparable relationship between male and female.[32] Jürgen Moltmann has extended Barth's relational model by emphasizing the relationship of persons within community. We reflect God's image by imaging Christ in the community of faith until we reach our full destiny with God.[33] In a similar vein, Wolfhart Pannenberg finds the *imago dei* in what he calls human "exocentricity," or the ability to transform relational constructions into new ones. Our relational uniqueness as humans is not limited to our present relationships, therefore, but is also characterized by what Pannenberg calls an "openness to the world" (*Weltoffenheit*). We humans reach beyond everything we experience in the world in order to find meaning and fulfillment. *Imago dei* is that aspect of our exocentricity that shapes our destiny toward God. It is an intrinsic part of our lives now but is only fully realized in the future in our final destiny with God.[34]

None of these major theologians understands *imago dei* or the concept of soul as separately existing entities, physical or non-physical.[35] Rather, the concept of the soul represents characteristics and potentialities that allow for interpersonal relationships. Moltmann is instructive when he notes the profound difference between an individual and a person, and the difference is radically affected by the variable of freedom. An individual who is totally without the capability or potential of

---

32. Karl Barth, *Church Dogmatics*, III/1: *The Doctrine of Creation* (trans. J. W. Edwards, O. Bussey, and H. Knight; Edinburgh: T. & T. Clark, 1958), 186ff; *Church Dogmatics*, III/2: *The Doctrine of Creation* (trans. H. Knight, G. W. Bromiley, and J. K. S. Reid; Edinburgh: T&T Clark, 1960), 77; 323–24.

33. Jürgen Moltmann, *God in Creation: An Ecological Doctrine of Creation* (trans. Margaret Kohl; London: SCM Press, 1985), 215–43.

34. Wolfhart Pannenberg, *What Is Man? Contemporary Anthropology in Theological Perspective* (trans. Duane Priebe; Philadelphia: Fortress Press, 1970), 7–8; *Anthropology in Theological Perspective* (trans. Matthew J. O'Connell; Philadelphia: Westminster Press, 1985), 63–74; *Systematic Theology*, Vol. II (trans. Geoffrey W. Bromiley; Grand Rapids: Eerdmans, 1994), 218–31. These are only a cursory sample of important theological interpretations. For a fuller study, see J. Wentzel van Huyssteen, *Alone in the World? Human Uniqueness in Science and Theology* (Grand Rapids: Eerdmans, 2006), 111–62.

35. Schenck's connection between the soul and breath should logically insist that if breathing stops, no human intervention with a machine should interrupt a profound divine decision to stop this connection.

freedom to form relationships with others cannot maintain his or her personhood.³⁶ It is not something one has but a capacity one enacts.

Finally, to say, as an abstract statement, that human life is sacred begs the question in today's world. It already assumes that one knows *what kind* of life it is that should be treated as sacred. Is mere existence life? In the end, the modern theological concept of sanctity of life must also include discussion about quality of life. This is no longer an either/or choice of pitting one against the other, with a stance for "sanctity" being conservative, biblical, and Christian, while a stance for "quality" is liberal, secularist, and pagan.³⁷ Mere living is not life anymore. We have now a new reality of human existence that is a medical and biological *fact*, and that fact makes it necessary for Christians to reshape the theological meaning of life and death. Today, the question is no longer, "When does death occur?" but "When should we allow biological existence to end?" This leads us to consider further the theological aspects of how we should respect life, the process of dying, and death itself.

RESPECTING, NOT WORSHIPING, LIFE

Going far beyond the U.S.A., the *Anthony Bland* case of a PVS patient in Great Britain directly addressed the "sanctity of life" as a principle.³⁸ The British court viewed sanctity of human life as a principle that has long been recognized as part of human rights conventions in the modern world. Yet, argued Lord Goff, "this principle, fundamental though it is, is not absolute."³⁹ Other considerations may trump the sanctity principle,

---

36. Jürgen Moltmann, *God for a Secular Society: The Public Relevance of Theology* (trans. Margaret Kohl; Minneapolis: Fortress, 1999), 156–57.

37. This is a dichotomy that both "pro-life" forces and pro-euthanasia philosophers such as Peter Singer make. But, as already seen, Christian theology rightly did not traditionally make such an either/or choice of values.

38. See note 17 above for a brief description. The *Baby "K"* case in Virginia later the same year (1993) included the mother's views that all life is sacred as part of their decision, but they did not deal with the "sanctity of life" in substance. Rather, they honored the mother's religious views as something against which Virginia law should not intervene, under the freedom of religious expression. The *Bland* case is substantially different in this regard. *In the Matter of Baby K*, 832 F.Supp. 1022 (1993).

39. *Airdale N.H.S. Trust v. Bland* [1993] 2 WLR 316, 5. See http://www.swarb.co.uk/c/hl/1993airedale_bland.html. Page numbers are from the online version, not the official court record.

for example, self-determination and the duty to act in the best interests of the patient. Lord Keith gives specific examples:

> The principle is not an absolute one. It does not compel a medical practitioner on pain of criminal sanctions to treat a patient, who will die if he does not, contrary to the express wishes of the patient. It does not authorise forcible feeding of prisoners on hunger strike. It does not compel the temporary keeping alive of patients who are terminally ill where to do so would merely prolong their suffering. On the other hand it forbids the taking of active measures to cut short the life of a terminally ill patient. In my judgment it does no violence to the principle to hold that it is lawful to cease to give medical treatment and care to a P.V.S. patient who has been in that state for over three years, considering that to do so involves invasive manipulation of the patient's body to which he has not consented and which confers no benefit upon him.[40]

The court crafted a careful line between allowing Bland to die peacefully and appearing to validate suicide or euthanasia. Some philosophers, such as Peter Singer, have tried to use this court decision to argue that the principle of sanctity of life is antiquated and that no distinction really exists between allowing dying and actively killing someone.[41] Even if this can be argued philosophically, in medicine and theology the distinction holds great weight. PVS patients should be allowed to die peacefully not because human life is less sacred now, but *because* of the sanctity of life *and* death. Further, arguments premised on the view that since the end result is the same—death—the difference is morally indistinguishable are questionable. Such distinctions occur all the time in reasoning about the validity of ethical choices.[42] Why attempt to disregard the crucial distinction here?[43]

---

40. *Bland*, 2 WLR at 3.

41. Peter Singer, *Rethinking Life and Death: The Collapse of Our Traditional Ethics* (New York: St. Martin's Press, 1994), 57–80. Singer points to the *Bland* case as the moment when the "old ethics" of Judeo-Christian values happily gave way. As we show above, this is simply not the case. Singer merely uses the case to declare as much.

42. For example, distinctions are made between killing and murder, starving and dying of hunger strike, and so on.

43. On this distinction and its importance in medicine, see especially Paul Ramsey, *The Patient as Person: Explorations in Medical Ethics* (New Haven: Yale University Press, 2002), 118–32.

Theologically, the sanctity of life is not an absolute that can be opposed to quality of life but *includes* quality concerns as essential to it. To preserve life for life's sake alone by any and all means available without concern for the quality of life is not a normative Christian view, historically or theologically. In 1587, the pre-eminent Spanish theologian Francisco di Vittoria delivered a yearly lecture to students in which he grappled with a contemporary ethical dilemma. Even then, prolonging life was already an issue. Vittoria delivered the following instructions:

> If a sick man can take food or nourishment with a certain hope of life, he is required to take food as he would be required to give it to one who is sick. However, if the depression of spirits is so severe and there is present grave consternation in the appetitive power so that only with the greatest effort and as though through torture can the sick man take food, this is to be reckoned as an impossibility and therefore, he is excused, at least from mortal sin.[44]

On using artificial means, namely drugs, to prolong life: "If one has moral certitude that drugs would heal and prolong life, then one should take the drugs himself or give them to a sick neighbor. If he does not, he would not be excused from mortal sin. But because a cure can seldom be certain, one need not utilize drugs even though very ill."[45] And regarding the withholding of specific foods, even if death would result, Vittoria maintained:

> It is one thing not to protect life and it is another not to destroy it. One is not held to protect his life as much as he can ... If one uses food which men commonly use and in quantity which customarily suffices for the preservation of strength, even though one's life is shortened considerably, one would not sin. One is not held to employ all means to conserve life but it is sufficient to employ the means which are intended for this purpose and which are congruous.[46]

---

44. Francisco di Vittoria, "Relectio IX; de Temperentia," *Relectiones Theologicia* (1587). Cf. *Relecciones Teologicas*, Vol. III, edition critica (Madrid: Imprenta La Rafa, 1933–35), cited in Kevin D. O'Rourke, "Development of Church Teaching on Prolonging Life," *Health Progress* (January–February 1988) 2. This extremely helpful article can be found online at http://www.domcentral.org/study/kor/korlife.htm.

45. Di Vittoria, "Relectio IX; de Temperentia."

46. Ibid.

So we see that already in the sixteenth century, Christianity was dealing with ethical issues about not prolonging life beyond benefit by feeding, artificial treatment, or eating special foods designed to extend life. In other words, prolonging life merely because it existed was not regarded as a Christian obligation.

This historic theological orientation continued into the modern era in mainstream Catholic and Protestant teaching alike. Its importance resurfaced when medical technologies brought difficult choices to the Quinlan and Brophy families. By then, Pope Pius XII had gone on record supporting considerations as to whether a treatment is effective for improving the condition of a patient or not.[47] Treatment without benefit was not obligatory. That is why the statements made by Pope John Paul II shocked most Catholic ethicists and health care professionals. In his speech the Pope stated: "[T]he administration of food and water, even when provided by artificial means, always represents a natural means of preserving life, not a medical act," and that it "should be considered, in principle, ordinary and proportionate, and as such morally obligatory." Withdrawing nutrition and hydration is therefore, he said, "true and proper euthanasia by omission."[48]

These statements stand in contradiction to the approach that had been developing since the sixteenth century. As early as 1996, John Paul II had embraced the four-hundred-year tradition. He separated euthanasia from decisions to forgo aggressive measures that are disproportionate to any expected results or are an excessive burden to the patient. Although his later speech at the conference (see note 2 above), an "allocution," ranks much lower than an encyclical, opponents of feeding tube removal have jumped on the Pope's remarks. Further, Pope Benedict XVI has announced that a new papal document on bioethical issues is being developed. If he heightens the level of this new stance to *ex cathedra*, a major shift in Catholic doctrine will have occurred and medical care will change dramatically.

For John Paul II to declare that a PEG tube is not a medical but an ordinary (natural) means of nutrition defies reason and medical fact,

---

47. Pope Pius XII, "Prolongation of Life," in *The Pope Speaks*, Vol. 44 (Congregation for the Doctrine of Faith, 1958), 343, cited in O'Rourke, "Development of Church Teaching on Prolonging Life," 4. Also helpful is Thomas A. Nairn, "Reclaiming Our Moral Tradition," *Health Progress* 78/6 (November–December 1997) 1–4.

48. Pope John Paul II, "Life-Sustaining Treatments," sec. 4.

as already pointed out. Theologians should be cautious about defining *medical* procedures as "ordinary care." Theology makes bad medicine. In a 1999 review, Michael Gauderer, one of the developers of the PEG procedure, expressed his concern that its use might raise unrealistic expectations, adding to the lingering signs of life of hopeless patients. He warned that its use should be controlled by demonstration that it truly benefits the patient to some appropriate medical goal. In no way is PEG intervention considered "basic healthcare that should never be denied to any patient."[49] A theological view, given by the Pope or by anyone else, should not attempt to redefine medical procedure. I doubt if the same logic would be applied to medically developed measures of contraception. Surely, if a PEG tube is a "natural" means to preserve life, then medically developed means to prevent life could also be seen as "natural"?

Karl Barth provides an appropriate theological starting point for reflection about proper respect for human life. His theology entails not only a deep respect for human life but also his own struggle to resolve such hard choices because of medical technology. He concludes that exceptions need to be made regarding prolongation of life. His theological focus remains clear: "Life is no second God, and therefore the respect due to it cannot rival the reverence owed to God."[50] To hold onto and maintain the biological functions of a moribund individual where there are no possibilities for improvement, no relationship remotely possible, no consciousness or self-awareness evident, nor any treatment that benefits beyond mere existence is not only medically unwarranted but also theologically unwarranted. The question of quality of life is an unavoidable element in shaping a humane dying process in our world today.[51] Theologically speaking, when life is preserved solely as an end in itself, so that quality of life is ignored, the result is an idolatry grounded in human arrogance.

---

49. Floyd Angus and Robert Brakoff, "The Percutaneous Endoscopic Gastrostomy Tube: Medical and Ethical Issues in Placement," *The American Journal of Gastroenterology* 98 (2003) 272–74.

50. Karl Barth, *Church Dogmatics*, III/4: *The Doctrine of Creation* (trans. A. T. McKay et al.; Edinburgh: T. & T. Clark, 1961), 342. Barth wrestles with the issue of prolongation of life. He calls both arbitrary euthanasia and arbitrary prolongation "human arrogance" (see esp. 423, 425, and 427).

51. Norman Cantor, "Déjà Vu All Over Again: The False Dichotomy between Sanctity of Life and Quality of Life," *Stetson Law Review* 35/1 (Fall 2005) 81–100.

A THEOLOGY OF PERMANENT EXILE OR OF RESURRECTION?

From a biblical, theological, and experiential perspective, what should function as the guiding light that shapes Christian attitudes toward living and dying? I suggest it is resurrection. The alternative, to defend the preservation of the last remnant of an individual—the physical, genetic composition contained in a body, is to argue for a "theology of permanent exile." Medicine speaks of PVS as being vegetative. The theological symbol for this tragic condition is exile from which there is no return. Artificially maintaining such a state is not defending innocent life but prolonging the delay of genetic death. The *person*, a psychological and theological concept, is already gone. The *individual* remains.[52]

Christianity has historically met dying and death with a theology of resurrection. This theological impulse understands that human biological life, while an essential part of our faith, *does not dictate its terms*. Ours is an embodied faith, not faith in the body. Resurrection faith takes death seriously, but death is not given ultimate standing against which we fight. It is the last enemy that has already been defeated by the resurrection of Christ. Thus we need not deny the reality of death and its impact of grief and sorrow.[53] Nor do we need to fend it off endlessly, grasping to keep any shred of life.

A theology of resurrection rejects permanent exile as a desirable fate and lives with the promise and confidence that God is always *with* us and *for* us, that the resurrection of Christ means that our destiny is tied to nothing less than *God*.[54] "Christian faith does not simply abolish fear of death and hatred of death," Eberhard Jüngel argues, "rather it takes away both the fear of death and the hatred of death arising from that fear, the blindness we have from death . . . It teaches us to understand

---

52. Barth, *Church Dogmatics*, III/4: *The Doctrine of Creation*, 327–33, speaks at length about seven features of personhood. One wonders why those who demand a theology of permanent exile stop at the point of whole-brain death. Why do they not demand cellular death? For after whole-brain death, "life" is still present in the cellular structures of the body.

53. Essential reading on this is Ernest Becker, *The Denial of Death* (New York: Free Press, 1973), who argues that humans live out of a universal refusal to acknowledge our mortality and develop culture to deny death its reality.

54. Thorwald Lorenzen, *Resurrection and Discipleship: Interpretive Models, Biblical Reflections, Theological Consequences* (Maryknoll, NY: Orbis, 1995), 248–95, esp. 255–59.

death. It illuminates death in the light of the gospel. Thus it brings light also into the darkness of death."[55] This is the theology of resurrection that must remain at the core of Christian faith.

Christian theology must think about the medical preservation of human life beyond absolutist, individualistic concepts. Christian sacredness is not about preserving biological functions at all costs but about how we can make our human lives holy. Christian sacredness must be *embodied*, to be sure, but the prolongation of fleshly existence is not its goal. Our sacredness is inter-relational and multidimensional. It is not mere flesh (*sarx*), which is one-dimensional, but "body" (*soma*), the concept St. Paul uses to speak about our transfigured nature in resurrection. The flesh is not the center of importance, but our integrated Self is woven into a new existence with nature and the cosmos as part of God's future. Medical "hope" concentrates on survival, and often on "beating the odds." Resurrection hope transforms our living *and* our dying. We see our bodies as a means to enact God's purposes for a brief moment in history. We "present our bodies" to God (Rom 12:1). As in life, so also in death. As Martin Luther said somewhat crassly, resurrection hope leaves Satan holding only shells in his *Nussknacker*.

Christian theology must also ask about issues of justice. Why is the medical maintenance of the biological functions of Terri and others like her seen as a necessity in technologically advanced parts of the world when it is not even an option elsewhere? Unless human life is more sacred in countries of wealth and privilege, Christians must extend the discussion to human beings who live in conditions that do not allow for such possibilities. One might wish that the President and Congress would rush back from vacation and stay up all night to pass legislation that would prevent 100,000 more civilians in Iraq or Darfur from dying. Even if we limit the question to rich countries, we must still face the wider issues of justice. As Fred Plum, one of the formative researchers into PVS, states, "We must some day face the brutal truth that the perpetual, demanded treatment of long term PVS patients is useless. It steals from the mouths of others who might have some hope."[56] The choice is not

---

55. Eberhard Jüngel, "Der Tod als Geheimnis des Lebens" (Munich, 1980), 338, cited in Hans Küng, *Ewiges Leben?* (Munich: Piper, 1984), 208 (my translation).

56. University of Minnesota, Managing Mortality: Ethics, Euthanasia, and the Termination of Treatment (Hotel Sofitel: Center of Bioethics, University of Minnesota, December 3–5, 1992).

simply a choice between an individual's life and death. We must reckon with the hard fact that others are dying because medical resources are busy maintaining PVS patients.

The three institutions constituting the social dynamics surrounding life and death are medicine, which maintains social understandings of good health, the law, responsible for maintaining good social order, and religion, which has functioned historically as the institution that watches over "good" dying. Entering this new millennium, these institutions overlap each other regarding end-of-life decision-making. Medicine, with advancing technology, is inclined to prolong biological life. Law, with obligations both to protect life and to the freedom of individual citizens, seeks to guarantee the rights of people to control their own lives within the boundaries of society's interest as a whole.[57] Theology, with its dissatisfaction with mere biological existence as the ultimate source of meaning, defends not only the sacredness of human life but also the sacredness of death. Sometimes death is the best that life has to offer, the moment when we return the gift of our life to God.

---

57. For a more extended treatment, see Dixon Sutherland and Rebecca Morgan, "Dying and Social Policy in the New Millennium," in *Advancing Aging Policy as the 21st Century Begins* (ed. Francis G. Caro, Robert Morris, and Jill R. Norton; Binghamton, NY: Haworth, 2000), 145–55.

Bibliography

Thorwald LORENZEN (Revd, Prof, Dr)

BOOKS

Der Lieblingsjünger im Johannesevangelium. Eine redaktionsgeschichtliche Studie. SBS 55. Stuttgart: KBW, 1971.

Resurrection and Discipleship: Interpretive Models, Biblical Reflections, Theological Consequences. Maryknoll, New York: Orbis, 1995. Reprint, Eugene, OR: Wipf & Stock, 2004.

Resurrección y discipulado. Modelos interpretativos, reflexiones bíblicas y consecuencias teológicas. Presencia Teológica 97. Santander: Sal Terrae, 1999.

Resurrection, Discipleship, Justice: Affirming the Resurrection of Jesus Christ Today. Macon, GA: Smyth & Helwys, 2003.

Toward a Culture of Freedom: Reflections on the Ten Commandments Today. Eugene, OR: Cascade Books, 2008.

BOOKLETS

Torture, a Moral Outrage: A Summons to Christian Action. Philadelphia: American Christians for the Abolition of Torture, 1984.

Baptists and Lutherans in Conversation: A Message to Our Churches. Report of the Joint Commission of the Baptist World Alliance and the Lutheran World Federation. Geneva, 1990. (Lorenzen was editor and chair of the Baptist representatives.)

Baptisten und Lutheraner im Gespräch. Eine Botschaft an unsere Kirchen/Gemeinden. Bericht der gemeinsamen Kommission des Baptistischen Weltbundes und des Lutherischen Weltbundes. Genf, 1990.

Die Kirche im zukünftigen Europa; The Church in a Changing Europe. Jugendseminar Impulse, Heft 11. Hamburg: Jugendseminar des Bundes Evangelisch-Freikirchlicher Gemeinden, 1990.

Auferweckung Jesu—Wahrheit und Wirklichkeit. Wiehler Herbstkonferenz, 1991 (2 Referate und 1 Predigt; 30 pages).

Freedom of Religion as a Human Right. EBF, 1995.

The Rights of the Child. Baptist Human Rights Booklet No. 2/1998. McLean, VA: Baptist World Alliance, 1999.

Freedom of Religion as a Human Right. Baptist Human Rights Booklet No. 3/1999. McLean, VA: Baptist World Alliance, 1999.

JOURNAL ARTICLES AND CHAPTERS
(*in chronological order*)

"Faith in the New Testament." *ANVIL* 2 (1970) 5–11.

"Ist der Auferstandene in Galiläa erschienen? Bemerkungen zu einem Aufsatz von B. Steinseifer." *ZNW* 64/3–4 (1973) 209–21.

"A Biblical Meditation on Luke 16:19–31: From the Text toward a Sermon." *ExpTim* 87 (1975) 39–43.

"Die Theologische Basis der Religionsfreiheit." *TZ* 33 (1977) 226–42.

"Ethical Problems and Christian Response." In *Towards A.D. 2000: Emerging Directions in Christian Ministry*, edited by John I. Durham, 57–70. Southeastern Studies 1. Wake Forest, NC: Southeastern Baptist Theological Seminary, 1977.

"Faith without Works Does Not Count before God! James 2:14–26." *ExpTim* 89 (1978) 231–35. In German: "Glaube ohne Werke zählt nicht vor Gott! Jakobus 2:14–26," *Theologisches Gespräch* (No. 5-6, 1978) 11–16, and also in *Der Gemeindebote* 57/5 (1979), Arbeitsblatt A.2.2.

"The Theological Basis for Religious Liberty: A Christian Perspective." *Journal of Church and State* 21 (1979) 415–30.

"Das Kind in der Gemeinde. Eine theologische Besinnung." *Der Gemeindebote* 56/11 (1979) 8–12, and 56/12 (1979) 5–8.

"Gott ist Liebe." *Der Gemeindebote* 57/9–11 (1979) 10–12 (in each number).

"Das Bekenntnis zum dreieinigen Gott." *Die Gemeinde* 2–4 (1980) 4–5 (in each number).

"Baptists and Ecumenicity with Special Reference to Baptism." *RevExp* 77 (1980) 21–45.

"Baptists and Ecumenicity with Special Reference to Baptism." *ER* 32 (1980) 257–73. (NB: This article is not the same as the previous article.)

"Baptism and Church Membership: Some Baptist Positions and Their Ecumenical Implications." *JES* 18 (1981) 561–74.

"Die Menschenrechte als Anfrage an die Kirche." *TG* 1–2 (1981) 1–14.

"Responsible Preaching." *SJT* 33 (1980) 453–69.

"'Evangelical' and 'Ecumenical': Alternative Approaches to a Theology of Mission?" *Foundations* 25 (1982) 45–66.

"Jesus Christ—The Hope of the World," *Baptist International Conference in Theological Education: Addresses and Papers*, 151–72. Washington, DC: Baptist World Alliance, 1982.

"A Baptist Response." In *Unity in Each Place— In All Places— : United Churches and the Christian World Communions*, edited by Michael Kinnamon, 25–34. Faith and Order Paper 118. Geneva: World Council of Churches, 1983.

"The Meaning of the Death of Jesus Christ." *ABQ* 4 (1985) 3–34; also in Japanese in *STR* 43 (1985) 85–126.

"Hebrews 7:1–10: God's Strong and Unconditional YES to US." In *The Way of Faith: Words of Admonition and Encouragement for the Journey, based on The Letter to the Hebrews*, edited by James M. Pitts, 81–92. Wake Forest, NC: Chanticleer, 1985.

"Theological Education between Church and World." *MF* 32 (December 1985) 11–26.

"Theologie und Menschenrechte. Kirchlich-theologische Zugänge zu den Menschenrechten," *Una Sancta* 41/1 (1986) 44–56.

"The Radicality of Grace: 'The Pharisee and the Tax Collector' (Luke 18:9–14) as a Parable of Jesus." *Faith and Mission* 3/2 (1986) 66–75.

"The Rights of the Child." Paper given at the EBF Evangelism and Education Conference in Rüschlikon, Switzerland, May 21–25, 1986.

"Die Rechte des Kindes." In *Gemeinde unterwegs* (Arbeitsblätter Januar [Teil 1] und Februar [Teil 2] 1987).

"Die christliche Hauskirche." *TZ* 43 (1987) 333–52.

"'Gerechtigkeit und Frieden küssen sich' (Psalm 85:11). Zur Theologie eines gerechten Friedens," *Initiative Schalom. Dokumentation Nr. 11.* Jahrestreffen der Initiative Schalom Baden-Württemberg, 10/11 September 1988, Reutlingen.

"The Rights of the Child: Introducing the *Draft Convention on the Rights of the Child*." Baptist World Alliance—Human Rights Commission, Zagreb, August 1989, *Journal of Study and Research* (1989) [no page numbers].

"Commission on Human Rights." In *Faith, Life and Witness: The Papers of the Study and Research Division of the Baptist World Alliance 1986–1990*, edited by William H. Brackney, with Ruby J. Burke, 241–43. Birmingham, AL: Samford University Press, 1990.

"Introduction: Human Rights and Baptists." *American Baptist Quarterly* 9/4 (December 1990) 198–204.

"Persecution in the Bible." In *Holman Bible Dictionary*, edited by Trent C. Butler, 1095–96. Nashville: Holman, 1991.

"Baptists and the Challenge of Religious Pluralism." *Review and Expositor* 89 (Winter 1992) 49–69.

"Die Glaubenstaufe—Ein Erfordernis für die Kirche? Baptistische Perspektiven." *Protokolldienst der Evangelischen Akademie Bad Boll* 32 (1992) 47–58 (nach einem Referat dort gehalten am 18. Okt. 1991); also in *Una Sancta* 48/1 (1993) 14–24.

"Freedom of Conscience as a Human Right: Freedom of Conscience as a Philosophical, Political and Social Concern Today." *Conscience and Liberty: International Journal of Religious Freedom* 4 (Winter 1992) 91–105. Originally delivered as a lecture, "Freedom of Conscience—Basis for Social Peace," as part of an international symposium at the University of Tirana, Albania, May 26–28, 1992.

"Resurrection and Discipleship." In *Festschrift Günter Wagner*, edited by the faculty of the Baptist Theological Seminary, Rüschlikon, Switzerland, 87–100. International Theological Studies 1. Bern: Lang, 1994.

"Christian Faith and Human Rights." *St Mark's Review* 156 (Summer 1994) 23–31; also in *ERT* 24 (2000) 63–76.

"Switzerland (German Speaking) (1847)." In *Baptists around the World: A Comprehensive Handbook*, edited by Albert W. Wardin, 209–10. Nashville: Broadman and Holman, 1995.

"The Life and Death of Jesus as Saving Event." *Reo: A Journal of Theology and Ministry* 2 (March 1996) 6–19.

"Resurrection and Discipleship." *St Mark's Review* 165 (Autumn 1996) 2–9.

"Jürgen Moltmann." In *A New Handbook of Christian Theologians*, edited by Donald W. Musser and Joseph L. Price, 304–16. Nashville: Abingdon, 1996.

"Baptist Heritage and Relevance in a Changing Society." *Faith and Freedom: A Journal of Christian Ethics* 5/3 (September 1996) 3–11.

"Baptist Heritage and Relevance Today." *New Zealand Journal of Baptist Research* 2 (October 1997) 3–23.

"Reconciliation: A Theological Meditation on 2 Corinthians 5:17–21." *St Mark's Review* 169 (Autumn 1997) 8–12.

"The Church as *Koinonia*." *St Mark's Review* 172 (Summer 1998) 7–13.

"Christ and Spirituality: The Foundation and the Structure of Christian Life." *Faith and Freedom: A Journal of Christian Ethics* 6/1 (April 1998) 5–11.

"Amt. Freikirchen." In *Religion in Geschichte und Gegenwart*. 4 Auflage. Band 1 (A–B): 433–34. Edited by Hans Dieter Betz, et al. Tübingen: Mohr/Siebeck, 1998.

"50 Years Universal Declaration of Human Rights—A Theological Appreciation." *Ethos: Official Publication of the Law Society of the Australian Capital Territory*. No. 170 (May 1998) 20–22.

"Some Reflections on Worship." In *Baptists in Worship: Berlin, Germany, October 1998*, edited by Tony Cupit, 35–42. McLean, VA: Baptist World Alliance, 1998.

"Die Reformation und die Baptisten—eine historische Analyse und systematische Folgerungen." *TG* 24/3 (2000) 75–95.

"Towards a Christian Theology of Religions: Christianity in Dialogue with Other Faiths." *Interface* 2/1 (May 1999) 39–55.

"The Universal Declaration of Human Rights: A Theological Appreciation." *St Mark's Review* 176 (Summer 1999) 11–17.

"'God Was in Christ, Reconciling the World to Himself' (2 Cor 5:18f.): A Theological Response to Conflict in Asia." Asian Baptist Federation publication, 2000.

"Mission and Discipleship." In *Baptist Faith and Witness Book 2: The Papers of the Study and Research Division of the Baptist World Alliance 1995–2000*, edited by Tony Cupit, 41–52. McLean, VA: Baptist World Alliance, 1999.

"Commission on Human Rights." In *Baptist Faith and Witness Book 2: The Papers of the Study and Research Division of the Baptist World Alliance 1995–2000*, edited by Tony Cupit, 213–14. McLean, VA: Baptist World Alliance, 1999.

"Towards a Theology of Human Rights." *RevExp* 97 (2000) 49–66.

"Theological Education at the Interface between Congregation and Society." *Reo: A Journal of Theology and Ministry* 18 (Spring 2000) 75–86.

"Saunders and Human Rights." In *Rev John Saunders: A Beacon Light and Some Baptist Reflections*, edited by Jill Sutton, 15–18. Melbourne: Baptist Union of Australia, 2001.

"Discerning the Signs of the Times! Culture and the Triune God." Paper delivered at the Seminar of the *Baptist Identity and National Culture*, 30–48. Baptist World Alliance, 2001.

"Die Zeichen der Zeit erkennen. Kultur und der trinitarische Gott." *ZTG* 7 (2002) 200–226.

(with Paul Falconer) "Baptists and the National Council of Churches of Australia." *Mosaic. The Quarterly Journal of the NSW Baptist Ministers Association* 4/3-4 (Spring/Summer 2002) 16–18.

"The Crucified Christ as Lord of the Church: Theological Reflections on 1 Corinthians 11–14." In *Prophecy and Passion: Essays in Honour of Athol Gill*, edited by David Neville, 83–125. ATF Series 5. Adelaide: Australian Theological Forum, 2002.

"Can War Today Be Just?" *Mosaic: The Quarterly Journal of the NSW Baptist Ministers Association* 5/1 (Autumn 2003) 1–5.

"The Call for a Contemporary Spirituality." *Mosaic: The Quarterly Journal of the NSW Baptist Ministers Association* 5/2 (Winter 2003) 6–8.
"Jesus Christ and Spirituality." In *Faith and Freedom: Christian Ethics in a Pluralist Culture*, edited by David Neville and Philip Matthews, 81–94. ATF Series 9. Adelaide: ATF Press, 2003.
"Ecclesiology." In *New and Enlarged Handbook of Christian Theology*, 140–43. Rev. ed. Nashville: Abingdon, 2003.
"Waging Peace Today." In *Gemeinschaft der Kirchen und gesellschaftliche Verantwortung: Die Würde des Anderen und das Recht anders zu denken. Festschrift für Professor Dr. Erich Geldbach*, edited by Lena Lybaek, Konrad Raiser, Stefanie Schardien, 251–60. Ecumenical Studies 30. Münster: Lit, 2004.
"Discerning the Spirits." *St Mark's Review* 195 (2004) 8–14.
"Christian Faith and Power." In *The Pastor's Bible Study*, edited by David Albert Farmer, 1:185–211. 5 vols. A New Interpreter's Bible Study. Nashville: Abingdon, 2004.
"Liberating Discipleship." In *The Pastor's Bible Study,* edited by David Albert Farmer, 1:213–50. 5 vols. A New Interpreter's Bible Study. Nashville: Abingdon, 2004.
"Baptists and a Theology of Mission." Paper presented at the Baptist World Alliance Summit on Baptist Mission in the Twenty-first Century. In *Summit on Baptist Mission in the 21st Century: "Reaching the World for Christ,"* edited by Denton Lotz, 31–37. Falls Church, VA: BWA, 2004.
"The Baptist World Alliance 1905–2005: A Centennial Overview of Its Missions and Programs. Freedom and Justice." *ABQ* 24 (2005) 41–52.
"Dietrich Bonhoeffer's Legacy." *Mosaic* 7/1 (Autumn 2005) 1–5.
"Dietrich Bonhoeffer's Legacy—60 Years On." *St Mark's Review* 199 (2005) 12–19.
"Ihr seid das Licht der Welt." *Die Gemeinde* 16 (24 July 2005) 4–5.
"Freedom or Security: 'Freedom of Religion' as a Human Right Today." In *Religions-Freiheit. Festschrift zum 200. Geburtstag von Julius Köbner*, edited by Erich Geldbach, Markus Wehrstedt, and Dietmar Lütz, 339–67. Berlin: WDL, 2006.
"Freedom from Fear: Christian Faith and Human Rights Today." *Pacifica* 19 (2006) 193–213.
"Find the Centre—Make it Known." In *"Into the World You Love": Encountering God in Everyday Life*, edited by Graeme Garrett, 227–43. Adelaide: ATF, 2007.
"The Centrality of Preaching in Christian Worship." In *Don't Put Out the Burning Bush: Worship and Preaching in a Complex World*, edited by Vivian Boland, 71–106. Adelaide: ATF, 2008.
"Speaking Truth to Power: The Theologian as Prophet." In *Embracing Grace—The Theologian's Task: Essays in Honour of Graeme Garrett*, edited by Heather Thomson, 69–85. Canberra: Barton Books, 2009.
"Justice Anchored in Truth: A Theological Perspective on the Nature and Implementation of Justice." *International Journal of Public Theology* 3 (2009) 281–98.
"Zumutungen. Baptisten und die Weltgemeinschaft christlicher Kirchen." In *"Die Bibel hat die Schuld daran . . .": Festschrift zum 175. Jubiläum der Oncken-Gemeinde in Hamburg*, edited by Dietmar Lütz, 424–45. Hamburg: WDL-Verlag, 2009.

PUBLISHED SERMONS

"The Mystery of God." *The Victorian Baptist* (July, 1977).
"Gute Nachricht für eine zerbrochene Kirche," *Die Gemeinde* 36–37 (1979) 4–5 in each.
"Good News for a Broken Church." In *Jesus Christ . . . for the Healing of the Churches*, 11–17. Washington DC: Baptist World Alliance, 1984.
"Der Flüchtling! Matthäus 2." *Der Gemeindebote* 65 (87/5, 1987) 2–4.
"The Meaning of the Resurrection of Jesus Christ." *Pulpit Digest* (March/April 1993) 49–52.
"Discipleship." *Pulpit Digest* (September/October 1995) 42–46.
"In the Beginning Was the Word—God's Yes." *Pulpit Digest* (January/February 1996) 21–25.
"The Church Is People." *Pulpit Digest* (May/June 1996) 38–42.
"The Secret Victory of the Crucified Christ." *Pulpit Digest* (September/October 1996) 33–38.
"Resurrection!" *Pulpit Digest* (March/April 1997) 35–40.
"The Ascension of Jesus Christ." *Pulpit Digest* (May/June 1997) 49–54.
"How Then Shall We Live?" *Pulpit Digest* (September/October 1997) 17–23.
"Baptism: The Necessity of Going Public." *Pulpit Digest* (January/February 1998) 51–55.
"Seek the Welfare of the City! To Build a Society of Justice." *Pulpit Digest* (May/June 1998) 41–48.
"When Our Prayers Are Not Enough: What God Has in Store." *Pulpit Digest* (November/December 1998) 57–62.
"The Calling God: Jonah, Part 1 of 4." *Pulpit Digest* (January/February 1999) 43–48.
"Jonah's Flight and the Providence of God: Jonah, Part 2 of 4." *Pulpit Digest* (March/April 1999) 48–54.
"The Joy of Repentance: Jonah, Part 3 of 4." *Pulpit Digest* (May/June 1999) 55–60.
"The Triumph of Grace: Jonah, Part 4 of 4." *Pulpit Digest* (July/August 1999) 45–49.
"Can These Bones Live?" *Pulpit Digest* (January–March 2000) 95–101.

THESES AND DISSERTATION

"The Prayer of Jesus: The Interpretation of John 17 in the Twentieth Century." Bachelor of Divinity treatise. Rüschlikon, Switzerland: International Baptist Theological Seminary, 1968 (137 pages). Major Professor: Günter Wagner.
"Die Bedeutung des Lieblingsjüngers für die Johanneische Theologie." Master of Theology thesis. Rüschlikon: International Baptist Theological Seminary, 1969. Major Professor: Günter Wagner.
"Johannes 21. Eine traditionsgeschichtliche Analyse: Zugleich ein Beitrag zur Johanneischen Lieblingsjüngerfrage." Doctoral dissertation. Zurich: University of Zürich, 1970. Major Professor: Eduard Schweizer.

Contributors

Isam E. Ballenger (USA)

Isam Ballenger was born in 1935 in West Palm Beach, Florida, and currently resides in Richmond, Virginia. With the Foreign Mission Board of the Southern Baptist Convention, he served as President of the International Baptist Theological Seminary in Rüschlikon, Switzerland, and as Area Director for Europe, the Middle East, and North Africa. From 1992 to 2003, he was Professor of Christian Mission and World Religions at the Baptist Theological Seminary at Richmond, Virginia, where he is now Emeritus Professor. He is married to Emma Katherine Ballenger and has three children and five grandchildren.

Keith D. Dyer (Australia)

Keith Dyer is Professor of New Testament at Whitley College, part of the Melbourne College of Divinity. Prior to that, he taught at the International Baptist Theological Seminary in Rüschlikon, Switzerland, with Thorwald Lorenzen, and for five years in the Solomon Islands. Keith's research interests include the gospels, eschatology, contextual hermeneutics, and ethics. His major work thus far is *The Prophecy on the Mount: Mark 13 and the Gathering of the New Community* (Peter Lang, 1998). He is married to Lynne, and they have four sons.

David Albert Farmer (USA)

David Albert Farmer is Pastor of Silverside Church in Wilmington, Delaware; Adjunct Professor of Preaching and Worship at Palmer Theological Seminary in Philadelphia, Pennsylvania; and Adjunct Professor of Humanities and Speech at Wilmington University in New Castle, Delaware. He was editor of *Pulpit Digest*, founding editor of *The African American Pulpit*, and general editor of *The Pastor's Bible Study*

(Abingdon). He is the author of four books and is presently working on a Web site for progressive preachers, homilynk.com.

Graeme Garrett (Australia)

Graeme Garrett is an Anglican priest and Senior Research Fellow at Saint Mark's National Theological Centre (also within Charles Sturt University's Public and Contextual Theology Strategic Research Centre). Before moving to Canberra, he was Professor of Theology at Whitley College in Melbourne. His major teaching and research interests are in contemporary theology, preaching, and ethics. He is the author of *God Matters: Conversations in Theology* (Liturgical, 1999) and *Dodging Angels on Saturday: Or Why Being a Theologian in the Twentieth Century Seemed like a Good Idea at the Time* (ATF Press, 2005), and editor of *"Into the World You Love": Encountering God in Everyday Life* (ATF Press, 2007). Graeme is married to Pam, and they have two daughters and four grandchildren.

Elizabeth Green (Italy)

Elizabeth Green studied theology at the International Baptist Theological Seminary in Rüschlikon, Switzerland, and the University of Salamanca in Spain. She has lived and worked as a Baptist pastor in Italy for many years. Her major field is feminist theology, in which she has published extensively in Italian. She has served as Vice President of the European Society of Women in Theological Research and as a consultant in the area of feminist theology for *Concilium*. Among her works are *Lacrime amare. Cristianesimo e violenza contro le donne* (2000) and *Il Dio sconfinato* (2007), and together with Mary Grey, she coedited *Ecofeminism and Theology—Ökofeminismus und Theologie—Ecoféminisme et Théologie* (1994).

E. Glenn Hinson (USA)

E. Glenn Hinson is Professor Emeritus of Spirituality and John F. Loftis Professor of Church History at the Baptist Theological Seminary at Richmond, Virginia. He has also been the David T. Porter Professor of Church History at Southern Seminary. He is the author or editor of twenty-seven books and more than 1,200 articles and book reviews.

He served on the Faith and Order Commission of both the World and National Councils of Churches.

David M. Hunter (Australia)

David Hunter was a doctoral candidate with Charles Sturt University, based at St Mark's National Theological Centre in Canberra (1997–2003). His PhD was awarded posthumously in June 2006. A person with wide-ranging interests and commitments, he was heavily involved in both Baptist and social-justice networks in Canberra. He contracted multiple myeloma in 2000 but remained active in social-justice advocacy and continued to work on his doctoral thesis until his death in December 2003. He was married to Jeanette Mathews and father of three sons.

Per Midteide (Norway)

Per Midteide is a Norwegian Baptist leader who studied theology at Oslo University and later taught pastoral theology at the Baptist Theological Seminary in Norway. He has served as pastor of three Norwegian Baptist churches, as General Secretary of the Baptist Union of Norway, General Secretary of Norwegian Church Aid (NCA), and has worked with NCA in southern Africa and Sudan. He was a member of the Baptist World Alliance Commission on Human Rights and chair of the Evangelism Committee of the European Baptist Federation. Now retired, he remains associated with Norwegian Church Aid in Eritrea and is still a member of the Baptist World Aid Committee.

Jürgen Moltmann (Germany)

A prominent theological voice of the second half of the twentieth century and author of many books, Jürgen Moltmann is Professor of Systematic Theology Emeritus in the Protestant Faculty of the University of Tübingen. He received his doctorate in theology from the University of Göttingen and then served as pastor of the Evangelical Church of Bremen-Wasserhorst. He became a theology professor at an academy in Wuppertal—*Kirchliche Hochschule*—operated by the Confessing Church, then joined the theological faculty of the University of Bonn in 1963. After a brief period at Bonn, Moltmann was offered the position of Professor of Systematic Theology at the University of Tübingen, where he taught from 1967 to 1994. He recently published his autobiography, *A Broad Place* (2007).

David J. Neville (Australia)

David Neville is Head of Charles Sturt University's School of Theology and lectures in New Testament studies at St Mark's National Theological Centre in Canberra. His research interests include the gospels, New Testament theology and ethics, biblical hermeneutics, and peace studies. He is the author of two books on the Synoptic Problem and editor of two collections of essays relating to Christian social ethics. He is affiliated with Charles Sturt University's Public and Contextual Theology Strategic Research Centre, within which he convenes a focus group concerned with Scripture and social ethics. He is married to Sonia.

Frank Rees (Australia)

Frank Rees is the Principal of Whitley College, the Baptist College of Victoria, where he has taught systematic theology since 1991. An ordained Baptist pastor, he previously served pastorates in Victoria and Tasmania. Frank is currently President of the Melbourne College of Divinity and has served also as President of the Australian and New Zealand Association of Theological Schools. His research interests include contextual approaches to Christology and ecclesiology. He is the author of *Wrestling with Doubt: Theological Reflections on the Journey of Faith* (Liturgical, 2001).

D. Dixon Sutherland (USA)

D. Dixon Sutherland is Professor of Religious Studies at Stetson University in DeLand, Florida. From 1983 to 1991, he was Thorwald Lorenzen's colleague at the International Baptist Theological Seminary in Rüschlikon, Switzerland. Much of his work in theology and ethics has been cross-disciplinary, resulting in publications in the *Journal of Aging and Social Policy* and the *Stetson Law Review*. He is coeditor of *War or Words? Interreligious Dialogue as an Instrument of Peace* (2005).

Tarmo Toom (Estonia/USA)

Tarmo Toom is a native of Estonia. From 2002 to 2008, he was Associate Professor of Divinity at the John Leland Center for Theological Studies, and he is currently Associate Professor of Patristic Theology at the Catholic University of America in Washington DC. He is both a member of the North American Patristics Society and a member of the Steering Committee for the Augustine and Augustinianisms Group within the American Academy of Religion. Toom is the author of two books: *Thought Clothed with Sound: Augustine's Christological Hermeneutics in "De doctrina Christiana"* (Peter Lang, 2002); and *Classical Trinitarian Theology: A Textbook* (T. & T. Clark, 2007).

Scripture Index

OLD TESTAMENT

Genesis

1	51
1:1—2:3	98, 106
1:3	82
1:3–4	107
1:6	82
1:9	82
1:14	82
1:20	82
1:24	82
1:27–28	237
1:31	59, 65
2:1	41

Exodus

3	114
3:13–15	114
4	134
7	134
20:8–11	98, 106
20:13	237
33:11	27

Numbers

11:26–30	37
12:2	36
12:4	37

Deuteronomy

5:1	42
21:22–23	106

Judges

13:2–7	112

2 Chronicles

20:7	27

Psalms

38:11	106
46:10	41
72	90
110:1	104
124:8	93
139:13–16	237

Proverbs

24:10–12	237
31:8	237

Ecclesiastes

3:1–3	237

Isaiah

	134
26	63
26:19	156
35:5–6	69
42:6	87
49:6	86, 87
58:1–2	175
61:1	174
66:1–2	54

Daniel

12	63
12:3	158

Joel

2:26	53

Micah

6:4	36
6:8	234

APOCRYPHA, SEPTUAGINT, AND PSEUDEPIGRAPHA

2 Baruch

50	75

1 Enoch

102–4	63

2 Maccabees

7	63
7:10–11	67
7:22–23	60
12	63

Book of Odes

5:19	156

Sirach

3:30	171
48:5	156

Tobit

4:10	171
12:19	68

Wisdom of Solomon

1–6	63
9:15	66

NEW TESTAMENT

Matthew

1:1–17	86
1:22–23	86
1:23	86
2:5–6	86
3:3	86
3:15	93
3:17	86
4:17	81, 90
4:19	88
5–7	88
5:3	174
5:7	171
5:8	174
5:10–11	89
5:13–14	87, 91
5:13–16	8, 83
5:14	86
5:17	86
5:20	93
5:42	173
5:43–44	28
5:46	222
6:1–2	170
6:9–13	83
6:10	57, 89
6:12	91
6:30	88
7:12	171
7:28–29	89
8:15–13	82
8:19–22	85
8:26	88
9:9	87
9:18–26	119
10:1	88
10:5	86
10:5–8	88
10:28	71
10:37–39	85
10:40	86
11:1	85
11:25–27	93
12:17–21	86
12:18–21	93
12:46–50	93
13:22	168
13:24–30	87
13:47–50	87
14:30–31	88
14:31	88
15:21–28	82
15:24	86
16:8	88
16:24–27	81
16:25	30
17:3–12	86
18:21–22	30
19:16–22	168

19:16–30	169	4:35	99
19:21	174	5:21–43	101, 119
19:23–24	168	5:42	111
21:1–46	118	6–8	121
21:4–5	86	6:17–29	101
21:11	112	6:29	101, 102
21:14	125	6:47	99
21:17	120	8:22–26	97
21:28–32	91	8:34	28, 45
22	63	9:3	104
22:15–22	185	10:17–22	168
22:30	62	10:17–31	6
22:34–40	83	10:21	39, 40, 174
22:36–40	224	10:25	168
25:31–46	91, 172	10:29–30	48
25:41	72	10:32	108
26:6	120	10:35–40	96
26:11	174	10:44	47
27:46	45	10:46–52	97, 119
27:53	140, 147	10:47	112
27:61	147	11:1—12:12	118
27:64	147	11:1—15:41	96
27:66	147	11:5	119
28:1	147	11:11–12	120
28:16–20	81, 82, 83, 84, 88	11:18	44
28:17	88	12:13–17	6, 7, 185
28:18–20	85, 87, 91, 93	12:28–34	95
28:19	83, 87	12:30–31	30
28:19–20	86	12:36	104
28:20	92	12:38	104
		13	148

Mark

		13:1—16:8	101
1:7	112	14:3	120
1:9	112	14:3–9	49, 97
1:10–11	96	14:7	174
1:14–15	97	14:9	50
1:16—16:8	96	14:17	99
1:22	44	14:27–28	108
1:24	112	14:28	105, 108, 109, 111
1:32	99	14:36	52
1:35	107	14:51	104, 105
1:44	110	14:51–52	104
3:6	43	14:62	104
3:7–12	97	14:66–72	109
3:27	112	14:67	112
4:19	168	15:16–41	96
4:20	49	15:34	45
4:27–28	41	15:39	106, 112

15:40	52, 106	19:1–10	6
15:40–41	96, 97, 98, 109	19:28—20:19	118
15:40—16:8	95–115, 96, 97, 114	20:20–26	185
15:40–47	98, 99	21:18	67
15:42–47	98	22:19	50
15:42—16:8	96	23:2	44
15:43	101, 102, 103	24:11	102
15:46	101	24:13–35	137
16:1–8	98, 99, 100	24:19	112
16:2	102, 106, 107	24:21	52
16:5	104, 105	24:35	x
16:5–6	104	24:37	68
16:6	53, 100, 101, 102, 112, 113	24:39	66, 68, 145
16:7	100, 108, 109	24:43	68
16:8	97, 98, 110, 111	24:50	120
16:9–20	98		
16:14	53		
16:20	98		

Luke

1:3	27
1:38	42
1:53	47, 168
2:52–53	43
4:16–30	174
4:18	174
4:34	112
6:20	174
6:24	168
6:30	173
6:31	171
7:1–17	119
7:22	174
7:44–50	174
8:14	168
8:40–56	119
10:29–37	49
10:25–37	28, 30
10:38	120
10:38–42	42, 119
14:13	174
14:21	174
14:33	47
16	119
16:19–31	119, 168
18:18–23	168
18:22	174
18:25	168

John

1:1–14	82
1:9–11	122
1:28	120
1:45	112
1:49–51	132
2:1–11	117, 123
2:3–4	132
2:4	122
2:11	122
2:13–22	118
2:23–25	132
3:1ff	132
4:14	128
4:46–48	132
4:46–54	117, 123
4:48	132
5–11	122, 123
5:1–9	117, 125
5:17	134
5:21	133
6	121
6:1–14	117
6:16–21	117
6:26–27	132
6:27	128
7:30	122
8:20	122
8:32	213
9:1–9	117
9:1–11	117
10	120

10–12	120	11:55	124
10:17–18	128	11:55–57	132
10:40	120	11:57	117, 134
11	116–135, 117, 118, 119, 120, 121, 122, 123, 124, 126, 127, 129, 130, 133, 134, 135	12:1–8	50
		12:7	133
		12:8	174
11–12	130, 134	12:9–11	125
11:1	120	12:16	122
11:1–44	117	12:17	133
11:1—12:11	131	12:17–19	125
11:3	118	12:18	117
11:4	117, 121, 122, 131	12:23	122
11:5–6	117	12:24	47, 60
11:7–10	121	12:25	48
11:7–16	117, 134	12:28	122
11:9–10	121	12:32	73
11:11	131	12:37–41	134
11:14	118, 131	13:1	122
11:15	131	13:31	122
11:16	121, 123	13:34	30
11:17	118	15:1	129
11:17–27	121	15:4	129
11:18	120	15:9	129
11:20–32	121	15:12-17	28
11:20–37	129	15:13	30
11:21	129	15:14	28, 31
11:21–27	117	15:15	28
11:25	117, 118, 129, 130	16:33	135
11:25–26	121, 134	17:1	122
11:27	132	17:1–5	122
11:28–44	121	17:4	122
11:32–33	117	19:10	45
11:33	118	19:12	44
11:38–40	117	20	123
11:39	118, 129, 132	20:9	67, 132
11:40–42	121	20:24–29	123, 132
11:43	134	20:27	53, 145
11:44	69, 118	20:30–31	122
11:45	132	20:31	127, 130, 132
11:45–46	118, 124	21:1–14	117
11:45–57	131		
11:47	117, 132	**Acts**	140
11:47–48	124	1:21–22	115
11:48	132	2:2ff	53
11:49–52	134	2:22–24	112
11:51	124	2:24	47
11:52	132	2:32	47, 115
11:53	117, 134	2:44–45	168

3:15	47
4:2	60
4:10	47, 112
5:1–6	168
5:17–42	6
7:48	54
8:9–13	168
8:32	45
10:4	171
10:31	171
10:35	170
10:38	112
17:31	60
20:35	169

Romans

1:4	140, 156
1:18	3
2:6	171
4	152
4:17	51
4:17–20	60
6:3–4	96
6:5	140, 156
6:8	141
7:24	69
8:2	69
8:10–11	68
8:11	53
8:18–25	154
8:19–23	55
8:19–25	58
8:21	73
8:21–23	73
8:22	53, 73
8:23	73
8:28	183, 234
8:29	62
8:34	104
9:1–5	149
12:1	245
13:1–10	6

1 Corinthians

1–4	152
1:2	149
1:4	149
1:5	168
1:23	141, 149
1:27–28	48
1:30	149
2:2	43
3:1	149
3:13	171
3:13–15	159
3:16	142, 160
4:8	144
4:10	149
4:15	149
4:17	149
5	144
5:3	142
6	142
6–7	144, 160
6:15	142
6:18	143
6:19	142, 160
7:4	142, 160
7:31	74
7:39	156
8–10	144, 151
8:6	53
8:10–13	151
9:27	142
10–11	142
10:2–4	152
10:27	151
11	144
11:27–34	143
11:30	156
12–14	142, 144, 160
12:18	143
12:27	143
13	160
13:3	142
15	63, 69, 71, 112, 115, 136–61, 137, 138, 140, 142, 145, 146, 147, 149, 151, 153, 154, 155, 156
15:1	155
15:1–2	149, 155, 159
15:2	148
15:3	155
15:3–8	111
15:3–11	155
15:4	136, 147, 157

15:6	158
15:8	137
15:8–9	145, 155
15:12	60, 136, 141, 144, 155, 156, 157
15:12–13	155
15:12–19	156
15:13–19	148
15:13	156, 157
15:14	46, 157
15:15	141, 157
15:15–17	155
15:16	157
15:17	149, 157
15:17–19	139, 144
15:18	153, 158
15:19	148
15:20	60, 147, 153, 155, 156, 157, 158
15:20–21	156
15:20–23	60
15:20–28	161
15:20–34	158
15:21	157
15:21–23	161
15:22	149
15:23	138, 147, 148, 156, 157, 161
15:28	138, 148, 152, 160, 161
15:29	152, 153, 157, 158
15:29–35	155
15:30–34	161
15:31	112, 149
15:32	157, 158
15:35	143, 155, 157
15:35–36	67
15:35–37	66, 158
15:35–41	154
15:40	142
15:42	155, 156, 157
15:44	68, 74, 142, 154, 159
15:45	68, 71, 147, 161
15:45–47	156
15:45–49	161
15:50	66, 145, 161
15:51	61, 68
15:52	153, 156, 157, 158, 159, 161
15:53	64, 68
15:53–54	161
15:57	112
15:57–58	149
15:58	155, 159, 161
16:24	149

2 Corinthians

1:17–20	140
4:12	47
5:2–4	72
8:9	168
9:6–11	169

Galatians

3	152
3:28	203
6:2	30
6:12	47
6:18	45

Ephesians

4:13	62

Philippians

2:3–6	39
2:6–11	37, 38, 39, 46
2:7	43
3:10	140, 156
3:20–21	60
3:21	69

Colossians

1:10	171
1:15	52
1:15–20	82
1:18	60
1:20	52

1 Thessalonians

4:14	60, 140
4:16	153
5:23	70

2 Thessalonians

1:11	30
2:17	171

1 Timothy

2:10	171
5:10	171
6:9	168
6:10	168
6:17	168
6:17–19	169

2 Timothy

2:11	60, 141
2:18	144
2:21	171
3:17	171

Titus

2:13	171
3:1	171

Hebrews

1:1–4	82
10:24	171
12:1	160
13:13	37
13:16	169
13:21	171

James

1:5	173
1:10–11	168
2:2–6	174
2:5	168, 174
2:23	27
5:2	168
5:16	30

1 Peter

2:13–17	6

2 Peter

3:13	57

1 John

2:29	170
3:2	56
3:7	170
3:10	170
3:18	171

2 John 211

1–6	211

Revelation

5:1–14	6
13:1–18	6
20	63
20:6	72
20:10	72
20:14	72
21	75
22:11	171

NEW TESTAMENT APOCRYPHA

Gospel of Thomas

77	54

APOSTOLIC FATHERS

Barnabas

19:8	169
19:11	173
20	174

1 Clement

2:7	171
13:1	168
13:2	171
30:3	171
33:1	171
33:7	171
38:2	171, 175
55:2	175

2 Clement

4:3	171
12:4	171
16:4	171, 173
20:1	168

Didache

1	168
1:5	169
2:7	173
5:2	171
11–13	174
13:2	173
	174

Shepherd of Hermas
Mandate

2.4.6	173

Shepherd of Hermas
Similitude

2	175
2.10	170
9.20	168
9.20.1	168
9.20.2	168

Shepherd of Hermas
Vision

1.1.8–9	168
3.6	168
3.6.6	170

Ignatius,
To the Smyrnaeans

6:2	174

Polycarp,
To the Philippians

2:3	171, 174
4:1	168

Author Index

Abram, Morris, 230
Achtemeier, Paul J., 121
Alewuya, Ayodeji J., 143
Allison, Dale C., 103, 110
Alfeche, M., 66, 68
Alsup, John E., 106
Ambrose, 169, 176, 177, 178
Anderson, Hugh, 92
Angus, Floyd, 243
Ankerberg, John, 138
Annas, George, 227
Anthony of Egypt, 169, 178
Aquinas, 237
Aristotle, 20, 21, 22, 23, 217, 218, 219, 220
Athanasius, 178
Athenagoras, 72, 73
Augustine, 31, 59–75, 172, 178, 179, 220, 237
Aune, David E., 114, 127

Balabanski, Vicky, 148
Ballenger, Isam E., 79–94, 253
Ballenger, John, 91, 92
Balthasar, 65
Barth, Karl, 11, 17, 34, 57, 237, 238, 243, 244
Basil of Caesarea, 169, 175, 176
Becker, Ernest, 244
Benedict XII, 61
Benedict XVI, 242
Bergman, Lorenz, 186
Bethge, Eberhard, 17, 18, 19, 20, 23, 24, 25, 27, 29, 30
Black, C. Clifton, 128
Bloch, Ernst, 55
Blumhardt, Christoph, 57
Bobert-Stürzel, Sabine, 27, 29
Boehme, Jacob, 55
Bonhoeffer, Dietrich, 17–34, 57, 58
Bolkestein, Henricus, 166
Borg, Marcus J., 138

Borgen, Peder, 204, 205
Bosch, David, 90
Brackney, William H., 204
Brakoff, Robert, 243
Brett, Mark G., 152, 154
Briglia, Sergio, 107
Broadhead, Edwin K., 113
Brophy, Patricia, 234
Brown, Raymond E., 102, 103, 120
Brown, Colin, 103
Brunner, Emil, 57
Bultmann, Rudolf, 11, 118, 121, 122, 124
Burke, Ruby J., 204
Burkett, Delbert, 98
Burnell, Peter, 70
Busch, Eberhard, 17
Bynum, C. W., 65, 66, 67, 69

Cadoux, C. J., 170
Calvin, John, 237
Camp, Claudia, 36, 37
Cantor, Norman, 243
Caro, Francis G., 246
Carter, Jimmy, 187
Carter, Warren, 93
Celsus, 166
Chrysostom, 172
Churchill, Larry R., 228
Cicero, 20, 22, 24, 167
Clarke, Thomas E., 73, 75
Clement of Alexandria, 120, 168, 170, 172, 173
Clement of Rome, 175
Collins, Adela Yarbro, 103, 105, 106, 108
Cooper, Lane, 218, 219
Copan, Paul, 138
Cornelius, 173
Craig, William Lane, 138
Cranford, Ronald, 230

Author Index

Crossan, John Dominic, 103, 111, 120, 125, 126, 138
Croy, N. Clayton, 98
Culpepper, R. Alan, 128
Cyprian, 171, 172

Daley, B. E., 61
Daly, Mary, 36
Danove, Paul, 96, 97
Davies, J. G., 65
Davis, Walter, 27
Decker, Rodney J., 137
de Gruchy, John W., 18, 19, 25
de Mello, Anthony, 40
DeLay, Tom, 227
De Mey, P., 32
Descartes, 54, 146, 154, 161
di Vittoria, Francisco, 241
Dobbins, Gaines S., 181
Dobson, James, 236
Dorrien, Gary, 3
Dunn, James D. G., 101
Dyer, Keith D., x, 136–61, 148, 253

Endsjø, Dag, 146, 150, 151
Eusebius, 173
Evans, Craig A., 105, 108, 112

Farmer, David Albert, 5, 206–24, 208, 253
Farmer, William R., 98
Ferguson, Everett, 151
Feuerbach, Ludwig, 56
Fiorenza, Elisabeth Schüssler, 36, 50
Flew, Antony G. N., 138
Ford, David F., 22
Fowler, Stanley J., 3
France, R. T., 108
Fredriksen, Paula, 124, 125, 126

Gandhi, Mahatma, 209, 210
Garrett, Graeme, vii, x, 17–34, 116, 254
Gauderer, Michael, 243
Gibbon, Edward, 177
Gibbs, David, 226
Gifford, Paul, 181, 182
Gill, Athol, 5, 10
Gingrey, Phil, 227
Goff, Lord, 239
Gonzalez, Catherine, 222, 223

Gonzalez, Justo, 222, 223
Gremmels, Christian, 18, 19, 20
Green, Elizabeth, 35–50, 254
Green, Joel B., 112
Greenslade, S. L., 175
Grenz, Stanley, 3
Griffith, G. T., 167

Habel, Norman C., 148
Habermas, Gary R., 138
Haers, Jacques, 32
Hampson, Daphne, 46
Hands, A. R., 167, 174
Hanson, K. C., x
Harvey, S. A., 40
Hatch, Edwin, 172
Hays, Richard B., 142
Heidegger, Martin, 212
Henry, Carl, 11
Heschel, Abraham Joshua, 222
Hinson, E. Glenn, 165–84, 254
Hitchens, Christopher, 210, 211
Hoestmaelingen, Njaal, 200, 202
Holmes, Michael W., 97
Holmquist, Hjalmar, 186
Homer, 150
Hooker, Morna, 103
Horsley, Richard A., 145
Hotchkiss, V., 65
Huber, Wolfgang, 18, 19, 20
Hughes, Charles, 103
Hunter, David, 114, 116–35, 117, 123, 133, 255

Irenaeus, 60, 172

Jackson, Howard M., 104
Jagland, Thorbjoern, 202
Jenkins, Philip, 181
Jennett, Bryan, 228, 229, 230
Jerome, 169, 172, 179
Jewett, Robert, 143
Johnson, Luke Timothy, 74, 112
John Paul II, 226, 229, 242
Josephus, 102
Juel, Donald H., 53, 101
Jüngel, Eberhard, 244, 245
Justin, 174, 175

Käsemann, Ernst, 9, 10, 11, 13
Keck, Leander E., 101
Kehl, Medard, 51
Keith, Lord, 240
Kelber, Werner H., 112
Kelly, J. N. D., 65
Kierkegaard, Søren, 28
Kim, H. C. Paul, 109
King, Martin Luther, 154
Kingsbury, Jack Dean, 80
Kirk, J. Andrew, 90
Kirshner, Howard S., 228
Klinger, Ross, 155
Konstan, David, 153
Kwon, Oh-Young, 152

Labahn, Michael, 119, 120, 122, 123, 124, 126, 131
La Mettrie, Julien, 54
Lama, Dalai, 221
Lamberigts, M., 71
Lampe, Peter, 63
La Due, W. J., 61
Latourette, Kenneth Scott, 85
Lee, Dorothy, 131
Lee, Michelle V., 136, 142, 143
Legrand, Lucien, 82
Levenson, Jon, 146, 147, 148, 152, 159
Levoratti, Armando J., 107
Lienhard, J. T., 65
Lietzmann, Hans, 186
Lincoln, Andrew T., 104, 105, 108, 111
Lindholm, Tore, 200, 202
Little, Graham, 22, 27
Little, H. G., 60
Lohmeyer, Ernst, 108
Long, Thomas G., 216
Lorenzen, Thorwald, vii–x, 1–14, 17, 52, 59, 61, 79, 92, 94, 95, 108, 116, 137, 138, 141, 158, 186, 203, 204, 215, 216, 244, 247–52
Lotz, Denton, 204
Lucian, 169, 173
Lüdemann, Gerd, 138
Luria, Isaac, 39
Luther, Martin, 89, 237, 245
Luz, Ulrich, 88
Lynn, Joanne, 230

Macquarrie, John, 41
Madigan, Kevin, 146, 148
Magness, J. Lee, 110
Malbon, Elizabeth Struthers, 102
Marcion, 172
Marrou, H. I., 62, 70, 74
Marshall, I. Howard, 112
Martin, Dale B., 136, 143, 146
Marx, Karl, 55, 56
Marxsen, Willi, 108
Mathews, Jeanette, 116
Matthews, Philip, 8
McCarthy, John 114, 127
McGrath, Alister, 3
McKnight, Scot, 112
McNamara, Marie Aquinas, 31
Meier, John, 119, 120, 125
Meilaender, Gilbert C., 28, 31
Meyer, Marvin, 103
Midteide, Per, 185–205, 255
Miles, M. R., 60, 62
Miller, Susan, 107, 111
Mitchell, Joan L., 110
Moloney, Francis, 131, 133
Moltmann, Jürgen, 11, 39, 41, 51–58, 52, 53, 138, 160, 238, 239, 255
Montaigne, 20
Moody, D. L., 84
Moody, Howard, 217
Moon, Brian, 215, 216
Morgan, Rebecca, 246
Morris, Robert, 246
Mott, John R., 84
Mourant, 73
Murphy, Nancey, 98

Nairn, Thomas A., 242
Neill, Stephen, 85
Neville, David J., x, 8, 95–115, 96, 104, 106, 150, 256
Nickelsburg, G. W. E., 63, 71
Nietzsche, Friedrich, 57
Nørregaard, Jens, 186
Norton, Jill R., 246

Obama, Barack, 154
O'Daly, Gerard J. P., 70
Origen, 171, 172

Author Index

O'Rourke, Kevin D., 241
Osiek, Carolyn, 102

Painter, John, 116, 132
Palladius, 177, 178, 180
Pannenberg, Wolfhart, 11, 238
Parsons, Mikeal C., 27
Pelikan, J., 65
Perkins, Pheme, 101, 104
Perrin, Norman, 97, 98, 108
Perry, Joshua E., 228
Peters, Ted, 52, 61, 63, 99
Pilch, John J., 125
Pius XII, 232, 242
Plato, 57, 145, 146
Plesner, Ingvill T., 200, 202
Plotinus, 63
Plum, Fred, 245
Polkinghorne, John, 101
Porphyry, 63, 64, 75
Ps.-Justin, 67, 70

Ragaz, Leonhard, 57
Rahner, Karl, 32, 33, 61
Ramelli, Ilaria, 153
Ramsay, Paul, 240
Rauschenbusch, Walter, 180
Rees, Frank, viii, 1–14, 256
Richard, Pablo, 107
Ricoeur, Paul, 114, 116, 117, 118, 126, 127, 128, 130, 133, 135
Ringe, Sharon, 109
Rist, John, 70, 71
Robertson, John A., 236
Robinson, John A. T., 143
Ruether, Rosemary, 38, 46
Russell, Bertrand, 222
Russell, Robert J., 61, 63, 99

Sabin, Marie Noonan, 97, 106, 111
Sataline, Suzanne, 216
Schenck, Paul, 236, 237
Schillebeeckx, Edward, 11
Schiller, Friedrich, 23
Schmidt, Ulla, 202
Schnackenburg, Rudolf, 90
Schweitzer, Albert, 143
Schweizer, Eduard, 88, 128, 129

Schwöbel, Christoph, 32, 33
Seneca, 167
Senior, Donald, 86
Sicouly, Pablo Carlos, 51
Singer, Peter, 239, 240
Smith, Morton, 120
Sobrino, Jon, 11
Sorabji, Richard, 75
Soskice, Janet Martin, 22, 24, 33, 34
Spong, John Shelby, 237
Steen, Reiulf, 200
Stewart, Robert B., 138
Suber, Peter, 212
Sutherland, D. Dixon, 225–46, 246, 256

Tacelli, Ronald K., 138
Tamez, Elsa, 107
Tannehill, Robert C., 147
Tarn, W. W., 167
Taylor, Vincent, 110
Terry, Randall, 236
Tertullian, 60, 64, 66, 67, 72, 169, 172
Theodosius, 175
Thiselton, Anthony C., 144, 153
Thompson, Jamie, 225
Thorkildsen, Dag, 202
Tomlin, Graham, 136
Toom, Tarmo, 59–75, 256, 257
Torrance, T. F., 171
Troeltsch, Ernst, 169
Turcescu, Lucian, 75

Upton, Bridget Gilfillan, 97

Valentinian, 175
Van Fleteren, F., 62
van Huyssteen, J. Wentzel, 238
Van Seters, Arthur, 223
Varro, 70
Vasile, Albert J., 213
Vattimo, Gianni, 34
Vischer, Lukas, 172
Visser't Hooft, W. A., 36
Volf, Miroslav, 154
Volpe, Rafaelle, 217
von Uexküll, Jakob, 55
von Weizsäcker, Ernst, 55
Vose, Heather M., 204

Wadell, Paul J., 21, 28, 33
Wallace, Mark, 114, 128
Walton, Jonathan L., 182
Warneck, Gustav, 84
Watson, G., 64
Weder, Hans, 89
Welker, Michael, 61, 63, 99, 101
Whitehead, Alfred North, 209
Wise, Michael O., 112
Wittgenstein, Ludwig, 98
Wolfson, Jay, 236
Wood, James E., 204
Woolf, Virginia, 42
Wright, N. T., 106, 137, 138

Yeats, William Butler, 35
Young, Ed, 215, 216

Subject Index

ACT Churches Council, ix
almsgiving, 170–77
ancestors, 151–52, 160
Apostolic Creed, 65
Augustine (*see* author index)
Australian Centre for Christianity and
    Culture, ix
baptism, 1–4, 93, 152
Baptist World Alliance, 7, 204
Baptist Theological Seminary (Norway),
    255
Baptist Theological Seminary (Richmond),
    253–54
Baptist Union of Norway, 255
Baptist Union of Victoria, 1
Beethoven, 23
body, 63–73, 142–43, 145, 159
Bonhoeffer-Bethge friendship, 17–31
boundary crossing, 35–50
Brophy, Paul, 233–34
Buddhism, 38, 40, 41

Charles Sturt University (Canberra),
    254–56
Christology, 8, 37–39, 43, 54, 112–13, 150
Christological spirituality, 1, 13
church-state relations, 6, 7, 21, 185–205
    Belgium, 193
    Bulgaria, 194
    Denmark, 195
    England, 192
    Finland, 195
    Germany, 193
    Greece, 192
    Iceland, 195
    Italy, 191–92
    Kosovo, 194–95
    Norway, 196–205
    Poland, 194
    Romania, 194
    Scotland, 193
    Serbia, 194
    Sweden, 196
communion (*see* Lord's Supper)
compassion, 221–22
conversation, 32–34
creation, 4–7, 41, 51, 53, 60, 74, 96, 105–8,
    210
Creed of Milan, 65
cremation, 137, 160

death and dying, 43, 56, 151, 225–46
dialectical materialism, 54–56
discipleship, 7–9, 11, 13, 87–88, 158
distribution of wealth, 165–84

earth, 56, 57–58, 148, 236
EBTTC, ix
ecotheology, 40, 51, 56–57, 74, 159
ecumenism, 1–2
Edinburgh (1910), 84
Empire of God, 4, 6–8, 31–34, 48, 51, 55,
    57–58, 66, 79, 81, 86–87, 90–91, 95,
    99, 102, 109, 114, 128–29, 168, 174
'empty' tomb, 12, 92, 100, 103–5, 111, 132,
    136, 145
ethics, 5–7, 13, 72, 94, 143–44, 149, 153–55,
    158–59, 165–246
ethos, 217–21
eucharist (*see* Lord's Supper)
evangelical sacrament/s, 1–4
evangelical theology, 3, 4, 11, 138
existentialism, 9, 10, 56
extremes of wealth, 166

faith, 5–7, 10–14, 132–33, 193, 234, 244
freedom, 8, 20, 25–27, 188–90, 204
friends, friendship, vii, 17–34

Galilee, 81, 108–10, 112, 124

globalization, 43, 56
glory, 56, 73, 122, 141
German Creed, 65
Great Commission, 83–86, 91, 93

heaven, 57–58, 81, 89, 90–92, 137, 148, 212
historical Jesus, 4, 9, 10, 12, 86, 92, 109–13, 118, 125, 127, 155
Holy Spirit, 4, 8, 12, 22, 38, 53, 55, 79, 82–83, 93, 142, 147, 158, 160
homiletics, 206–24
human rights, viii, ix, 6, 7, 90, 165, 185–205, 222–24, 239

IBTS (International Baptist Theological Seminary at Rüschlikon), vii, viii, 5, 216, 253
infant exposure, 167
Islam, 185, 191, 204–5

Judaism, 42–43, 171, 213
justice, viii, 8, 11, 13, 39, 80, 91, 94, 142, 148, 149, 154, 159, 161, 202, 203, 217, 223, 245

kenosis, 37–40, 45–46, 49
Kingdom of God (*see* Empire of God)

Lord's Supper, 3, 4, 50, 143
Lorenzen, Jill, ix
Lorenzen, Thorwald
    birth, vii
    BWA work, ix, 204
    conference speaker, viii
    denominational responsibilities, viii, ix
    ecumenical activities, viii, ix, 2,
    education, vii
    friend, vii, 17
    family, ix, x
    human rights work, 7, 203–4
    life story, vii–x
    marriage, ix
    ordination, vii
    pastoral service, viii, 8
    preaching, 1, 5, 79–80, 215
    publications, viii, ix, 59, 61, 95, 141, 247–52
    table fellowship, ix–x

teaching career, viii, 59, 137, 158
theologian, 8, 11
United Nations work, ix, 80, 203–4
love, 23, 28, 30, 33–34, 44, 50, 83, 129, 160, 171–72, 209–11, 221–22, 224

Mark's ending, 95–115
marriage, 21–22, 25, 31, 62, 220
Martha, 42, 119–21, 129, 131–32
Mary/s, 12, 36, 42, 47–50, 67, 119–21, 133
Melbourne College of Divinity, 152, 253, 256
Miriam, 36–37, 43
mission, 10–11, 79–94, 109, 131, 141
money, 6, 167–70
Morling College (Sydney), vii
Muslim world, 185, 191, 204–5

narrative hermeneutics, 117–35
new Earth, 51–58
Nicene Creed, 58
Niceno-Constantinopolitan Creed, 65

Oslo Conference, 190

Palmer Theological Seminary (Philadelphia), 253
parable and metaphor, 128–30
patriarchy, 36, 46
persistent vegetative state (PVS), 225–46
philanthropy, 166, 180–82
poverty, 10, 13, 165–66, 170–77
power, 6–7, 37–38, 42, 44–48, 54, 104–5, 138–40, 154
prosperity "gospel," 181–82
Quinlan, Joseph, 232
Quinlan, Karen Ann, 231–32
radical discipleship, 5, 177–80
reciprocity, 24–25, 28
reign of God (*see* Empire of God)
religious liberty, 185–205, 223
resurrection, 10–14, 46–49, 51–58, 59–75, 91, 95–115, 136–61, 244–46
Rüschlikon (*see* IBTS)

Sabbath, 41, 52, 57, 98–99, 106–108
sacraments (*see* ordinances)
sacredness of life, 235–43

Subject Index

Saint Mark's National Theological Centre (Canberra), 254–56
Schiavo, Terri, 225–46
SEBTS (Wake Forest), viii
Sermon on the Mount, 88–89
signs, 117–35
slavery, 134, 183
Southern Baptist Convention, 181, 253, 254
soul, 59–61, 63–66, 70–74, 136–38, 142, 144–46, 151, 237–38
spirituality, 7, 8, 13, 45, 46, 49, 57
Sturm, Ursel, 29

Thyrd, Jill, ix
Trinity, 32–34, 75, 79, 82–83, 114–15
truth, 208–13, 216

Universal Declaration of Human Rights, 165–66, 188–90, 201
University of Bonn, 255
University of Sydney, vii
University of Tübingen, 255

wealth, 167–70
women and resurrection, 52–53, 97, 99, 102–3, 110–12
Whitley College (Melbourne), 116, 137, 253–54, 256
Wilmington University (New Castle), 253
worship, 7, 12–13, 171, 188–90, 220